Shelter for the Night

Shelter for the Night

On Afghanistan, Language, and Detours

FATIMA MOJADDEDI

DUKE UNIVERSITY PRESS *Durham and London* 2026

Project Editor: Livia Tenzer
Designed by Matthew Tauch
Typeset in Garamond Premier Pro and Degular
by Westchester Publishing Services

Library of Congress Cataloging-in-Publication Data
Names: Mojaddedi, Fatima, [date] author
Title: Shelter for the night : on Afghanistan, language, and detours /
Fatima Mojaddedi.
Other titles: On Afghanistan, language, and detours
Description: Durham : Duke University Press, 2026. | Includes
bibliographical references and index.
Identifiers: LCCN 2025028028 (print)
LCCN 2025028029 (ebook)
ISBN 9781478038535 paperback
ISBN 9781478033622 hardcover
ISBN 9781478062141 ebook
Subjects: LCSH: Anthropological linguistics—Afghanistan |
Language and culture—Afghanistan | Sociolinguistics—Afghanistan |
Violence—Social aspects—Afghanistan | Afghanistan—Social
conditions—21st century
Classification: LCC P35.5.A3 M653 2026 (print) | LCC P35.5.A3 (ebook) |
DDC 306.44209581—dc23/eng/20251120
LC record available at https://lccn.loc.gov/2025028028
LC ebook record available at https://lccn.loc.gov/2025028029

Cover art: Shaheer Zazai, *Real Surreal Unnatural Sky*, 2018.
Acrylic on panel, 14 × 11 in. Courtesy of the artist.

In loving memory of Monena.

For my parents, and for Krystyna,

who made writing possible in different ways.

Contents

Prologue

Open Windows and Houses

The house will also fall to dust.
—LE CORBUSIER, *Towards a New Architecture*

We have long forgotten the ritual by which the house of
our life was erected.
—WALTER BENJAMIN, *One-Way Street and Other Writings*

Houses, lines of houses, streets, miles of pavements, piled
up bricks, stones. Changing hands. This owner, that. . . .
Shelter for the night.
—JAMES JOYCE, *Ulysses*

Nadia, who believes she is now in her eighties but isn't sure, liked to open the windows of our sixth-floor apartment first thing in the morning, because she proclaimed, "The sun is cleansing," and she liked to look out at the street and city of Kabul below.[1] It was not so much a habit as a sense that what is true and good can be both outside and inside. It was a sovereign moment like the kind Walter Benjamin describes as the sudden courage to look through an aperture "for the tiny spark of contingency" and find the undefined point where "the future nests so eloquently that we, looking back, may rediscover it."[2] It was a moment about living life on her own terms, and the open window set her free: "Ah! That's so much better. It opens my heart."

In "A Berlin Chronicle" Walter Benjamin describes the city from a nostalgic, sometimes melancholy distance, and from the perspective of his own discontinuous past in which the "imprint of a collision" between society and self was clear.[3] When I think of my childhood in Hanover, I mostly think of the German winter and of lush piles of snow against the gray sky, but also of Herrenhäuser Gärten, with its magnificent fountain that spouts water eighty feet high at its center, and in our neighborhood next to it, a small children's sandbox and an imposing brick archway that led to our block. From Nadia's perspective, starting the day with light and air was about joy from within. Looking out at the city did not owe itself to a physical crossing. When I asked her if she had visited the terraced Gardens of Babur, where the first Mughal emperor is entombed, or the ancient Bala Hissar fortress she asked, "Why would I go there?" Looking out at the city was more like a "voluptuous hovering on the brink."[4] The light would flood the room, and she would lie down in the one space on the floor that she proclaimed as hers. It was as small as her petite and hunched body. There was no balustrade or trellis framed with climbing vines, no pictures on the windowsill to stand in front of, and no paneled shutters to create latticed lines or interfere with her light. Put differently, there was no *punctum* (Roland Barthes's term) in front of her, only the kind of new direction and clear symmetrical arrangement Le Corbusier praised in a different era for its equality and modern openness. Unlike mere holes in the wall, which make a room unempathetic and dismal looking, like an enclosure, he wrote that windows must "serve to admit light . . . and to see outside."[5]

Nadia talked of spiritual, moral, and medical changes, and about hearts that break and stop suddenly, but not from inevitable decline. "When they cannot take any more," she said, "they just stop." She yearned to travel far away, but most days she was content to stay home and lie in the sun. She had been told sunshine possesses curative powers and that the air it passes through should move through windows and pervade the inside of homes and rooms, into the smaller rooms where wet clothes are hung to dry, and therefore onto bodies and furniture and tabletops, extending its cleansing and healthy effects to homey, familiar things.

Nadia's kind of faith in the world, like the willingness to convince and "conquer without conception,"[6] is matched by her fiery sense of justice and her discourse on reason and the importance of writing, reading, and sharpening one's mind. "Did you ever want to learn to read?" I asked her one afternoon. She didn't really answer, but she said that in old age, the more one attempts to understand exactly how the world works and why people disappoint us, the more one feels defeated. She confesses her own mind is less agile than it was, she cannot read or write, she never could, and now her patience for new and different things has diminished. There is also no room for calamity in her life. If a single tragedy transpires, she says, her heart will immediately stop. More generally, she has a proclivity for candor.

And because she did not tell me why she wanted to lie down first thing in the morning or how she slept at night, I did not ask about her dreams. In a routinized, less keen, and more obtuse way, I only asked if she was physically comfortable—knowing her back, legs, and rheumatic hands bothered her—but never if she actually enjoyed having her own private bedroom where, as Le Corbusier said, one could "walk at ease," stretch oneself, and where "each thing can be put at once in its right place."[7]

The things we asked each other and answered were more like zigzags. We found ourselves in the space of a shared mother tongue and in the grip of words and silence, but also in the rough outline of an undecided relationship. I had hired her to come to my apartment to sleep at night, so I would not be alone. She once told me she had never had a room in her life, not in her father's house nor in her husband's, where she knew she could not dream of it, and that not many people in the country had a room of their own. But now, like a *Bibi*, lady of the house, she is on the high floor of a new concrete apartment building close to the Kabul River with views of the Hindu Kush Mountains and their undulating foothills, the green-domed local mosque, and the bustling neighborhood of Qala-e-Fathullah.

She said sometimes at night in bed, she would lie and imagine herself lying in her bed in her bedroom on the sixth floor of the apartment building in the center of Kabul and feel like a queen. Living there made her feel different, better about herself, and she told everyone about the apartment *emirates* (towers) that were new and modern, in stark contrast to the Soviet mass-built gray and dreary apartment blocks in the neighborhood of Microrayan. She said she used to admire those, years ago, but now she can see they are plain and ugly. Her perspective is different. She tells everyone who calls or visits her about the windows, tiled and heated floors, her own bathroom, electric heating, and her general sense of well-being. She tells them about the elevator that goes so fast but makes her nervous because there could be an electricity blackout while she is inside—or worse, what if a man is stuck with her? "Oh, Allah, you are the true protector," she says. One morning, she was at the elevator door with our next-door neighbor, a kind man in his forties, but she would not go in when the door opened. He kept asking her to go in first, and she would say: "Oh no. No, I could not possibly sir, please you first" and he would reply: "No, mother, you first, please I insist, you are my white-haired elder," and so on. She seemed to enjoy this back-and-forth for a bit, then abruptly grew tired of it, threw on her long flower-embroidered headscarf, and ran down the stairs. He took the elevator. "You can never *truly know* another person," she would say.

....

In his prologue to *The Kingdom of This World*, Alejo Carpentier proposes that European surrealism produces the marvelous "by means of conjuring tricks, bringing together objects which would never normally meet: the old and fraudulent story of the chance encounter of the umbrella and the sewing machine on an operating table, which spawned the ermine spoons, snails in a rainy taxi, and the lion's head in a widow's pelvis of the surrealist exhibitions."[8] His point is that surrealism is both customary and absurd, and it cannot evoke the power of the marvelous or the transformation of reality, whatever that might be. The artistic representation and discourse of the marvelous fails to account for the extent to which the belief in "the marvelous in the real" is already an enormous, transformative power. Carpentier is also saying that miracles are not only about the enlarged domain of expectation but also the willingness to see in some previously ordinary, even banal fact of social life, a new and energizing potential, and thus, a kind of joy and "amplification of the measures and categories of reality, perceived with peculiar intensity due to an exaltation of the spirit which elevates it to a kind of "limit state."[9]

Nadia told me that those who do not believe in saints and angels cannot reasonably expect them to later intervene on their behalf when they are in trouble. Belief and expectation cannot be too far apart from each other. But the home has a certain dignity, and the miracles and blessings inside it, she said, are revealed if one believes a home is different from everything outside it. The room and the street are not the same thing: One could look out at the street from a window, but those on the street should not be able to look back in. "One must never let any stranger into the home or reveal the affairs of the home to the outside world. Every window needs curtains," she instructed. A home is not marvelous, but it also is not merely a structure with windows or just another thing to build or possess; it touches on matters of the imagination, the heart, and therefore life and death. After being stuck in a torrential downpour in Berlin, reminiscent of a "primeval forest," and having no direction at all, Benjamin stumbled upon the same truth and recalls the life-giving feeling of reaching "the bronze lions' mouths on our front door with their rings that were now life belts."[10]

And when Benjamin writes about the confidence and prosperity in the bourgeois person's house, he describes the opposite impulse as a street-facing openness: "The domestic interior moves outside. It is as though the bourgeois were so sure of his prosperity that he is careless of façade, and can exclaim: My house, no matter where you choose to cut into it, is façade. . . . The street becomes room and the room becomes street. The passerby who stops to look at the house stands, as it were, in the alcove."[11]

I think my home and her room were a kind of escape for Nadia: her inside and outside, a place where she slept, left during the day, and returned at night; she once quipped that the best part of the day was coming home to her new room, her shelter for the night. Relative to other commodities, houses stand not on their feet but on heads full of ideas. In the late 1950s, my mother would play "house" with her friends. They would play with their dolls using the trees in their long, terraced garden in Kabul: One large, beautiful tree was their doll's father's house, and the other, smaller surrounding trees were all future husbands and their homes. House, husband, and father were the same thing. In turn, each of them would bequeath one of the dolls to a tree, pushing it in a wooden wheelbarrow to her fate, and they would fake tears of separation, lament, and then sit under the tree alongside the newly married doll in her new "home." On one impassioned occasion, my mom's doll divorced after a few minutes, telling the tree, through my mom's voicing: "I've had enough of you! You make my heart feel closed. I want to return to my father's house." She ran back to the father tree with her doll and told it all her marriage woes.

Nadia's childhood, a decade earlier than my mother's, was a time of hard, concentrated modernity, especially in Kabul, where iron, steel, and great public works were more visible than ever before. Between 1943 and 1946 the Royal Afghan Public Works Ministry placed "urgent" orders for fifty tons of dynamite for road building in the mountains, heavy-duty power and drag shovels, pile drivers (from Chicago and Milwaukee), crawler-mounted power shovels from Ohio for canal construction, 315 tons of reinforced steel, building materials (there was a global scarcity of wire nails at the time), and seismological and meteorological instruments.[12] The earlier suspicions of European government officials that factories in Kabul were secretly being used for bombmaking by Bolshevik agents like Dr. Abdul Hafiz had largely dissipated, and imports were skyrocketing so much that more goods were being ordered than could be supplied by the United Kingdom, United States, or India alone.

The dreams of modernity and of a modern city filled with new and more solid, but also smaller, delicate things pressed on. They were part of a growing expectation. New objects began to fill homes and businesses

FIGURE P.1 The austere form of this fort-like house echoes architectures of defense and endurance, evoking the house as not just a shelter but a philosophical and material threshold. Kabul. Photographer: Burke. Source: Album photo 430/3, photo 174, India Office Records, British Library.

too: hedge cutters, wall sockets, white enamel bathtubs, Bakelite and porcelain ceiling roses, stainless steel cutlery from Thomas Turner and Company (Sheffield), table knives with ivoried handles, meat choppers, sugar tongs, ice-cream freezers, household scales, letter scales (also used for income tax purposes), Wilkinson's tailor scissors, and Vulcan hair clippers. The furniture factory in Kabul ordered one hundred saw blades, twenty-four mortising machines, and sixteen chisels with core drivers.[13] The total weight of items ordered was more than two thousand tons. But perhaps most tellingly, because the house is never severed from the desire to look outside, and thus to be elsewhere, there was a surge in the demand for windows and for sixteen thousand yards of green window screens.[14] These made the difference between inside and outside, and between a home and an ordinary house.

Color and paint were everywhere. Spanish brown, bright red ochre, deep blue, mid-green, jet black, burnt sienna, lemon chrome, sweet yellow, straw, and middle Chinese green were ordered in dozens of tons for painting homes. White oil paint was used on ceilings, factories, buildings, schools, and government ministries. Copal varnish was used inside mosques. One government school in Kabul, the War Ministry, and a sugar factory 160 miles away in Baghlan were all painted exactly the same shade of ultramarine blue.[15] Nadia grew up in this vivid, more open era surrounded by color, the building up of the city, and the promises of modernity. And today as well, the city is still in the same process; the building of workplaces and neighborhoods gives people a sense of closeness-in-change. The detached, windowed homes—ranging from modest to gilded, gated monstrosities—reflect the desire for a private life with the possibility of looking out at others on the street. Like before, for those who want to live in modern and secure homes, the materials for building, furnishing, and segregating come from abroad, previously as glossy images in magazines and now on television, which Nadia watches whenever she can.

But no house or social relation between things could have prepared her for the growing unease that came with old age, or the divide between literate and illiterate people that determined fortunes and lives. She told me it was now, in 2013, common to hear that people were producing papers against one another, even within families. Kids were producing false documents, birth certificates, and counter-deeds, usually to take their parents' home or money from them. It was not quite the world of Nikolai Gogol's *Dead Souls*, but for her it was close enough. There was a lot of scheming and deception, and the added power of the written word made these more violent. And it was not just a matter of writing, even though writing intensified these patterns. She said bad words also played a role because bad words come from bad thoughts that are at the origin of the evil plans later put in motion.

Violence, Hannah Arendt argues, is different from strength and power because it needs implements, and because it "harbors within itself an additional element of arbitrariness."[16] Those implements include writing and people's words. The violence of old age and illiteracy is the unknown quality of Nadia's future. She accepts that her own body will increasingly betray her, that her body will slow down and fall apart, and that these infirmities are part of the obvious changes of life in this world. Nadia grapples with the fact that we always live in our bodies ("I accept death but I do not want to suffer in pain") and in a society with others, some of whom have money, power, bad thoughts, more powerful bodies, and mechanisms to kill and destroy with, meaning that evil is always possible. She does not take for granted that any of her relationships will last for the rest of her life. For her it seems that with age the small spaces between people are eventually "lit up by an almost intolerable, piercing clarity in which they are scarcely able to survive."[17]

Nadia's husband, severely hunchbacked and illiterate like her, died around the age of one hundred in 2016. "I've seen all the kings," he said. When I called Nadia in Kabul from New York to give my condolences, she told me she wished that all the years he lost (how many was she thinking?) would be added to the lives of her friends and to mine, and she said if I was feeling up to it, I should come around for a mourning lunch. In the last years of his life, he worried about his daughter, who can read and write. He feared she would steal the deed to his house or produce a counterfeit copy of her own. He slept with it at night, fearing she would bribe a government or court official or corrupt judge and put "everything, the whole of it, everything in our life" in her name. If she didn't do it of her own volition, they feared her husband would drag her into it. The hardest thing to understand, he would say, is another person. One afternoon he visited me after the bodies of a mother and daughter were found, beaten to death and barely covered up, in an alleyway behind their neighborhood. "These things happen," he said. I asked if he truly believed his daughter would betray him after a lifetime, owing simply to the fact that she could write. "What do you know? For the sake of a house," he said, "people do anything!" Then he asked me for a Coke.

Loneliness and old age, like family and the inside of a home, are about language and silence. There are exactly two courses of action: one can speak or not. And writing, Freud proposes "in its origin is the voice of an absent person."[18] When I asked Nadia what she thought about her daughters reading and writing (all three of them are literate), she turned the question around and asked why I do it so much. When I was in Herat a year prior to meeting Nadia, a little boy of five or six saw me writing in my notebook and asked, "So do you walk around with that all day and write everything?" In Nadia's case the matter is simpler and more personal: There are too many words in language, and they are more difficult when they are arranged on paper like the teeth on a comb.

If she could become literate magically or through one act of sheer will-power, she would do it in a heartbeat. It would give her latitude and connect her to the world and to many more people. But the neatness of what is put on paper does not match the way the words occur to her in her mind or resonate with her general style of life. I offered to read on her behalf whenever she needed it, but she said she is never involved with paperwork and that even when she is, it does not corrupt her, because her thoughts and memories are full of good things and good people. I took this to mean that if alphabetic writing baffles her, she has recourse to her own mind and to the memory of language, which she believes to be more reliable. Besides, she said, paperwork is the problem of young people and the rich.

Different kinds of voices reach her. She often proclaims that she loves living in a modern society. There is mass media: ninety-six television stations, sixty-five radio stations, her favorite Turkish soap operas, and more than nine hundred print publications she cannot read. She does not know these numbers, but it is their proliferation she claims to enjoy. And she is glad other women are reading, and doing much more than that; she sits within an inch of the television screen, almost attaching herself to it, to take it all in and see their lives up close. We regularly watched the Turkish soap opera *Öyle Bir Geçer Zaman ki* (Time goes by) in which Captain Ali Akarsu, the husband, cheats on his wife, Cemile, with a blond European woman. "A fool in a funny hat if there ever was one!" Nadia said. She hated Ali. These were moments when I thought of the television as an extension of her "whether of skin, hand, or foot," and I was convinced it affected her "whole psychic and social complex."[19] During the news hour, she would sit farther away and curse under her breath. She told me the politicians were old and useless. They walked around with pens, signed their names on everything, and tore up bits of paper when it suited them, and they took all the money and land. But even during periods of high inflation, when cash was tight and talk of corruption was omnipresent, she redecorated and painted her home.

The sense of a plan and detailed scheme for achieving something was circulating in the city and across the country; it was winnowing with and without the details, facts, and numbers through television and radio into homes during the noon and 6 p.m. newscasts as the promise of a new government and social order. Nadia was buoyed by some of these forecasts, but on other days knew better than to believe that having a plan meant either peace after war or peace during war. Huge swaths of the country were not under government control, which made the plans more important, secretive, and ambiguous than ever before. Nadia said the problem is that nobody knows where to begin because other people cannot be known to us, and this has been true for all of time in "all of history" as she sees it. I imagine that for her, individual memories of a grievance are like persons figured in a photograph and drifting, as Sartre writes, "between the shores of perception, between sign and image, without ever approaching either."[20]

Her possibly violent son-in-law mistreats her favorite, literate daughter. Her daughter has the power of the word, and he is irresponsible and contemptible. Her daughter would run away to her parents' house, then return to him soon after, leaving Nadia confused but determined to come up with a plan of her own to put an end to it.

NADIA: She is better off in her old hunchback of a father's house!

AUTHOR: Yes! How should we do this? We can also bring her here to the apartment. We will hide her.

NADIA: No, that is a terrible plan. Look at me asking a girl who has never married how to run away from a man's house!"

Most days would start for her with natural light and boldness but then, like clutter in her path, an inertia and rethinking would set in and change her aim and outlook. She changed her mind when she wished. She proclaimed how difficult her life was because of her illiteracy. Then she said she wanted nothing to do with the new way of being she saw all around her, which included reading and writing. She would become cautious, baffled by the old habits of killing, revenge seeking, and bad words. She was happy her grandsons were in school and learning to read and write, but given the numerous suicide bombings in the city, what, she asked, would she do with herself, if they were killed? To me it seemed that if there was a bold opening or radical perspective—something like the call of the other and the city in the grand sense, evoking the vivid "panorama of dialectical images" Benjamin associates with his vision of Paris as a scene of possibilities—that the event lost its excitement and left her behind to discern its remainders.[21]

AUTHOR: Do you speak to your children about the things you fear?

NADIA: Some things I tell them. Some things I do not!

AUTHOR: What kind of things?

NADIA: They don't have much time. Running here and there. They are making a living.

AUTHOR: Yes, they work hard.

NADIA: Work! Work! Work! It is like you and all your writing. What about taking care of their parents? Why do you think people bring children into the world, then?

AUTHOR: What do you most want in life?

NADIA: For my children to live long, prosperous lives, of course!

. . . .

Thinking about windows and outlook Walter Benjamin also wrote: "The interest of the panorama is in seeing the true city—the city indoors. What stands within the windowless house is the true. Moreover, the arcade, too, is a windowless house. The windows that look down on it are like loges from which one gazes into its interior, but one cannot see out these windows to anything outside. (What is true has no windows; nowhere does the true look out to the universe.)"[22] Thinking about her window and the happiness of others, the Iranian modernist poet Forough Farrokhzad wrote: "If you come to my house, friend / bring me a lamp and a window I can look through / at the crowd in the happy alley."[23]

Windows are not only about light but also perception and truth and the return of the other. The panorama reveals the city that lies within, in the arcade, behind the door, in passageways and alleys and in the windowless house as the enclosure of a reality. The truth of the city hidden in its interior does not seek our gaze. But the window reveals the street, the crowd, the other, and the facade that is everything and has its own truth revealed but only through the gaze and the help of the gift of light and an opening.

For Nadia the truth is not enclosed or removed from the world of the window or gaze. Seeing the truth is a question of interpretation not as a distortion of reality but an image of that distortion in her mind's eye: She sees her world, city, and relations for what they are, mutable phenomena she cannot control or prevent from becoming something else. Husbands die. Children grow distant. Elevators get stuck. Kings vanish; politicians replace them. Neighbors become violent. Her open window onto the city street; her recommendation to close the curtains; the inside of her room; the inviolable sanctity of the home; her concerns and ambivalence about her children, her mind and body, the future, the government, the paperwork, betrayal and dirty hearts, Captain Ali Akarsu from the soap opera— all of these are an introduction to how to think about the other and the problem of interpretation in collective life, but also about the other side of truth and knowledge that reveals itself in the gap between self and other, speech and writing, the breakdown of collective thought and the transcendence of that failure in order to gesture, dream, sacrifice, and say something other than this.

These are flashes of memory and history but also a history of language-encounters that transform how she views her life. In Nadia's imagination of others, there is a sense of indeterminacy whereby the people in her life, and their subjectivities, agendas, and desires, become other than they are. This indeterminacy has nothing to do with text or discourse, but it is nonetheless discernable to her through their words and actions and exemplifies a textual practice in the broadest, most dynamic sense. In her encounters, through her language and shared memories, the deferral of meaning enables her to keep open a space in her mind—an ethical choice rooted in the recognition of the impermanence of life, relationships, and even language itself—and it transcends mere ambivalence or her belief in kismet. This improvisational openness embodies an ethic of transgression rather than conformity, enabling her to encounter those she already knows anew within the realm of language, where the fantasy of identity is repeatedly displaced by a metonymic and radical otherness.

Seen in this light, a language-encounter, as the concept of arche-writing also suggests, encompasses knowing the other and recording memory, historical events, desire, death, translation, and absence. In this way, the release she envisions becomes a more radical freedom of existence. It is a way of living that continually redefines itself through her pursuit of understanding others and the difference in historical time such that she is always writing, *sous rature*, but still writing. For me, this constellation of concepts is best approached through detours and by demonstrating the discontinuous process of thinking and knowing the other and its implications for our understanding of symbolic life. It is also best captured by a mode of ethnographic writing that draws on the insights of literary and psychoanalytic theory to accomplish a close reading of those realities where the fantasy of self and knowing come undone; in other words, a perusal of traces, cracks, and detours that operate as the principle of collective consciousness in a world with a terrifying void at its center.

To pursue these detours is to approach them as an open-ended text, full of ambiguities and, as Roland Barthes describes, a world of voices and words ad infinitum, a "tissue of citations,"[24] through which the idea of signification is displaced by the counter-theological practice of reading the phenomena through which all identity, including that of subjects, authors, and concepts, is lost. Encounters within and between ethnographic openings are marked by a caesura in meaning such that the question of who and what the other is in relations of love, absence, historical memory, and practices of translation is radically undone. Yet, it is precisely in this undoing that a symbolic order emerges and suggests to us that collective life depends on the ability to arrest meaning and identity. For me and my process of writing, Nadia's relentless insistence that things can always be other than they are opened a series of questions and quilting points that move through the chapters and hold together a dialogue between two dimensions of this project: the place of subjectivity in language and the new forms of social violence that raise the question of how to imagine collective life amid profound upheaval.

Cracks and Detours

What we cannot reach by flying we must reach limping.
. . . The Book tells us it is no sin to limp.
—AL-HARIRI OF BASRA, from the *Maqâmât* (translation by
Friedrich Rückert)

. . . to diverge ever more widely from its original course
of life and to make ever more complicated *détours* before
reaching its aim of death. These circuitous paths to death
. . . would thus present us today with the picture of the
phenomena of life.
—SIGMUND FREUD, *Beyond the Pleasure Principle*

The topic of this book can be envisaged in the image of a crack rising to
the surface of collective life and consciousness in Afghanistan. It moves
across subjective relations, forms of speech, and action characterized by
loss, not knowing, ambivalence, and sometimes a tragic arc where a social
bond was hoped for instead. How far it will grow is impossible to say. It
emerges as a historical dilemma, and in the contemporary moment it fissures through the transformative, difficult relationship between language
and being. *Shelter for the Night* pursues this crack through a series of what
I call *language-encounters* in the domains of war, interpersonal betrayal,
and translation, and it reveals how these bear on possibilities of collective
existence. I invoke language-encounters because the content of my ethnographic stories is myriad and complex, ranging from deception to love,
sacrifice, and accusation. Yet, each story shares the sense that the place of
language in social life is marked by rupture and discontinuity rather than
coherence or shared meanings. In other words, by thinking of language as
a space of encounter, where the words, discourses, and interpretations of
others shape possibilities of being, I seek to bring to the surface the idealism

and violence my interlocuters experience in their lives and the cascade of domino effects they struggle to contain.

The unifying theme of this project emerges in relation to a larger post-structural analysis of the forms of sociality no longer defined by the cohesion of symbolic life but by its rupture and discontinuity; that is, the play of representations, signifying practices, decentered political forces, insurgency, urban life, multiple crossings, and interpretive anguish that mark the experience of subjectivity and new, often devastating forms of social violence that unexpectedly enable collective life and survival.[1] The image of a crack captures the fact that these two sides are not separated. It also connects a series of encounters and sites with my larger question of how the difference separating the speaking (the symbolic) from an immediate identification (becoming, possessing, and embodying) can be imagined. In a sense, the political and subjective problem of becoming other, estranged, fungible, or dead is also a moment when this gap—across which language ideally would facilitate communication and understanding—fails to hold the symbolic and real apart.

Conceptually, I approach this failure in two ways: my interlocuters' experience of life and society closing in on them (the closing of the gap), and the opening of something beyond that, a crack or fissure in which social life remains possible.[2] In 1952 Frantz Fanon wrote about the terrifying logic of the former, a nightmare of waking life, in his description of the Malagasy people, who dream of pathways, guns, and oxen, among other things. The nature of collective trauma is such that Fanon suggests even in the oneiric world, the rifle is not a symbol for something else (it is not power, the phallus, and so on). Instead, the rifle is merely denuded of its own symbolic capacity as an ambiguous sign.[3] It is a weapon of death, and its emergence is how the real interrupts the dream rather than the dream being an escape from the real. Some of this logic will appear in the pages of this book and suggest to us that when the metonymic quality of a signifier fails (that is, when a sign does not defer its meaning to another sign) ambiguity cannot be tolerated and we are no longer insulated from the real. In other words, when language fails to enable communication, mediate between individuals, or represent a shared reality, the nature of social violence also radically shifts. It becomes intensified and deadlier in ways that are tragic and often difficult to contain. In the chapters of this book, social violence occurs as one dimension of all the ethnographic encounters I seek to mediate. Examples are the story of Sami, a failed suicide bomber, who is betrayed by his mother almost to the point of his death; the urbanite translators whose condescension in relating to rural persons becomes deadly for both sides; and the place of translation in modern, cosmopolitan thought, in real-world, irrational violence, and even in the realm of love, which gives us more than we expect.

As an analytic device, language-encounters include the obvious aspects of linguistic life, such as the place of dialogic speech in establishing or destroying social relations, practices of translation and intelligence gathering, testimonial strategies, illiteracy, and rhetorical life in general. But I invoke *encounters* because there is a dimension beyond dialogic speech that touches on questions of life and death, what it means to know something, *how* we know, new forms of accusation, and the complex mediations that transform subjectivity from the fantasy of being into the most primal place where we experience difference and signification (what Jacques Lacan describes as a signifying cut) even as that experience cannot always be put into words.[4] When I think about this, one poignant moment rises to the top. During his trial, Sami was asked about his intention and willingness to die, and he replied: "Oh, I cannot say what I mean!" And yet, Sami later did speak, perhaps most strikingly when he addressed me directly in court to say he was tortured by the Afghan police with a glass Coke bottle. Why does he address the judges through me, and why does he call me "sister"? What is he unable to say?

The unsayable captures what Benjamin describes as "not only the flow of thoughts but their arrest as well" and the inevitable but generative failure of signification. By this I mean the failure and impossibility of signs and meanings totally coinciding between the sayable and the said, intent and reception, sound and mishearing, the hard blows of life and blowing up one's life, translation and its others; in other words, the kind of coinciding that would bring the communicative act and the movement of signs to a point of rest and felicity: a kind of death, really. For me, this noncoinciding captures the crack where Sami is both defeated by language and turns to it in a fateful bid to make his condition known to others. The crack is marked by a caesura in thought and expression whose force of immobilization and excess leads to a metonymic opening: sometimes to a halt or stutter, at other times to voice and the outpouring of words and catharsis.

In 1920, when Freud formulated his theory of the uncanny, the psychic rupture that constitutes the foundation of subjectivity, he also introduced the concept of Thanatos, or the "death drive," as distinct from Eros, the life-affirming drive rooted in pleasure. Freud arrived at this idea through his study of dreams, accidents, and child's play. He wrote that the death drive does not reveal an impulse toward literal death or destruction but is instead a fundamental principle of movement, a flow of "ever more complicated *détours*" and "circuitous paths" through which the subject creatively lives, evades, dreams, and pushes back against the specter of total dissolution.[5]

This alternation and movement, including toward an elsewhere both past and future, is a radical but essential dimension of language irreducible to the uncertainties of interpretive life. It includes that but is fundamentally more. It is about the persistence of a life-sustaining and aporetic opening that recurs, creates detours, haunts us, holds knowledge in suspension, and emerges when we least expect it to include people we may or may not be able to entrust with our lives; and it suggests that desire for a particular kind of "Other" in collective life only operates through deferral and movement.[6] In this book, alternation and movement are the groundless ground on which a series of events and pharmakonic worlds emerge in relation to new forms of political action, intersubjectivity, global imaginaries, and translational power.

SHELTER FOR THE NIGHT

Shelter for the Night started as an attempt to grasp the formation of a highly speculative economy and to understand the notion and transmutation of value as it enabled new forms of exchange, extractive violence, and modes of living in Kabul. In Afghanistan the spectacle of war gripped the national imagination as a source of fantastic power, a kind of theater where war created spectacular value even as it destroyed so much through intensive bombing and combat-related damage. In this context, from 2010 to 2013, I witnessed a collective fantasy about value creation in the hydrocarbons and minerals underground and the commodification of linguistic and cultural expertise, translation, spoken English, and literacy, all of which were incorporated into the apparatus of a US- and NATO-led counterinsurgency campaign.

But through the detours of fieldwork inside courtrooms, mosques, the Green Zone, government ministries, national and colonial archives, security compounds, corporate headquarters, and people's homes, I encountered a different kind of dilemma: the tension between engaging with others through a shared language and the recognition that a more general failure of representation is part of the experience of collective life when communication cannot be taken for granted. And yet, the other side of this predicament is that, even amid a military and political culture of intensified surveillance, arrest, and interrogation with far-reaching and devastating effects, my interlocuters spoke freely with me. They asked me what I had come to learn through them and how my thinking evolved, and they shared either insights they felt they understood or questions that continued to elude them. The majority of my interlocuters were incorporated into facets of a war economy ranging from governmental to the corporate and scientific worlds of mining and linguistic translation. Others worked inside the militarized Green Zone in Kabul's Wazir Akbar Khan neighborhood as security guards, cooks, cleaners, or drivers, or they were entirely removed from this scene, living in poverty-stricken neighborhoods where they were unemployed, subject to restrictions on mobility into central Kabul, and usually illiterate. Still others I encountered through a dialectic of observation and the gaze, mediated by two distinct experiences of the law: those within the dangerous reach of its corporeal and punitive practices; and my experience, observing these practices unfolding within courtrooms and high-stakes tribunals—spaces where I, too, was subject to observation and judgment and to address without dialogue.

As I will show, the predicament of these trials is not only the violence of veridical or regulative ideals but the fundamental problem of knowing, encountering, and communicating with others. When both the judges and defendants presume these others are dissimulating their "true" (*asli, raast*) selves, this raises questions about the place of "reality" (*haqiqat, vaqiat*) in social life. This predicament reflected a general sentiment about the nature of political life, in particular distrust in the notion that through representation by the state or national politicians, recourse to political violence could be supplanted by dialogue and mediation. More specifically, in the lead-up to the 2014 presidential election between Dr. Ashraf Ghani and Dr. Abdullah, delayed for months by widespread fraud, a pervasive sense of falsehood shaped views of Afghanistan's future. This distortion reflected a new, pragmatic judgment of others and the social milieu, which emerged alongside crime, insurgency, counterinsurgency tactics, heightened security, and black-market profiteering.[7]

To many Afghans, the state was an ineffective entity mired in corrupt or criminal schemes; it was on the verge of collapse, complicit with insurgents, or controlled by an oligarchy in Kabul and Dubai. People believed the Taliban were biding their time in places like Logar or Ghazni, awaiting an opportunity to take the city but hindered by poor and unpredictable road conditions. Other rumors suggested the Taliban used their own currency in villages; administered a parallel system of justice; operated legal and illegal mines; negotiated with foreign governments like those of Qatar, Saudi Arabia, Pakistan, and the United States (a rumor that turned out to be true in the lead-up to the Afghan government's collapse in August 2021); and executed Afghans for crimes that included being translators or soldiers in the Afghan National Army.

The fluctuating prices of commodities like oil, gas, land, housing, and food became part of a discourse of speculative yet reasonable truths that gained epistemological force. Rumors circulated that government ministers had transferred their funds to foreign banks in Dubai and Abu Dhabi and were preparing to flee the country. People lined up at Kabul Bank, Afghan International Bank, Azizi Bank, Afghan National Bank, and other banks to withdraw their money, fearing a collapse like the one in 2012, when deposits worth $900 million were embezzled by bank officials and people with government ties, including former President Karzai's brother.[8]

Corruption (*fesad*) and fraud were suspected to underlie every aspect of economic life and were braided into a discourse of the other that addressed violent forms of gain and the fundamental dissonance between one's outward appearance (*zahir*) and inner truth (*batin*). Precisely because language and representation are defined by a signifying function, it follows that political disillusionment was not limited to abstract critiques of governance but also shaped collective consciousness and the struggle to render oneself or others legible. People experienced this representative failure within contexts of social violence, where attempts to find answers, others, and connection seemed to produce the opposite effect: People dissimulated, conned, betrayed, and condemned one another without clear intentions or narratives. Here, subjective life was carried out through rumor, narrative, fantasy, and accusation—not through knowing but through a continuous *working-through* in which language generated referents and spectral effects that were reasonably present but never fully manifest.

In this negativity, new social phenomena came into existence that were hard to communicate or "represent" and might even refuse to be contained by language. And yet through all this, people continued to narrate stories, to translate their experiences into words, and in the process helped to create worlds that were fundamentally different but that also made sense. When Sami said, "Oh, I cannot say what I mean!" he was also saying that the nature of saying can signify something altogether different from what seems to be said or expected or experienced. On one level we can think of this communication breakdown as being due to the putatively exceptional state of war and upheaval, but on another level, war reveals truths that were always already existing, making it possible to talk about things that were before invisible and unsayable.

On that threshold of translation, I reflect on language-encounters as a relation between representational failure and a collective unconscious in which deferral, play, and detours converge. How do we witness and translate moments when language fails to deliver or delivers something other than what we hoped for? How do we move in a pharmakonic world where the erratic aspects of language coincide with the formation of collective life and its unannounced "elsewhere"?

WRITING IT DOWN

Cracks, gaps, and fissures in the symbolic and in the fabric of knowing and living with others—who carries them and how do they bear on people's lives? What is at stake in writing about this era of Afghan society as a site for the examination of symbolic and psychic life? How does a certain form of equivocation become the basis for collective life and relationality? Inspired by a psychoanalytic ethos of listening attuned not only to what is said but also to what is not said or is stuttered or misheard, I draw on the idea of ethnographic concepts and ethnography as a "concept-making genre."[9] Together, these perspectives inspire a mode of anthropological writing that invites dialogic voices, primarily those of my interlocutors but also those of the theorists of modernity and psychic life who inform my thinking. Drawing on both philosophical and psychoanalytic thinkers and a rich body of works from a poststructural canon, my approach emphasizes the fragmentation of collective life not as a clash of opposing ideas, forces, or discourses but as fractures embedded within their very conditions of possibility.[10]

The book centers on four ethnographic stories and one historical narrative, exploring the uneasy relationship between forms of social violence and living made possible in language, including, historically, the language of modernity in the colonial world, versus a more ambiguous equivocation that, while not undoing this violence, signals possibilities for recuperating and recasting possible futures. In the realm of experience, the violence of this duality is vivid, especially when signification is displaced by direct violence, but it has another dimension where forms of deferral and uneasy knowing and living-with gesture toward other forms of social life. On one hand, this dimension is about subjectivity in language and the sense, intuition, political frustration, and social reality of psychic and social fragmentation, in other words, those moments when people cannot be shielded from the violence of the nightmare. And on the other, it is about persons and dilemmas that are open-ended, expressed as the problem of writing or speech, understood as violence or love, sometimes tragic but always about the way signification creates new, arbitrary sites and ways of being that render social life imaginable. This, I think, is the dream.

The analytic encounters in the chapters trace the twists and detours my interlocuters experience in a period of national disillusion, following the deferrals, betrayal, and engagements that reveal how a social imaginary and political unconscious emerge in linguistic encounters with others. For example, a false abduction in chapter 1 becomes the problem of a real accusation of abduction between husband and wife in chapter 2. The unexpected arrival that becomes deadly in the story of Zia in chapter 4 is contained through the exchange of an enigmatic gift for his friend Matin in chapter 5. I situate these stories within a dense and fraught political and economic context in which individuals find themselves separated not only by the power of their speech or the lack of power of speech but also the binaries of inside and outside that characterize social life amid an insurgency: inside or outside of the law; on one side or another of moving battle lines, interrogations, or scenes captured in a photograph; in or out of love, with or without the power to write. I suggest that in these stories, ordeal and hope each appear, like a trace that cannot be explicitly described but that we follow through descriptive writing in different places. In essence, my aim is to engage in the kind of exploration that ethnography does best.

Chapter 1, "What's the Use Between Death and Glory?" mediates a series of knowledge gaps; the aporia resulting from illiteracy, gossip, and the breakdown of a local symbolic order that are not only sources of confusion but also catalysts for action, often with tragic consequences. In the dramatic court trial of Sami, a young man who attempted to carry out a suicide bombing at the Intercontinental Hotel in Kabul, a crime initially assumed to be tied to insurgent politics, we encounter a desperate act of love and sacrifice grounded in misunderstanding and the relationship between a man and the social norms he feels obligated to violate. Sami's story and testimony reveal his complex motive. He agreed to carry out the bombing in exchange for the release of his sister Mina, who had eloped with her lover but whom Sami falsely believed had been abducted by the Taliban. But his defiance of norms stems from a misunderstanding rooted in the limitations of language to convey shared meanings while also reflecting the simultaneous nature of *linguistic being*, in other words, he embodies both the rupture and sense in signification, the *différance* of meaning that is not fixed but deferred, without a final interpretation or ground to make his actions legible.

At the same time, I demonstrate that his action is not the consequence of a lack of true knowledge so much as it is fueled by the desire to know and take seriously the discourse of the other. Thus, his story unfolds in the space of juridical reason and its normative categories of good and evil, but also in two domains of language: the realm of speech, including his own, and the absence of writing that, through a profound distortion, is taken by others to mean he does not understand the nature of events and signs around him. It is here, in the collapse of knowing, being, and doing—in the idea that Sami, a simpleton, is exactly as he appears—that an ethic of radical devotion is informed by the knowledge found in the discourse of others.

Chapter 2, "Rumors of Love" is about the gift of love and the conceptual problem of the other amid the breakdown of social exchange. It follows the story of Sohrab, a young policeman whom his wife accuses of abducting her. I trace the emergence of desire both in the world of dialogue and in Kabul, the scene of intensified forms of insurgent and counterinsurgent activity, social anomie, and demilitarization. In this context, love, accusation, sacrifice, and absence recur as the problem of how to know the other: again, it is about the difference my interlocuters refer to as the *batin* (essence) and *zahir* (appearance) of subjective life as it is mediated by uncertain exchanges and speech. The second part of the chapter considers the nature of the accusation against Sohrab and the place of images, photographs, and testimony amid the loss of representative capacity and its unexpected recurrence.

Together, these two chapters trace multiple incoherencies and the idea of action and accusation each being mediated by the other. What do we know? How do we encounter a speech without writing and, sometimes, a speech without recourse to the fantasy that one can escape in the city, in love, in dialect, or in the interior world? I take up these concerns again in the second part of the book but in relation to translation as a metaphor for modern history and a form of engagement across historical lifeworlds and persons, and in rhetorical and dialogic life. In these chapters, the problem of the prior and the Afghan hinterland, imagined to be a linguistic scene that bears on the being of its inhabitants, guides my attempt to understand the status of wartime linguistic translation as a symbolic act of mediation inseparable from the gap between urban and rural life, logos and its mimesis, and the fear of the future as a return to the past.

Chapter 3, "The Alternation of World and Word" marks my conceptual turn toward the place of translation in the historical and contemporary experience of social difference. I take a broad perspective to consider the historical problem of translation as a concept-metaphor for global transformation, as Walter Benjamin and the nineteenth-century Afghan thinker Mahmūd Tarzī perceive it, as well as in the imperial experience of the Afghan frontier as a site of ideological danger and excess. This modernist history is crucial to mishearing, misinterpretation, and intersubjective violence in Afghan provinces, where translation is deployed as a cultural weapon in the Afghan War but is mired in the perception of Afghanistan as a hinterland in the global imaginary. By tracing the historical, conceptual, and ethnographic place of translation in encounters between places, lifeworlds, and persons, I illustrate how the nature of translation determines encounters with social difference—for example with the stranger, the "brute," or the outsider—and is a reflection of historical and national experience. I also examine how the violence of translation is the ideological heir to an earlier global moment when a fixation on oral culture and politics was inseparable from the fear that in an oral culture, where written propaganda is of little use, political momentum and rebellion against empire could be as straightforward as harnessing the most resonant and passionate forms of speech.

Chapter 4, "Discourses of Another Other" is about a scene of speaking and mode of being in language as commodified linguistic expertise. It examines translation as a porous, mobile form of relation that is about mediation, social difference, and existential violence. I trace the experiences of Zia, a wartime translator from Kabul, and his fear of the Afghan hinterland and its population. This is a population he is hired to represent as a translator but that he also perceives as an itinerant, irrational threat to purity and order in Kabul. I attempt to understand his anxiety in relation to the spatial and conceptual frontier he reckons with as a translator as well as in the idea of Kabul coming to terms with its own history as a center within peripheries. I limn a series of representational and narrative practices through which Zia inscribes the other as lacking reason and being prone to thievery, invasion, itinerancy, and impulsivity while constructing his own speech and subjectivity as the ideal. Through Zia's experiences, translation is caught in a crisis of representation that emerges through the metaphor of the stranger as an object of fear and is symptomatic of a crisis that unfolds as much in rural space as in certain voices and rhetorical lifeworlds that he deems strange and foreign. How are those voices spoken and heard? What is the price for his mediation? How does translation reveal a dangerous fixation with social difference?

Chapter 5, "Between Ground and Sky" follows the experiences of Matin, Zia's childhood friend and a fellow translator. I extend the analysis of translation to consider its symbolic mediation in the form of play, mimesis between insurgent and state security forces, uncanniness, and the complexity of gift exchange in lieu of violence. In expanding the idea of translation, I consider the mobile crossing of reason and its absence or perceived mimesis as part of the work and failure of translation but also as what opens the possibility for the gift. Again, what structures this chapter is an urban translator seeking out the rural persons on whose behalf he seeks to translate, while also narrating the fear of a return to the past in the future of his city. This chapter follows the logic of a chase in discourse and dialect and in the forms of reason, unreason, and symbolic activity that characterize life and the possibility of communication amid a grueling counterinsurgency campaign.

The epilogue, "A Vita Detoured," considers the vita (biographical sketch) as a text but also a path in life alongside the ethnographic phenomenon of sistering. I illustrate the ways of being, knowing, and calling on the other that defy the enclosure of tragic downfall and instead insist on new conditions of possibility to come.

DETOURS, ENCOUNTERS, CRACKS

At the heart of this book is the idea that the collective experience of language harbors an incessant desire for elsewhere, a drive toward something beyond the immediate, the said, or even the thought-image we take for granted as the thing in itself. This movement is intrinsic to signification, and it has profound consequences for the nature of collective life in which encounters with oneself and others (in dreams, translation, desire, and haunted action) are always incomplete and full of zigzags. What matters profoundly in this regard is that fissures emerge within this detour, without a transcendental ground, and that signification is not about the presence or absence of meaning but rather how it is *not where we expect*, or better yet, how it is precisely where we fail to look.

These detours, elusive and beyond our full understanding or control, are described by Michel de Certeau as both "the deceptive mask and the operative trace of events that organize the present."[11] They reveal how language, irrespective of the ways we intend to inhabit or use it, works through us "to signify something altogether different from what it says."[12] They suggest that the attempt to grasp modes of living and being must first confront the idea that consciousness and subjectivity are seized in the aporia of time, language, and the distortions of psychic life, a stratified terrain Freud compares in *Civilization and Its Discontents* to an ancient city of ruins governed by endless displacement and erasure, a place of metamorphosis without a map.

If Freud's ancient city of Rome is characterized by ruins and the buried buildings and strata that double as a metaphor for psychic life—the place where thought is concealed rather than consciously constructed—the same is true for the nature of psychic life and its forms of knowing and not knowing. Knowledge, especially in relation to the other, arises not in moments of deliberation but precisely when we do not know we are thinking. In this sense, speech, thought, intention, and consciousness are fundamental failures born from the psychic and trace structures that bring them forth, each an "act of homage to missed reality" that remains unresolvable "for an anthropology which is not freed from the naive realism of the object."[13]

To demonstrate this erratic dimension of language and its "elsewhere" requires engaging with the pharmakonic worlds that emerge from the fact that language, whether spoken or written, is fundamentally structured by the movement of difference it seeks to overcome.[14] At the same time, I look at how this gives rise to a series of atmospheric figures like uncanniness, ruin, sabotage, rumor, illiteracy, and excess and how these push on, tear, and linger at the edges of interpersonal and political life. And yet, there is an incompleteness in these spaces that, I argue, shows us the crossroad between the deferral of meaning as a condition for sociality, one that allows people to act, mediate, love, and speak into the void, and a renewal of imagined futures.

THE SIGNIFYING CUT

Detours, encounters, cracks: These terms anchor my engagement with the idea that language is never fully comprehensible, and that relations between people, including in desire or representation, are driven by displacement and what Lacan identifies as the discourse of the Other in unconscious life. In this sense, I want to reclaim the conceptual and philosophical legacy of psychoanalytic and literary thought to understand subjectivity in collective life as a site of fundamental incoherence where desire "envelops the pleasure of knowing" but is still "caught in the rails of metonymy, eternally extending toward the desire for something else."[15] For Lacan the elsewhere, the same idea he mobilizes against the bourgeois and conciliatory discourse of American ego psychology, is fundamentally topographic. It is a site of ontological insecurity I try to capture in the image of a crack that transforms subjectivity into a scene of radical undoing fractured by the same signifying chain that subverts knowledge and moves in unforeseeable ways to transform who we love, speak for, and sometimes destroy in the process.

But wherever there is a crack there is also psychic labor that spans the oneiric world of dreams, the work of culture (*Kulturarbeit*), and even processes of mourning and detachment, enabling us to find new objects and to give the world another chance. This labor is inherently psychic, collective, difficult, and occasionally dangerous; it forms the backbone of the stories in this book. These stories reveal encounters that belong to a symbolic order which might otherwise make translation, love, and trust possible but which is somewhere on the run. Yet, they also suggest that this very loss is deeply regenerative: It enables established, emerging, and approximate ways of thinking, relating, and working through in place of the agony of symbolic collapse or the paralysis of not knowing.

Although this book is not structured by the kind of rich dialogic relation João Biehl prioritizes in *Vita*, it is inspired by his poetic devotion to a proliferation of words, writing, and testimonies that inspire people to rethink "the literalism that made possible a sense of exclusion," and to "demand one more chance in life."[16] In this I am also in conversation with Stefania Pandolfo on the forms of ambivalence that constitute both psychic drives and the ethic of an ordeal to which "the subject is called to respond." Pandolfo situates this ordeal as an ethical break in the context of symbolic disorder and cultural pain, when generalized despair results in the spiritual condition of "soul choking" but remains part of a "pedagogy of the imagination . . . aimed at creating conditions in the heart for a renewed receptivity to the divine message."[17] This concept is partially reflected in the metaphor of hearts tightening or opening (*dil tangī* or *dil e bāz*) my interlocuters invoke as the process of either turning away from the social or giving it another chance. Seema Golestaneh reveals that such openings of the heart involve gnosis, or "unknowing" (*ma'rifat*), at the beginning rather than the conclusion of the life of the mind. Writing on Iranian Sufism, Golestaneh frames unknowing "as a fundamentally generative enterprise . . .

moving forward into the "nothing" until all life is lived at the level of an improvisatory gesture."[18]

Language-encounters begin with stories, words, dream-images, and rumors but encompass issues of desire, life and death moments, and the politics of the drive: the doing, acting, loving, sacrificing, and killing that produces excess in every relation and every effort to convey to others what a person means or intends to be.[19] But how do these encounters, including the forms of knowing and ignorance they entail, enable people to live with aporia? To compromise with each other during political and cultural upheaval?[20]

In the tragic stories of Sami and Sohrab, the uncertainty over what forms of knowledge and action to pursue become part of the encounter with others in language where narrative, rumor, and falsehood fragment subjectivity along a path of deferred meanings, meanings that expose new desires but also the old violence of how to constitute the self in relation to others. Both men are constituted, violated, and potentially violent amid voices, narrative gaps, rumors, and the words of others. And later, they are summoned and reconstituted through their own words in court, where dialogic exchange moves them through another interrogatory and truth-finding "itinerary of a signifier."[21]

When Sami learns that his sister, Mina, is missing, he relies on his mother to understand what eludes him because he is illiterate. The "meaning" of Mina's absence is produced later through his mother's discourse, a discourse that determines her own place in the story and reflects her fear of collective speech in the form of rumor and gossip in their local village. This fear of gossip generates the need for a story of "abduction" to circumvent the more vexing questions of What will people say? or Where has Mina *really* gone? This story, in turn, becomes the answer to Sami's desire to know and do more: to become the kind of subject who knows how to act in the world of rumors and who can return Mina to her rightful place in their home. His mother says his sister has been abducted, so he must do whatever it takes to free her.

Mina's absence and his mother's dialogue encompass the way action and desire are relayed through each other such that no single intention is legible to others and no single person is capable of controlling the outcome. Mina is possibly unaware of her mother's fabrication, Sami does not know Mina is in love and has eloped, and their mother cannot foresee the consequences of her words. The Taliban, who use their local knowledge to manipulate Sami into a suicide bombing by pretending to be Mina's captors, do not know if their dangerous gamble will pay off. The people in the Intercontinental Hotel that day had no idea what had almost befallen them.

For me, these moments of narrative and speculation mark the excess of social and intersubjective life that emerges in language but attaches itself to forms of action that are politically oriented but are not confined to the political sphere as such. I imagine that as words are exchanged, and the meaning of this story unfolds, so does Sami's internal conviction that he must sacrifice his own life and kill others that Mina may live. The more willing he becomes to sacrifice and kill, the more easily he is co-opted into a suicide bombing against the Afghan state. The disappearance of Mina is not only about where she might be but also about a moving predicament between subjects that is foundational to political and social violence; thus, these moments of blowback and nearly blowing up are also when symbolic disorder performs its most brutal, unforgiving violence.

RUMOR HAS IT

The absence of persons and reliable narratives, and the fact that being missing and being talked about as missing are not the same thing, open onto different forms of action and retaliation, onto different notions of symbolic return to one's "rightful" place. This is an order of speech that owes no loyalty to the truth. It is a two-faced kind of speech that, despite the collective understanding that it is not true (after all, we all know not to believe rumors) continues to accumulate power through its retelling.

In the ethnographic stories in this book, the deferral of meaning enables rumors to proliferate, not as falsehoods or deceptions per se, but as narrative drives that possess and compel individuals in powerful, sometimes violent ways. Where does a rumor begin and end? And how does it transform desire relative to fantasies of love and heroic action? In the criminal case against Sohrab, the threat of spreading rumors was one of the charges his wife raised against him: She accused him of forcibly abducting and marrying her on the threat that if she refused, he would spread rumors and put photographs of her up on walls and billboards around Kabul. In turn, Sohrab, who maintained his innocence and claimed he rescued her from her abusive mother through marriage, fears that rumors and gossip will circulate about him in the aftermath of his trial if word gets out that he, a former police officer, was arrested and charged with the abduction of a woman.

The alternation of rumors that are spread and deflected raises the question of the Other not as a predicament of desire or lack but as a dimension of knowledge irreducible to truth or logos. As a matter of historical and political experience, particularly during the acquisition of new communication technologies (such as the telegraph, telephone, and radio), this tension between the expressed and unexpressed, and between truthful discourse and deception, took on added significance. It shaped the collective consciousness of what it meant to communicate with the so-called third world, a world perceived to be overdetermined not by forms of communicable truth but by a proclivity for dissimulation. In other words, there is a world of alterity that does not disclose itself but moves dangerously through signifiers on the loose.[22]

In the contemporary moment, language-encounters, including the experience of love, reveal the limits of representation and the fluid tie between desire for a certain kind of self and other versus the absence or deferral of understanding of who one is, who one falls in love with, or what a shared future might entail. In this context, rumors and whispers are not the excess or remainder left behind by logos but its inviolable double, its other face and atmospheric manifestation. As Mladen Dolar provocatively suggests, this is the place where our fantasies of the "big Other" are met with something else entirely: "It is as if we have to do here with two opposing faces of the big Other, with no common measure: on the one hand, the big Other that can (and should) provide the epistemological foundation of proper knowledge, based on logos and aiming at truth; and, on the other hand, another big Other based on nothing but hearsay, on the wind, but nevertheless standing fast and sticking."[23]

Despite this porosity, rumors are powerful and possess a coherence ordinary language struggles to achieve such that "the other big Other is more powerful than the official and celebrated one; rumors, trivial and unfounded as they are, have the capacity to outwit logos, which seems to be no match for them."[24] Isn't this the appeal of gossip and rumors: the knowledge that they will achieve some effect irrespective of how untrue we know they are? This is an example of language and the word achieving the power not only to produce referents but also to "produce (the specter of) something that isn't there."[25] And once in motion, it is impossible to make a clean break because no matter how "untrue" the rumor is, it follows its object like a shadow. How can Sohrab defend himself against the rumor that he wanted to spread rumors? The point, as we will see in chapter 2, is not that either Sohrab or his wife lie to the court but that all speech is gossip insofar as there is no speech that lacks the cannibalism of untruth and is free from this "other" side of logos. Perhaps this is why, in response to the judge's questioning, Sohrab simply replies that he should have known better than to believe in Razia's declaration of love, to believe, in other words, in the one-sided truth of her words.

And yet there is another, more open-ended way of understanding this structural imbrication that is not one or the other but always dual. Desire that unfolds in response to the speech of the other is crucial to subjective undoing and to political and social violence. After all, these are stories of a failed suicide bombing of a hotel and an alleged abduction of a wealthy woman. And yet, each story bears the trace of something that cannot be contained by the narrative of abduction or violent sacrifice; each marks a moment when the ambiguities of meaning and claims of truth open a space of equivocation as the condition rather than just the violence of social life. After all, these are not simply stories of a failed suicide bombing or an alleged abduction; they are also a call to the other and the search for love.

DREAMWORK AND THE REAL

How else can we think about this kind of uncertainty? And where does it leave us? When Zia returned to Kabul from his translation missions in the countryside, he worried that his face would be recognized and that he would be killed in an act of revenge. Being seen for who he was and what he had done meant getting caught, and getting caught meant he was a dead man. His actions and the way he treated others elsewhere, in the places he always described in the language of distance and anachronism, followed him to Kabul, the city where he fantasizes that reason holds sway in lieu of blood codes and honor but where his eyes, facial expressions, clean-shaven face, sunglasses, and hats all become elements of danger. These were his urban means of camouflage and deception but no matter how hard he tried to hide, he still felt he was being seen without being able to return the look.

He only saw clearly in his dreams: He had a vivid nightmare about being recognized by a burly man who had previously encountered him during one of his "missions" and was now out to kill him. Fear and dream and repressed actions were part of the same overdetermined drive, a drive to kill that could only be seen, in other words condensed, into signs in the dream-world where the violence of the real was not experienced but translated through the symbolic language he woke up to and interpreted as a deadly serious warning to alter his appearance in Kabul.

In psychoanalysis, most clearly in Freud's *The Interpretation of Dreams*, the perpetual detours of understanding, and on occasion, their distillation in moments of knowing, serve as principles not only of psychic life but also of collective experience. The interplay between language and the deferral of knowing finds a powerful echo in the realm of dreams, where Freud's insights reveal how the enigmatic quality of a dream's manifest content (the memory we wake up with) stems from the simultaneity of effects formally articulated through the rhetorical tropes of metonymy and metaphor, a kind of rebus that uses images and symbols to translate abstract thought through *condensation* (metaphor or distillation) and *displacement* (metonymy or contiguity). The simultaneity and playfulness of effects operate as a structural grammar of the unconscious that translates, subverts, and distills the diversity of the dream into overdetermined signs. Thus, the idea that the structure of language exists in the unconscious, later theorized by Lacan, also means that subjectivity and common sense, knowing, and dreaming are all transformed by language.

It is that transformative split, not the event itself, that necessitates a mode of interpretation which reaches beyond the division of psychical and "real" in order to account for aspects internal to language and its translation. Zia's dream is an eruption of the real into the symbolic order that speaks to the mimesis, blowback, and backstabbing we find in language to reveal, as Fanon theorized, an experience of embodied and ontological disorder. This demands a theory of the subject (and the gaze) that exposes our dependence on an experience of language in such a way that it is impossible to escape its inscriptions, body schema, codes, and entrapments or to fully articulate the real.

To understand this theory, I also draw on Michael Taussig's idea of a "space of death" as a threshold of meaning and consciousness where terror illuminates and extinguishes a lifeworld.[26] Taussig's approach to conceptualizing terror reveals not only the dislocations of colonial violence but also the displacement of signifiers from their referents, echoing Gilles Deleuze's notion of the perpetual misalignment between an itinerant "occupant" and a "slot" that accounts for the structural genesis of signs.[27] In this sense, a "space of death" is also a space of floating signifiers and meanings; it is "the admission that there is always indeed something more meant than (or in) what we say; the mode of insistence of the unconscious in the conscious" and in collective life.[28]

The disruption of dreams and bodies, and the crack between a representation (including how one sees or dreams of oneself) and the worldly experience of a "flaw that prohibits any ontological explanation" is part of the deeply embodied encounter with the other's racialized gaze, one Fanon experiences in the colony, while riding in trains, and in every place where "a slow construction of myself as a body in a spatial and temporal world" becomes the dialectic between self and world.[29] But the crack is also a product of the failure of a certain dream of representation, a failure that becomes most apparent in moments when surface agreements, bodies, contact, skin, games, gestures, play, and cheap words collapse under the weight of what they cannot hold or convey through exchange alone.[30]

Consider another nightmare, this time a real one: Before returning to Kabul, where I met him, Matin and his military unit initiated an improvised game of soccer with local men in the province of Kandahar, in exchange for safe passage through their village. As the game and its putatively shared rules unfolded, the local men stumbled and fell over the makeshift ball, and the soldiers began to take photographs and videos to capture the funny but soon-to-be-deadly moments. They laughed and ridiculed, a cruel enjoyment, a *bazi* (game) that was meant to be in fun but got elevated by the jouissance of the invader. The following morning, local men, presumably those who had been humiliated, planted an enormous roadside bomb that nearly killed Matin and the soldiers. This is the kind of serious play that is real; it is not funny. Instead, it is meant to deliver the final laugh and blow, a blow directed within an atmosphere of surfaces, where literalism almost prevails: Falling over is just falling over, so what's the big deal? But in the mimesis of play as violence, where every sign and gesture assume the force of a weapon, nothing is just play; every laugh is a sovereign blow, becoming both gift and death. This is what escapes the rules of the game and cannot be defeated. It is the excess that is not symbolized or articulated and can only be "said" through the unsayable explosion—"take that!"—to end all talk. Yet, Matin unburdens himself when he talks to me about these experiences, saying, "Sometimes I feel myself *dil tang*, you know, like my chest is closed, but I feel better when I talk to you."

BEFORE THE WORD, VIOLENCE

These moments, when hard blows and harsh reality violently intrude into the symbolic, are inflicted to silence the other and put an end to dialogic reply. Insults, mockery, and the laugh of the invader foreclose exchange:

Dreams feel close, kidding is deadly, talking back becomes explosive. Nobody is kidding. Yet, these closures are rarely final; instead, they generate more shocks and blows, replies, and new forms of inscription. (Zia carved the date he was caught in a roadside bomb attack, May 9, 2010, into his bedpost, and Matin told me about the scars on his leg from the incident after the soccer game.) Stories like this one, which Matin conveys as an instance of violent cannibalism, are a botched jeu where bodies eat up sensemaking and words in the most brutal way.

But to me, this exchange in which forms of speech collide and people seek out, play, and hit one another through semantic distortion illustrates not the failure of social relations but rather the condition James Siegel describes as a failure of "socially determined thinking" projected onto the question of linguistic power precisely at the "points where no definition of social reality can take place—where, therefore, phantasms and, often violence occur."[31] These points are not about the failure of relationality but rather a failure intrinsic to language itself. And they exemplify the pharmakonic aporias that result from the fact that language, whether in speech, writing, dreams, blowups, or laughter, is always marked by the structure of difference and violence it attempts to surpass. Thus, its practices are constituted by the same arabesque detours of meaning they seek to ground.

That we are fragmented subjects, divided by the limits of knowing and lost to traces of memory and new forms of repression, must also account for the presence of a crack in the experience of written language versus speech. For Nadia, writing is a source of freedom she does not possess. It is part of the desire for proximity to others and to a global cosmopolitanism she cannot access because she has never lived outside of Kabul. Being in the world and with others is the same unified movement as writing, the same completion and decisive escape. It is not that Nadia feels disconnected from the world or is incapable of understanding how it works; rather, she believes that if she could read and write, she could put that understanding to work in a meaningful way.

But if writing is an escape, this break is redoubled insofar as writing also enables the archiving of memory and reveals the "extent to which memory and thought can be said to belong to the possibility of repetition, reproduction, citation and inscription."[32] Writing escapes the attempt to restrict it in form; that is, to frame and therefore restrain it as a material or alphabetic inscription—as a technical dimension rather than an indeterminate process of substitution whereby meaning, others, and knowing are constantly deferred. In this sense, as Derrida famously contends, speech and writing never stay clear of each other; writing is not a secondary medium of inscription but an elsewhere. It is an undetermined site where signification is perpetually deferred, exposing the arche-violence of language that unfolds both in writing and in speech, each taking from and interrupting the other through traces and difference.

But where in collective life do we encounter this interplay? How do the absence of writing and the power of speech become limits to fantasies of knowledge and action? In Sami's trial, like other cases involving illiterate defendants, case files acquire an air of mystery and power, but the law is truly written on bodies through torture practices fantasized as a means of obtaining the truth through oral confessions otherwise deemed unreliable precisely because the defendants are illiterate. If you cannot write and support what you speak of, then the truth is not in what you say but somewhere deeper, in the mind, the body, maybe the soul, and as Elaine Scarry brilliantly observes, truth becomes part of a strange inversion in which every question is a motive and every answer a betrayal: "It is only the prisoner's steadily shrinking ground that wins for the torturer his swelling sense of territory. The question and answer are a prolonged comparative display, an unfurling of world maps."[33]

Sami finds himself somewhere in this map when the Afghan police sexually assault him with a Coke bottle during his initial interrogation. I will return to this event as a startling moment of revelation in court, but aside from its raw violence, it also reveals how the valorization of writing and the idea of terror as the latent, irrational desire for violence find their dialectic bond, becoming part of the notion that men like Sami are inherently beyond the law and language, and that the pain of torture inscribes truth into a speech otherwise devoid of testimonial value.[34]

Sami is defenseless in the face of a law not accountable to his speech and to the writing on his body, a mythical machine that moves between a collective fear of primitive violence, crimes against the state, and the extraction of "truth" in a confession.[35] Law, word, silence, bombing, question, answer, and torture are all examples of what Fanon describes as the eruption of the real in the domain of symbolic mediation, those moments when ambiguity and openness (even in speech and writing) become the nightmare of the body and mind.[36] As Fanon describes it:

> The Senegalese soldier's rifle is not a penis, but a genuine Lebel 1916 model. The black bull and robber are not *lolos*, "substantial souls," but genuine irruptions during sleep of actual fantasies. . . . Sometimes there are *black*

infantrymen; sometimes there are *black* bulls speckled with white on the head; sometimes there is actually a very kind white woman. What do we find in all these dreams if not this central idea: "To depart from routine is to wander in pathless woods; there you will meet the bull who will send you running helter-skelter home again."[37]

To this I would add that sometimes Coke bottles are the most powerful weapons of all. And yet, in this world of literalism, there remains the possibility of what Pandolfo calls a "testimony in counterpoint" that moves through the encounter between self and other, speech and writing, knowing and not knowing and, most dramatically, between action and self-sacrifice.[38] The complexity of this encounter, including in Sami's life and trial, requires us to think about concepts not as theoretical forms but in terms of how they are made and unmade in the worlds they play out in.

WHEN A VOICE GETS THROUGH

The fact that writing is a "strange invention" and material practice that can be denied to some persons does not mean speech fares any better. Illiterate individuals, especially the young men implicated in terrorism, offer a different perspective on speech compared to Derrida's critique of phonocentric bias.[39] In rural areas on the fringes of state or insurgent control, their speech becomes another pharmakon, unable to convey the coherence expected of it. Perhaps this is why Sami acknowledges his illiteracy at the start of trial and states that he does not know how the world works, presenting himself as an antiheroic figure who refrains from seeking knowledge or acting.

Our voice and our exposure to the voice of the other entail vulnerability. What else can account for our fear of public speaking or of hearing our recorded voice or its source of power: the influence, authority, charisma, and ability to access knowledge in transcendental or intersubjective life? The voices of prophets, oracles, healers, and witches (including the voices they hear) testify to this primordial power. For Sami, it was his mother's voice, the first voice and dialectical tie, that turned her speech into his mission of radical self-sacrifice. Because he believes his mother's understanding of events surpasses his own, he cannot disregard her speech or what she makes clear to him is his responsibility toward his sister. Sami took her story as the ultimate command to do whatever was necessary to bring Mina home.

Reflecting on this transformative moment, I return to the question of what it means to hear a voice as an irreducible demand. For me, these tensions reveal the alternative metaphysics of voice Dolar describes, something overlooked both in the phonocentric bias of Western thought and in deconstruction, which cannot account for the other, darker histories of discourse, speech, and voicing as sites of inviolable danger and passion that are difficult to control. For Dolar "there is a history of the voice receiving a metaphysical vote of no confidence. Not just writing, but also the voice can appear as a menace to metaphysical consistency and can be seen as disruptive of presence and sense. Lacan did not have to invent the ambiguity of voice and its perilous reverse side; metaphysics has been well aware of it all along."[40] In my book, the same disruption of presence and sense occurs repeatedly, but the consequence of an "ideal" voice covering up the existence of a destructive or "lawless" voice is never just conceptual; it is deeply imperial-historical and ethnographic, forming a critical juncture between the experience of reason and its other(s), truth and dissimulation, and ultimately between life and death.

In the historical and geopolitical context of Afghanistan, the meaning of this tension, the emergence of the "other" voice as both disruptive and uncontrollable, transforms the ambiguity Dolar highlights from a metaphysical problem to one of historical belonging. This more ambiguous opening is articulated by the nineteenth-century Afghan intellectual and writer Mahmud Tarzī. Tarzī's poetic invocation to "listen to the telephone" because "the time of speechlessness is over" grounds this duality in a specific historical moment at the beginning of a fraught global modernity irreducible to any single place or tradition of thought. For Tarzī, the problem of collective life and language is bound to the place of Afghanistan in the world as it is transformed by its "peripheries." And in the contemporary moment, the same dialectic between global forces and the experience of the power of language, including thinking about what constitutes its power, is a crucial feature of life and why Afghanistan is crucial for rethinking our present moment.

TRANSLATION: FRAGMENTS OF A VESSEL

What is the language one calls one's own? And what does "possession" of this language mean? When I first met Matin and Zia, two childhood friends and Persian-speaking translators from Kabul, they each remarked that they trusted me like a sister.[41] This became the opening between us and, because we share a mother tongue, the possibility of our dialogic exchange. But outside of Kabul, where their linguistic and translational expertise was in demand as part of a larger counterinsurgency effort across the country, one that commodified linguistic expertise into a weapon for winning "hearts and minds," this kind of opening was rare. The illusion of monolingualism, the idea that we fully inhabit and know our own language, takes hold of Matin and Zia precisely when a desire to master, know, assess, narrate, and translate the other confronts fragmentation in language. This fragmentation takes the forms of gaps or partial meanings, deceit, rumor, and senseless talk. In their narratives, translation undergoes a transformation, attempting to contain two functions it cannot reconcile: On one hand, it is part of the endeavor to decode rural subjects who do not possess a command of language (who are illiterate, clumsy, speak in strange dialects, live dangerously, and so on) and whose subjectivity threatens the future. On the other, their own lifeworld (literate, settled, urban, fully ontologized) must first dissolve this threat to survive in the modern world, where they believe rationality, truth, and prosperity go hand in hand. These contradictions perpetuate each other: The belief in translation is upheld by the social body that translation also seeks to read and dissolve, while the specter of social disorder (in Kabul, where they live) is intensified by the presence of the other on whose behalf the translator is summoned to speak but cannot erase.

In part this problem is a historical one. In Afghanistan, for much of the nineteenth and twentieth centuries, the anxiety over being seen and heard (and overheard) was about the place of the global other in the experience of technology through telegraphic, telephonic, and radio connectivity, each of which contributed to cosmopolitan consciousness among Afghan government officials and the elite. These technologies were gained and interwoven with the latticed dream of global belonging; the experience of contact, images, letters, calls, and travel; and the feeling of being part of the world. This was a response to something large but still undefined in the cultural imaginary and was part of a general desire for global belonging. And yet, in the colonial imagination, Afghan political discourse communicated via those channels was characterized by deceit and a lack of grounding in truth or moral judgment; this deceit was made worse by technologies of mechanical reproduction whose authenticity could not be assured in a predominantly oral culture, where political speech was thought to covertly disseminate Bolshevik, pan-Islamist, and pan-Asian ambitions.

In this history, the problem of voicing and communication assume yet another dimension: Again, speech (over the telephone or radio) and writing (in telegrams) are not loci of truth or revelation but threats to political order and the global sphere.[42] During the conflict in Afghanistan, this idea still informed attempts at translation during deadly encounters between Afghan translators and civilians, encounters in which mishearing the words of the other is inextricable from the fantasy that translation should enable transparency and persuasion, that illiteracy can be a target of translational labor, and that the other's speech and its political force can be contained. Matin and Zia carry this fantasy and the violence of linguistic commodification with them on their missions, and these are part of what they later reveal to me in their narratives of what they saw and experienced on military missions, in Kabul, and even in the oneiric world of their dreams.

What begins to feel impossible in their translational encounter extends itself to social life more generally. Matin and Zia talk about national decay, invasion, dirt, poverty, economic crises, empty factories, heat, smell, illiteracy, broken speech, unfathomable dialects, and a sprawling and poor hinterland; they hear an uncanny and chthonic discourse of the stranger through which the other engages in the mimesis of intellect as a means of dangerous play. They discover that the other side of translation is not the articulation of fragmented meaning but a topographical and subjective scene that is impossible to surveil and formulate as anything other than madness unbound in speech. Borrowing from Julia Kristeva, these are the descriptions and moments of symbolic collapse when translation is met with the fantasy of monolingual power: "A signifying sequence, necessarily an arbitrary one, will appear to them as heavily, violently arbitrary; they will think it absurd, it will have no meaning. No word, no object in reality will be likely to have a coherent concatenation that will also be suitable to a meaning or referent."[43]

Matin and Zia enter a scene of nonrelation. They recall to me the experience of uncontrollable encounters, moving closer to death, and feeling bewildered in the places where they hoped their words could facilitate truth and understanding. At times consciously and at other times without knowing what they project, they are immersed in the old political fantasy that the other is the source of phantasmatic, dangerous speech, removed from the guarantee of writing and slated for self-destruction. And yet, behind these moments of closure and symbolic breakdown are deferrals of meaning that unexpectedly surface and make an alternative possible. These are the moments that vividly reveal how translation is not reducible to an act of linguistic exchange but is a metaphor for the experience of disjunction that is internal to meaning and difference.

For Benjamin, the figure of the translator gives up the idea of transcendental meaning to embark on a more ironic journey, like a critic, to reveal the original as incomplete rather than the self-same or an origin to be preserved. He describes this in different ways. He writes that the translator stands not at the center of the language forest but "facing the wooded ridge." The translator's aim is a totality that is an "echo of the original" and is "midway between poetry and doctrine." And finally, a translation is recognizable just like the fragments that "are part of a vessel."[44] I read an opening in these descriptions that can allow us to trace possibilities other than symbolic disintegration or the breakdown of meaning that Matin's and Zia's encounters suggest as the place of translation in ideological and actual scenes of battle. Through these images Benjamin tells us that the work of translation reveals an original in need of a supplement. This logic, between the "original" and translation, the familiar and foreign, unfolds in a metonymic way that is always partial and never a sovereign point we can describe as pure or original. Fragmentation and retroactive meaning defer the fantasy of a whole farther and farther beyond, carrying it away not to "home" but to a permanent state of exile that inhabits all languages "especially the language one calls one's own."[45]

Where do we draw the line between the urban and rural populations whom Matin describes as being as distinct as "ground and sky"? The more they seek to translate this concept, the more they grapple with the place of textuality in their own life and its absence in others' lives. They are in doubt over what thoughts and actions to pursue. They are uncertain of what they know and of their own prospects for life in Kabul, where ideally, they should be free to speak and live but are afraid to. The deeper this division pushes, the more they become other to themselves, perhaps most dramatically when Matin hides in the mountains where insurgents typically take cover, becoming and living like the barbarian in the ultimate act of mimesis. Then in a later, more poignant moment he mistakes a bomb for a gift, only to realize it was indeed the gift of a bomb defused by the giver out of concern for Matin's life.

The collapse of stable meaning in these encounters allows us to see the fragmented but radical dimension of translation Benjamin alludes to through the metaphor of the vessel. In Benjamin's hands, the vessel is a palimpsest of traces, voices, and remnants that can exist only in a continuous realm of transformation. In seeking to find out and know about the other, Matin and Zia know less than they did before and less than what they need to know in order to negotiate their encounters without violence. After seeking to preserve and build up the dream of a modern future in Kabul, where they speak their mother tongue, including with me, they return to find a city in material and symbolic ruins. In seeking to speak and live only in the world of their mother tongue, Matin and Zia encounter others who, to borrow again from Kristeva, are "foreigners in their maternal tongue."[46] This alternation between self versus other, discourse versus madness, and the place of signification in social life versus its wanton violence are crucial to the social world of translation; it underlies symbolic life and signification, in some instances exerting pressure until forms of exchange erupt into unconditional sacrifice, the appearance of a radical gift, or betrayal. It is precisely these unpredictable detours, I argue, that enable individuals to inhabit aporia—sometimes but not always tragic—and still give gifts, trust they can be listened to, love others, fulfill their duties, and allow the symbolic order to sustain rather than inevitably condemn them. Finding and following this meandering crack through collective life is the goal of this work.

PART I   SUBJECT TO OTHERS

In the first part of this book, I trace the problem of accusation as it emerges both in relation to suicide terrorism as a crime against the Afghan state and, more uncontrollably, in the world of intersubjective knowledge and desire. My goal is to understand the stories of two people—Sami, a failed suicide bomber (chapter 1), and Sohrab, a young man accused of abducting his wife (chapter 2), both tried for their supposed crimes in the spring of 2013—as language-encounters occurring in a dense, politically fraught context but also in relation to the place of misunderstanding, gossip and rumor, illiteracy, and the discourse of others. I move between describing situation and place, including the role of insurgency and counterinsurgency, in upending social life, and describing the nuanced moments in which the problem of knowing and acting is undone in the relationship of one's own language to the words of others. How, in the contexts of testimony given in court and also of interactions in collective life, do we respond to a speech that cannot be verified by writing? How do we understand the epistemic place of rumors and gossip in new forms of accusation, understanding, and political action? What do we know about the other and how in turn do others read us? In short, how in language and its world of multiple meanings, deferrals, and signifying gaps can we be sure we've hit the mark of conveying our intended meaning?

On one level, the experience of social violence is part of the dissolution of a symbolic order that might otherwise make sacrifice, trust, and love possible between people. However, it is also irreducible to this dissolution because it creates a series of openings and forms of understanding and action (like sacrificing one's life or falling in love) that are enabled by the loss of faith in meaning. Thus, the gaps in knowing and the collapse of the symbolic order are never experienced by my interlocuters only as such. Interpretive intervals are the pivots on which the stories and ethnographic concepts turn; for example, the decision to undertake a suicide bombing or to elope. The obscurity of meaning—those moments when language reveals its own intractable, ambiguous functioning—operates not as the eclipse of knowledge or interpretation but as its cause. Taken together, the first two chapters trace these effects to understand how love and loss, presence and absence, and sacrifice are mediated by language and the other; they also trace how language, which we fantasize to work as a mechanism for the revelation of meaning, is always haunted by *its own others*; namely, deferral, spacing, and masking.

CHAPTER ONE

What's the Use Between Death and Glory?

There is a history of the voice receiving a metaphysical vote of no confidence.
—MLADEN DOLAR, *A Voice and Nothing More*

You have seen how difficult it is to decipher the script with one's eyes; but our man deciphers it with his wounds.
—FRANZ KAFKA, "In the Penal Colony"

It is being written after us, they write behind us.
—SALAR (failed suicide bomber, spoken at his trial)

In this chapter I follow the trajectories of knowing, sacrificing, and acting as they are mediated by the discourse of the other and the place of language in collective and psychic life. Sami, a man in his twenties, attempted a suicide car bombing at the Intercontinental Hotel in Kabul in the summer of 2012. Like Antigone's, his devotion is both a matter of universal duty and a response to a subjective desire he does not entirely understand. His decision emerges from a complicated web of familial obligations, rumors, and misunderstanding but also the ambiguities of language: the kind that arise when language falters and meanings are deferred or entirely distorted, leading to actions that likewise defy straightforward interpretation.

In court, where I witnessed his trial in spring 2013, Sami's story initially seemed like a case of a crime against the Afghan state. I assumed he was a member of the Taliban or Al-Qaeda insurgency for political and ideological reasons, a presumption that unraveled once he testified on his own behalf. As I show, the attempted bombing was not a crime against the state so much as it was the culmination of the pluralization of meaning and of deceptions between family members; however, this deceit, achieved through stories and words, especially the story Sami's mother told to him, which I learned about through his testimony and from the court, also enables an ethic of sacrifice beyond collective and symbolic recuperation. For Sami, it meant killing others and himself in order for his sister, Mina, to live. Where in this ethical call to the other do we situate misunderstanding? How does Sami embody the deferral of and quest for understanding? And how do we account for a form of sacrifice that defies all symbolic convention even as it emerges from the scene of collective discourse?

Sami's sister Mina, a Sunni Muslim, eloped to Pakistan with an older Shia man.[1] Sami did not know about their relationship and came home one day to find her "missing." Initially, there was no explanation of her disappearance but later, when the absence became obvious to neighbors and stirred rumors about her whereabouts, his mother told him and others that Mina had been abducted from the village center by a group of "unknown and strange men." The news of Mina's supposed abduction spread. Neighbors and acquaintances began to drop by Sami's house to offer support but also to satisfy their own curiosity. Why had Mina been taken? Where was she? Would she ever return? A few days later, undoubtedly because someone in their village or close circle tipped others off, Sami received a phone call from Taliban fighters in Pakistan posing as the abductors; they claimed that they had abducted Mina and offered to release her if he agreed to undertake a suicide mission. Because he loved Mina, he agreed. Sami was caught on his way to the Kabul Intercontinental Hotel with a car full of rudimentary but powerful explosives. His case was heard in the special tribunal in Kabul, inside a high-security military camp, where his story and its deferrals and fault lines unfolded.

PART 1: WITHOUT LETTERS

Sami was brought before the special tribunal that convened weekly to sentence the country's most aberrant criminals. At the start of the trial, held in a military camp in Kabul's Police District 9, Sami was uncertain of what to say. He presented himself as illiterate and unworldly. At this time, social violence and crime were peaking across the country, while in Kabul the surge of urban bombings, suicide attacks, and cold-blooded murders made the task of prosecution more desperate than before. The law was fierce in the face of what the public perceived as a new kind of primitive irrationalism. The sporadic, violent reprisals had the impossibly large objective of tearing apart the social body and collective life. In turn, the representation of that violence was met in the cultural unconscious with an equally unreasonable fear of a wild, aimless compulsion ranging at large across the country and particularly in Kabul. It was not just that the situation was dire but also that the desire to inflict death had become more indiscriminate and purer, a simple goal that had been distilled and honed over years of conflict and could no longer be contained through the law or relations of symbolic exchange.

Inside the makeshift courtroom Sami stood in brown plastic sandals across the bare room from the judges and said: "I do not know what has become of this country or the world or why it is this way." It was not that he was ignorant or confused but that he had found a limit to his power of speculation. By "world" he meant the global political sphere and his ability to understand it or be a good observer of its geopolitical tumult. Interpreting it was beyond what he envisaged himself as capable of. It was not that he positioned himself against the world or in dialectical opposition to its transformative phenomena but that he had given in and stood before it, feeling like he was not really a part of it. Instead, he had the love of his family and an inviolable work ethic that helped him provide for his mother and sister; and these were the things he felt could not be corrupted or taken from him by others.

He presented himself as possessing a transparent and earnest relationship with his family. In an almost Kantian sense, he was bound to them by moral obligation and the fundamental principle of treating them as ends in themselves. He had a reticent, drooping posture and kept his head down, as if he were looking inward or seeking shelter from the grim, depleted courtroom that had none of the carnivalesque atmosphere of a murder trial in the city but was instead spare and nearly empty. He had curly hair and looked cold in his prison uniform. He spoke with a soft, clear tone but in a manner that suggested he was at a loss for words or that he was unaccustomed to being asked direct, successive questions that were purposeful and suggestive, since he came from a very rural place where he always tried to "keep his head low and himself to himself."

When he addressed the judges, he did not plead for his life but simply tried to convey the sudden changes that had swept him up. He suffered unbearable thoughts about his sister's ordeal "night and day," and these thoughts transformed his experience of others in ways beyond his control. He also understood that he was constrained by the world of question and answer: "If I may say something. It is hard for me, all these questions. I do not know very much about how the world works. I am illiterate and plain, but I know right and wrong. I am not used to so many questions and answers, but please hear me when I say I am a good person" he explained. At other times he was more direct and clearer. He announced that he loved his sister, Mina, more than anyone in this world.

He looked at the judges and said: "I am illiterate, but I love my sister more than anyone in the world. She is the only person I talk to." Mina was singular in kinship and in language. In describing himself as illiterate but loving he invoked the representational violence of a radical simplification in which the materiality of writing operates as the trace of reason while its absence is condensed into violent and spontaneous passions. He loves Mina and is illiterate, and thus his desire is part of his oral lifeworld and its transcendental bind. He loves Mina despite being illiterate and despite what he imagines is the judges' perception of him as violent and irrational and incapable of love.

In 2012–13 basic supplies like drinking water, fuel, and firewood were hard to come by, especially for the poor, and a long, snowy winter drove inflation and economic anxiety to an all-time high. People were worried about the future of the government and the insurgency closing in on the city of Kabul. For those without work or struggling to pay debts, family ties faltered, giving way to tenuous alliances viewed by some as parasitic and dangerous, and by others as a conduit to new people and breaking free from the past. At the same time, anxiety over the place of language in social life was distilled in the issue of illiteracy, at first in the narrow sense of the letter, then, much more dramatically, as a dynamic metaphor for how to interpret the entire realm of subjective behavior and action.

The distinction between literacy and illiteracy became a critical and hostile factor that determined people's experience of danger and collective existence. It emerged in the translation of languages, on the front lines of battle, amid legal proceedings, and in quotidian life. The distinction was about access to symbolic capital but also about a new divide between groups of people and ways of being; it reflected different ideas of what it meant to encounter others and what actions to take to be able to live with them. This was coupled with a widespread preoccupation with the status of rural individuals and new forms of social violence, ranging from oral expression and illiterate men who did not speak the "language of the body politic" and were deemed volatile, to the emergence of a new social truth: that subjectivity is best understood through the interplay of rational thought and broken madness, and that the latter often stems from an inability to read and write.[2]

In Sami's case, it was believed, perhaps most crucially by his mother, that he lacked the capacity to perceive things beyond their surface appearance and that, as a result, he earnestly accepted people and their words at face value. In this sense, he was seen in the same light as the defendants who stood trial before and after him: as a simpleton incapable of rational thought and beholden to a more primal world. For the judges this was the fundamental principle that connected his predicament to his reliance on speech and the tendency toward simple, literal thinking that culminated in his fateful decision: "Look at him, the poor soul, let us take pity on him," a judge remarked at one point. Sami and Mina's story occurs in the space of juridical reason and its normative categories of good and evil, but those categories are embedded in the two domains of language at stake: the realm of speech, in particular his speech, and the absence of a support for it (through reading and writing) that is otherwise seen by the judges and in the collective imagination as the supplemental link between signs and rational thought. Like passion and drive, speech could only indicate a deeper, latent desire for excess and death; it signified, through a profound distortion, the inability to reason and understand the nature of events and signs, signs that others assumed reached him without any mediation but that he did not *really* understand.

This is the first elsewhere Sami encounters, a place of knowledge he cannot access through his speech alone, but as his trial progressed the status of alphabetic writing was part of yet another adaptation in which speech (in particular, his mother's) became the site of intuitive power and delineated a space of necessary, ethical action. Despite the long-standing presumed innocence of speech and the idea of writing as a supplement to speech, people also readily invoked the idea that in the absence of writing one can only rely on intuition to read people and circumstances. In this way, they still lived with the seduction of signs, except those signs are re-formed as part of the abstract reading of people and discerning the difference between their appearance and true being. Law, justice, fear of others, and social violence all became part of a deeper battle over *how to understand* (how to read) the place of reason and violence in social life. The connection between writing and access to the techniques of reason turned speech into the domain of an inner sense and, depending on the person, a source of wisdom. Ideas of difference, sameness, ethical action, and the play of meaning were all part of this collective quest to understand more clearly. This is not to suggest, as we will see in Sami's case, that knowing and living became features of literacy while not knowing and dying (or killing) were the mark of its absence but rather that language was understood to work best and refer most accurately to an actual, "real" state of affairs precisely when it could be affirmed by the guarantee of the written word.

Cellblock, Coke Bottle

I would watch the old gray bus pull up slowly and park by a small dirt clearing outside the only courthouse window. It loudly sagged when the ignition was turned off, then the prisoners followed one another out the front door in their plastic sandals and old jumpsuits. Some of the men chatted idly while others looked aloof or uncertain of what to expect; they shifted in their heavy chains and looked down or tried to peer into the window. Usually they were individually shackled at their ankles and wrists, or sometimes were chained together at the waist. The heavy chains pulled down on their uniforms and gave them a droopy and misshapen look like what John Berger describes as the appearance of hardened peasant bodies in suits: "the clothes look less absurd, less 'abnormal' than the men's bodies which are in them."[3] As the prisoners stepped out of the bus they were immediately confronted by their grim surroundings and the isolated, mysterious neighborhood where the tribunal was being held, one in which they most likely had never set foot before.

To look in the direction of the small but high-profile neighborhood of Shash Darak from an ordinary civilian block or road is to try to see a place that is somehow not there. The streets, security cameras, asphalt dividers, and military roadblocks hide it, separating this flat area from normal life and helping it achieve its isolation. They are part of the battle over who can move freely and secure access to resources and who is shut out and forced to make do with the city's arbitrary divisions. Shash Darak is in eastern Kabul next to the former Green Zone and the Soviet-built neighborhood of Mikrorayan, which was popular with the intelligentsia and professional class in the 1970s and 1980s but has since become a varied hive of urban life. Unlike Mikrorayan, which borders it on two sides and is filled with imposing concrete "Khrushchevka" apartment blocks and local markets, Shash Darak seems to stand alone and without lifeblood; it is a lonesome, stark part of town that feels isolated and impenetrable. At night, when it is typically empty, its narrow alleyways and dirt roads, where cars are mired in muddy ground after even a light rain, make it feel eerie and add something mysterious to its blunt facade.

On the inside, along the main and side roads, are various walled-off security compounds that locals and military personnel call "camps." They are foreign, highly weaponized sites of fear and intrigue as well as brutal violence. The materials used for building them usually come from elsewhere. The concrete barriers; barbed wire; large, stackable boxes of smaller mesh filled with dirt or sand known as "HESCO" (used to line the entries to camps to blunt the impact of explosives); portable toilets; and consumer goods are all imported and sometimes objects of local desire. When approaching the area on the main dirt road, the first things to become visible are the numerous signs prohibiting photography and videography with the short captions "No Jammers" and "No Photography." Inside its fortified walls, which house the US Embassy, the former NATO headquarters, and the Afghan National Directorate of Security, the posture is harsh and unforgiving. The sensible logic is one of obeying every rule.

In the camp where Sami was tried, there was a small, inconspicuous structure at the end of a long gravel road, which was being used as a makeshift courtroom. The white door was flimsy, with a simple plastic handle, and the floors were bare. It was a stand-alone structure in a stand-alone part of town. There was a small adjoining room with a rudimentary squat toilet. The room had a single small window that let in a cold draft and looked out on the rest of the grim camp and its prefab structures. A large, heavy, wooden desk was placed in the center of the back wall, with two long tables on each side of it and a few chairs behind the desk and in the corner of the room. From the outside the building looked like an ordinary makeshift structure that I initially mistook for a large storage unit. Belying its nondescript appearance, movement into and out of the building was subject to an additional security screening performed midway between it and the guarded main entrance. Part ramshackle and part a place of mystery, it was a liminal and disguised space between a barely understood or even agreed-upon notion of the law and the sources of social and political violence. I sat in the corner of the room by the window.

Every Wednesday from noon to four o'clock the sole purpose inside was to prosecute the most violent cases that had rocked Kabul and raised the political and moral question of how to punish a successful insurgency in the name of the faltering Afghan state. In part, the very idea of punishment was not a penal or juridical concern but a symbolic act that was part of a larger series of signals to a beleaguered public ranging from televisual propaganda to new surveillance practices and attempts to bolster the Afghan National Army and security forces. At the same time this sense of order distinguished the neighborhood from surrounding provinces, where sites of resistance and sabotage continued to flourish, and the idea of the state was not so much a fantasy or fear of power but another name for what people flat-out refused to accept as an authority in their lives.

Sami was gaunt, presumably not because he had always been thin or unwell but owing to his time in a notorious prison on the desolate outskirts of Kabul where food, sanitation, and medical attention were scarce and where he was incarcerated among other irrational "wild men," estranged from the social body and civil society. He was sexually assaulted on at least one occasion with a glass Coke bottle during his interrogation: "Sister, I am sorry to speak you like this," he proclaimed to me, not to the judges: "but you must know that in prison they forced me to sit on glass Coke bottles!" This was one of the few moments in which his voice attracted unmitigated attention. It was like a disembodied force that spoke through him rather than his being able to speak or control it. A silence fell over the room as he shifted his feet, looked around as though unable to make up his mind, then turned toward the presiding judges, uncertain but waiting for some kind of response from them. Then, when it did not happen, he proceeded to talk more:

> It is no place for humans. It is not for life. They punish you and beat you inside like the animals. They beat you with pipes and sticks and shock you. For the love of God, try to understand! They forced a glass Coke bottle inside of me! Everything is over. There is no society here. There is no law. Nobody believes in anything. We are illiterate people with nothing and because we have nothing, they put us in prison. I cannot make any promises about tomorrow. Nobody can vouch for tomorrow. But what I have been through is enough to make me feel there is no life or hope.

Owing to the torture, he shuffled in a self-conscious way and I had initially thought he had a limp. In court, he stood before everyone with a blank face and absent demeanor like he was neither present nor capable of fully transporting himself elsewhere. Prison, he described, was a place of wanton brutality and the ruthless interrogation he recollected through the experience of the Coke bottle was one part of that violence, part of the pain and instruments that were his immediate experience of power. Moreover, the possibility of an "elsewhere" outside of his experience seemed impossible. Because he was so self-conscious about how he spoke, and so overdetermined by language (question, answer, another question, another answer, getting everything right, getting the words out right), the idea of giving testimony and speaking or arguing on his own behalf seemed like another cruel punishment rather than a formal opportunity to be heard in the presence of others and the law.

And yet, this moment constitutes a radical opening in what is otherwise the series of closures he faces because of his illiterate "plainness." Why, in a story and dilemma about his sister, does Sami refer to me as "Sister" before he can tell the court about being tortured? Where in this moment can we locate the power of his speech? "Sister" emerges not as a "sign of" but as an absence and a substitute that becomes a condition of possibility for him to understand that he *must speak of the truth of certain things*. His words confirmed what everyone in the room already suspected about the violent conjunction of archaic and modern justice. He testified to his pain but also to what Andreas Gailus describes as the "mythical machine" of the law. This is a machine founded on violence that acquires the additional power to write and reiterate that violence without symbolic mediation and leave its marks on the body.[4] The judges stand outside of this violence of writing, they are immune to its immediate form of inscription even as they reinscribe what they cannot experience by embodying the idea of law as an ideal process rather than the instrument of violence. Yet, like a phantasmatic door, Sami's words took us to the other side of the law, to the space Walter Benjamin calls the origin and essence "of all that is transmissible." That space emerges in the same moment as the state's self-image of justice and order collapses, but it also raises a question about the place of language and speech in its unfolding: What kind of speech can be heard here, and to what end?[5]

Up Against a Wall

Sami stood at the end of the room, his body slumped away from the drab concrete wall. Like the other defendants, he unexpectedly found himself on swift trial. And like them, he was mixed up and desperate, at times confused and in other moments mentally sharp but alienated from whatever he had previously taken for granted. He had wanted to die as a suicide bomber but failed to reach his target. His punishment and trial, like the bombing he nearly carried out, seemed to come from elsewhere: To him, they seemed to emerge from beyond what he understood as the quotidian space of his being and actions and through the unexplained intercession of forces he sometimes referred to as his fate.

When he looked at me, I had the impression he was not holding a gaze but looking through me toward something indefinite. He was listless, but when he spoke about certain events or about his younger sister Mina, he passionately reconnected with the room. He spoke across an intangible divide of presence and absence, moving from one to the other with words that were sometimes direct and clear and at other times filled with regret. His faith in others had been destroyed. He admitted that he had people in his life, including a few decent neighbors, but he refused to rely on them, and he had a growing desire to isolate himself and avoid others as much as possible. He sometimes took back roads to avoid running into people and making small talk; and it was precisely that sort of thing—idle talk, gossip, and hateful speech—that he said made him feel depressed in society.

Sami was a prisoner in Pol-e-Charkhi, an infamous, high-security, eleven-cellblock prison on the outskirts of Kabul. In the 1970s and 1980s, a period when Afghan men readily "disappeared," the prison was associated with the violence enacted on the bodies of the state's ideological opponents as part of a larger and uncontrollable domain of unreason that was crucial to the discourse and violence of the socialist People's Democratic Party of Afghanistan coup d'état and later the Afghan Civil War of the 1980s–90s. It was known as a site of mass detention and death but also a place where the most modern of political ideologies could not stay clean of brutality and its own irrational excess. For decades, but especially in the aftermath of the coup, when hundreds of Afghan men were executed by government forces in the prison's large central courtyard, Pol-e-Charkhi has been a place closed off both from view and from the public imagination, cordoned by large walls and barbed towers, and a key signifier of torture, mass death, and the reach of the state.[6]

I imagine that prior to his arrest Sami only knew of Pol-e-Charkhi from stories that other people told, if he knew of it at all. Now he was on the inside, and the difference between being dead or alive had become marginal. "Every day I wonder," he said, "if I am dead or still among the living." His sense of loss, too, and his expectation of dealing with staggering forces had become part of how he imagined living in society: "Everything and everyone," he said, "can abandon you."

Society is violent. But it is the interpretation of its power, and the uncontrollable nature of events and signification, that inheres in this fear. The abandonment he experiences reveals a peculiar kind of terror. It is not the material, incendiary kind he was charged with attempting to inflict on others but a form of fear that has no specific object and is tied to the totality of one's social relations and experiences. It is a fear that moves in larger, ever-widening circles and belongs more to language than to the realm of events, even as the intuition and experience of the social body is marked by its scale as the uncontrollable scene of transpersonal affairs.

SAMI: I know that everything will be very, very bad for me.

JUDGE: What do you mean, everything will be very bad for you? Are you referring to this case or to your life or to some specific thing or . . . what exactly? You must speak clearly and say what you mean. All your words matter.

Sami experienced people not merely as strangers but as volatile ones. As we will see in chapters 4 and 5, this is the form representational violence takes when translation becomes part of a violent relation to the other. But there is also a simpler reality to the failure of his words. They exemplify a fear that he cannot fit into any familiar categories of understanding precisely because those categories have come undone. Sami attempts to speak about, and live with, the most intense kind of predicament possible: one that transpires in relation to the words of the other and, thus, to a chain of different significations that are irreducible to a single discourse or mode of sense-making. After all, how do we know what others intend to mean and do based on what they say?

The relationship between speech and meaning also raises the question of voice and of where in language its power is located. In contexts where the voice achieves the power of speaking or referring to nondialectical possibilities, when it expresses, as in the case of the witch's speech, a thoroughly "foreign power," it also raises the question of what it means to speak through a "voice," or collective articulation, that is not strictly one's own. But whose is it? In instances of witchcraft, this is the voice of the witch but also the voice of collective healing and magical speech that are the product of a division of the self that occurs through traumatic force and the power of collective desire.[7]

What is Sami afraid of? As we will see, his fear relates to his mother's words and the power of her speech, particularly the absence (of Mina) it presents to him as a crime he must rectify. This is something he could not comprehend on his own. Thus, their discourse is dialogic but not shared, because only her speech has the capacity to speak on behalf of the reality he cannot fathom alone. More importantly, she speaks to express not her thoughts but information that could not be known in general by others and especially not by Sami; she speaks of a nondialectical truth and on the side of mystery.

In responding to the judges, Sami expresses the idea and experience of a social body marked by an impossibly large scene of uncontrollable factors. This is the complex scene, the world, that his mother's voice and that speech must clarify for him. When his mother spoke of evil and a fate that could not be avoided, it led to the kind of prejudice James Siegel describes as "stemming not from prior belief but from unbearable curiosity and desire that there be a mighty and uncontrollable power available for them to be witness to."[8] The power of her speech lies not in the political action it generates or in the insurgent tactic it triggered through Sami's decision, but rather in the collective and intersubjective fascination with indefinable and general powers at work. And yet, it is her own split subjectivity as both Sami and Mina's mother and Mina's co-conspirer that gives her words the power to intensify rather than resolve his predicament.

Claude Lévi-Strauss, in his analysis of the sorcerer's cure, and Siegel, in interrogating the sorcerer's speech, call this the "composite voice." Her voice is not only her own but speaks through her to gesture toward the structural deficit and surplus of meaning internal to the possibility of signification rather than a stable meaning. Following Siegel, we can say that "the power of curing is the capacity to form a composite voice," a voice that turns pain into collective experience or meaninglessness into signification.[9] The fear of disorder is mitigated by the composite voice that can speak on behalf of realities and powers that others do not yet understand and that cannot be expressed in a dialogic way. But those realities are still there.

Sami's experience of fear exists in the small and diminishing space between his perception of others and the volatile reality that structures collective life in his village and province. But I believe he also expresses an anticipatory anxiety tied to his imagination of what might occur in various situations or chance encounters. Whatever ground he felt he could stand and count on quickly came undone, and he was constantly "keeping my head low and myself to myself." The more uncertainty he experienced, the more his understanding of the place of violence in his milieu extended behind the manifestation of events, or "behind the scenes," as he put it, a scene that is its own elsewhere and is inseparable from the itinerant place he occupies in a symbolic order of meaning. In other words, his place is at the same time a being out of place that illustrates how language, symptom, and desire articulate with each other, and in doing so remove Sami from any possible world in which things are familiar or known to him.

. . . .

Sami's trial took place in the spring of 2013, when the Taliban's "spring uprising" against the Afghan government was in full swing. One of the Taliban's strategic aims was to take control of major cities and provinces and precipitate chaos in Kabul, the city most associated with the ingress of foreign control and influence in the collective imagination. In a sense, the goal of these trials was to ascertain the place of tension between an insurgency and foreign or state control in different parts of the country. More generally, people were ambivalent about social relations and the government and fearful of practices of death, torture, underground economies, temporary alliances, distribution of goods and services, road access, aerial firepower, bombings, and the power of words. In the news media, predictions of an imminent American military withdrawal circulated widely and filled the world of talk in markets, in mosques, and on the street with pervasive anxiety about the future. A vicious cycle erupted as the Afghan military became increasingly keen on demonstrating to a doubtful public that it had the forces and firepower to defeat the insurgency despite the announcement of American withdrawal by December 2016. Inside the tribunal, doubt about moving lines of combat became part of the objective structure of the hearings and moved in two directions, shaping the perception of the defendants as either "wild" irrational men or pitiful subjects caught up in the collective upheaval of US military operations, widespread civilian death, limited movement from provinces to the capital, and a booming black market in weapons, precious gems, and drugs.

As the fighting intensified in urban areas, hundreds of poor men were arrested for suspected involvement in a series of grisly bombing campaigns. Those who were involved were recruited from all over the country. These men (often young and illiterate, but not always) came from working-class and impoverished neighborhoods or were picked up from skeletal construction sites where they were looking for work. Within months, the bombings turned the city on its head: The young men targeted government ministries, public gatherings, mosques, military bases, politicians, exclusive restaurants, small markets, large shopping malls, airports, crucial roads, traffic circles, houses, courtrooms, business headquarters, and other random sites. Some of the men were attracted to the idea of danger but others were embroiled in plots and dangerous underground networks, what locals called *daseeseh* (schemes), without fully understanding what they had become part of.

Between 2006 and 2015, approximately 1,052 suicide attacks occurred in Afghanistan, killing 4,845 people and wounding 12,079. These numbers are not only the highest of any country in the world but also represent a twelvefold increase over suicide attacks carried out within Afghanistan between 1982 and 2006, a span that includes the Afghan-Soviet War (1979–89), the Afghan Civil War (1992–96), and the first six years of the American War in Afghanistan. This stunning increase also entailed a dramatic surge in attacks with civilians as primary targets. While 820 attacks against foreign military and security personnel resulted in 3,214 deaths, a mere 67 attacks against civilians resulted in 632 deaths, a lethality rate of almost 10 percent. Equally telling, and perhaps shocking, is the weapon of choice. Car and belt bombs accounted for 893 of these attacks, which killed 4,227 people and wounded 10,497.[10] It is hard to imagine any other phenomenon touching on the raw nerve of a populace the way the bombings did. For the Afghan state, which was still in control of large cities but quickly losing ground in the provinces, the suicide bombings became the most visible signifier of its powerlessness and the most serious of the crimes against the state, which included ordinary bombings, trafficking, and weapons dealing but was especially exemplified by the erratic horror of the body.

The Work of the Drive

Walter Benjamin describes violence that is "crowned by fate" as both the foundation of law and the exercise of power over life and death.[11] In this courtroom, or anywhere in the modern world, violence and force serve to reify the law and its distant origins, while also shaping the distribution of cause and effect and notions of just punishment, including execution. Sami was clear about his duty toward his family. He was caught one afternoon by the Afghan National Police driving an older-model white Toyota Corolla up the steep and winding hill that overlooks the entire city of Kabul, atop which sits the historic Intercontinental Hotel. It was a particularly violent and hot summer in 2012, and the fighting and intelligence-gathering campaigns between the Taliban and the Afghan National Army were intensifying across Kabul. People talked about foreign powers and schemes; they talked not about trauma but about the orchestration of violence as part of the structural upheaval of a larger geopolitical shift in the global distribution of power and resources. It was about America, China, Russia, India, and the Gulf States.

As he drove up the hill, Sami recalled being worried his car could break down at any moment. Was he hoping it would? Most people were used to cars breaking down on paved and dirt roads, in the middle of long journeys—dangerously on the Khyber Pass or the Mahipar Highway cutting through the Hindu Kush Mountains—and at awkward moments. But on this day, if his car broke down, that would mean the end of his mission.[12] His car did not break down, and in the back he had a large water heater compressed with various readily found explosives that were rudimentary but compact and extremely powerful. I often wonder if he knew about the chilling and common practice of handlers remotely detonating explosives from afar if the driver got cold feet, but regardless, I know he kept driving up the hill.

Like the Kabul Serena Hotel, constructed in 1945, the British-built Intercontinental Hotel has been popular since 1969 among the elite and with foreigners. On a clear day, the view from the hotel's terrace and courtyard onto the patchwork of urban life below is panoramic. Clad with gilded walls, marble columns, chandeliers, and gold-tasseled velvet curtains, containing several restaurants, and with a storied rooftop pool overlooking the city, the hotel hosted everything from aristocratic wedding galas to disco parties and concerts. In more recent decades it became a place of faded grandeur when it fell into total disrepair during the Afghan-Soviet War, but then, after 2001, it became one of the few places available to host professional events, journalists, military contractors, and international aid organizations.

Sami's aim was clear: He was to continue driving up the hill through the final, white-tented checkpoint at the top, then straight into the hotel lobby, detonating his car and body on impact. His intended target was imprecise: a large gathering of government officials, contractors, and international business leaders. He was not a part of them, but neither was he ideologically opposed to their presence nor particularly concerned with the ingress of foreign life and values or even an economy in which value production was increasingly experienced as a feature of war and social violence. And in any case, he would be dead. But instead, by chance or owing to a tip from an informant (who else could have known?) he was intercepted by the Afghan police at the last checkpoint; he was wrestled out of his car, probably beaten, and arrested on the spot.[13]

Typically, these kinds of attacks have a signature in a broader milieu of symbolic-material violence, a pattern that, Jean Baudrillard argues, is a form of address in a world where the "real" of political violence is deferred by symbolic exchange and virtuality. He writes about the World Trade Center attacks as a fascination that is "foremost the fascination by the image (the consequences, whether catastrophic or leading to jubilation are themselves mostly imaginary)."[14] Like in the First Gulf War (1990), this violence is not only "real" and historical (of course, it is real and historical) but also part of a symbolic exchange that generates singularity and fascinates people through "the white magic of movies and the black magic of terrorism." Terrorism is a violence that is in part fictive and located in the virtual and imaginary circulation of the images that "consume the event" or make it resemble an "image-event."[15]

Modern violence and terror are marked by the loss of the principle of reality. The material violence of the First Gulf War was displaced by the symbolic power of its real-time images and around-the-clock news coverage, but it was also a surplus event, a violence made possible in language and representation.[16] In Sami's case he attempted to commit an act he otherwise would not "dream of," as he put it. There was no image in his mind for it and no fascination or black magic. He did not demonstrate any awareness of the prior attack on the hotel in 2011 or of the hotel's significance in Kabul as a modern landmark. His act was not about the hotel or the people inside. Thus, he presents us with a case where the violence of the real is added not to the image, as Baudrillard contends, but to a symbolic slot opened by discourse and the desire of the other: This is a slot that awaits reply, and this opening becomes the condition of possibility for the material violence that follows to be a fascinating addition.

Sami was facing the confusing prospect of a death sentence from the Afghan government, which likely wanted him and others like him dead, but he was overwhelmed and perplexed about how to judge the phenomenon of suicide bombings. To die and kill in a suicide-murder is to make everything end but, in this instance, it is also about storytelling, ambivalence, recurrence, and the place of language in comprehending events that are otherwise too dense or senseless to understand. Sami grew up in the countryside, but people around him would come and go from Kabul, sharing stories about things that happened in the city and about urban life. He knew that city people had more money than he did, and that they wanted more money than they had. Like most Afghans, he had heard about the corruption in Kabul, and he associated greed and perhaps even godlessness with the city and its troubled population. But he didn't dwell on any of this; he simply made a judgment of the profane in passing.

Other young men who moved to Kabul for work or love confessed a similar feeling of alienation in the city they had long fantasized about as a place of happiness and wealth. They described their old, poorer lives as small, most of them having grown up in stark rural villages or small towns with meager resources where they claimed close-knit persons and strangers alike fought over arable land and basic commodities. When I spoke to them, I had the sense they wanted to be part of the momentum of the new. At the same time, these young men were part of the unexpected movement of persons and desire in pathways difficult to predict or corral. Existential doubts about life or family, the excitement of new lovers, old loyalties, and the quest for quick money merged with a growing sensibility for the bold and unknown. It set them on a path of detours.

Sami recalled how his heart dropped at thought of his task. At one point, he said he thought his heart would burst. He knew what had to be done, but he didn't really understand his target or the city he was in. He pronounced the name "Intercontinental Hotel" correctly but with a noticeable trace of self-consciousness. In his hometown of Kunar, stories about life in Kabul were shared like bits of foreign intrigue. The small but influential anecdotes led him to understand the city as the epicenter of foreign influence and economic corruption, a place where foreign words like "World Bank," "IMF," "development," and "subcontractor" were casually used; in other words, a city that felt like it was much more a part of the world than the rest of country could be.

When the judges mentioned the hotel by name, Sami looked alert and tried to stand taller. On the day of his attempted attack, being so unfamiliar with the place, he did not know where exactly in the hotel the large group might be assembled. He did not know anything about the Intercontinental, its history, the kinds of people inside, what purpose hotels in general served, or if they were earnest, good places. He knew the people inside were usually rich, powerful, or foreign, and it was only in that sense that he understood the hotel as a serious place. I imagine him looking up at the structure—the rows of windows, multiple doors, and terraces—and being in awe. Or maybe he didn't look up at all but kept himself to himself.

The Breakdown of Local Order

A large province in the northeast of the country, approximately 140 miles from Kabul, Kunar was restive in 2012. The three-hundred-mile Kunar River and its numerous tributaries cut through the province and flow into the Kabul River near Jalalabad. In the deadly aftermath of the Communist Saur Revolution of April 1978, resistance in Kunar against the oppressive and indiscriminately violent government in Kabul became a prolonged source of military and political upheaval, resulting in both the massacre of local men in the village of Kerala in 1979 and a legacy of formidable defense against further military ingress or state violence.

For years Kunar has been a crucial province both in the imagination of many Kabulis, who envisage it as one center of the Taliban insurgency, and in the Afghan government's discourse on the importance of the US/NATO counterinsurgency as a buttress to its own sovereignty. In recent years, violence in the area peaked to the point that the lush, forested Pech Dara Valley was referred to as the "valley of death" by locals, who were inexorably caught in the middle of the fighting and subject to missile, bombing, and 81 mm mortar high-explosive rounds of fire. At the same time, the province was deeply marked by a new form of social violence: accusation and interpersonal sabotage, including the dissemination of false rumors about terroristic activity, which led to a surge in civilian deaths and arrests. Neighbors, former friends, close relatives, and sometimes people who simply envied what others had, found a new avenue for settling scores.

The gathering of intelligence, submitting of "tips" to NATO military bases or Afghan intelligence agencies, arrests, interrogations, and deaths by airstrikes had become part of a web of rumors and the violence of being unable to verify the truth of what others said.

In rural provinces across the country, especially in the south and east where the insurgency was strong, entire populations found themselves caught between the wanton violence of Afghan, NATO, and Taliban fighters who, depending on the alternation of power and sabotaging of strategic supply routes between them, controlled or lost territory. This transpired alongside deadly nighttime raids across the southern and eastern regions of the country.[17]

The frequency of accusations between civilians made violence an omnipresent part of people's lives, and terror became both the object of discernment (something to see in the behavior of others) and a general anxiety that emerged from the social body itself. Terror turned the social fabric into an extended scene of uncertainty and therefore into a collective fascination with why and how misfortune comes to overwhelm some people while sparing others. People asked the same questions of each other and themselves: What if I am wrongly accused of something? Who has it out for me? Do I have recourse to set things right?

As far as I know, Sami's family home never came under direct fire. He didn't mention any such event in court, and the judges did not raise it as a mitigating factor that could reduce his sentence or clarify his motive. But he had witnessed the dramatic upheavals that transformed the material conditions for survival all around him as much as they transformed an entire symbolic order. He had seen bad and disheartening things happen and believed they were all rooted in the desire for power or money. Usually, such events ended either in the death of people—sometimes entire families—or the feeling that the triumph of evil was unstoppable. He spoke with compassion about other people from his local village and the wider province who suffered from military and insurgent assaults. He said that times had dramatically changed with a ferocity he had never experienced before, and that nothing could be taken for granted.

He lived with pragmatic caution. "I just kept myself to myself," he said. On occasion, he cried over the state of his country. He also knew about the abuse of locals by American soldiers and the intense fighting between Taliban fighters and the Afghan National Army: "Brother is killing brother," he said. The people he lived alongside had transformed from individuals he could befriend or even marry to dangerous strangers. He kept a wide berth: "I always knew I had to keep away from people. The more I thought about it, the more I realized that it is with other people that you are never safe. You can never know them; you never know who they truly are. You do not know what they can do. The only person I really had in my life was my sister."

....

A propensity, like an urge or instinct, carries the notion of being out of control. It has no direct object or goal. Over time, as murder and revenge became more common in people's personal and political lives, the idea of a deep inclination for violence became part of how people imagined one another. They became criminals, strangers, crowds, paramilitary forces, and opposition groups to each other. This notion tightened and gave rise to social panic and brazen campaigns of urban bombings, political assassinations, suicide missions, and insurgency operations against the other. There was unprecedented use of force, and the very ideas of conviction and action increasingly came to mean a willingness to do whatever it takes to achieve one's end.

From all that I could gather and comprehend about Sami and his life, I understood that he saw conviction not just as something he took seriously, such as when he faced an ordeal or test, but as a crucial aspect of survival and collective life more generally. It was a form of *survivance*; it was part of the will to live, and in its absence the specter of disintegration and chaos was not only more real and frightening but so all-encompassing that it was impossible to see through the fog.

I think Sami did not see desperate moments, events, or encounters in life as situations that might resolve in time but simply as ongoing features of living in the world or, as he put it, of living in "this world." Circumstances moved like quicksand, and local men who had run into trouble often decided it was safer to leave their entire lives behind rather than risk retribution. Money, insurgent connections, black-market dealings, and revenge killings were always possible, making it easier to vanish than to resolve conflicts that usually involved large sums of cash, stolen land, illegally mined gemstones, drugs, or even timber harvested from the valley's lush forests. These men were among the "missing" who went on a *hijrat*, or pilgrimage, and cut communication with their families, usually leaving behind a web of desperation and, on the part of those they owed money or favors to, an appetite for revenge.

People were being killed with alarming regularity in both cities and the countryside. In Kabul disappearances were part of an urban discourse of fear about rural people closing in on the city in dangerous, primitive abandon. But the act of killing to achieve one's goals was no longer solely associated with ideological warfare and insurgency. Instead, it had become intertwined with much more pragmatic and material objectives, including the aim of avoiding being killed.

Confusion and disorder shifted from the targeted violence of typical warfare to a more open-ended relationship to others who pose danger or unwanted demands. Danger was understood more broadly too. It was not just the specter of death or bodily harm, both of which frequently occurred, but something more abstract and transcendent that was intertwined with the understanding of social life as the violent quest for profit and gain, on one hand, and a willingness to retaliate against others who gained, on the other. Thus, with equal rapidity, people became resources and means for one another or deadweight when no longer needed, and violence began to occur in situations where people either thought they stood to gain something or were able to cut a tie without regret. The idea of social cohesion and bonds that could transcend situations gave way to the assumption that people, like political orders, entire countries, or kings, come and go in life.

To be able to read this situation meant understanding that violence was not necessarily attached to specific events or objects of destruction.

It was uncertain and more powerful, vacillating between something that might occur and something that would transpire no matter what but at an unknown time or place. It was a shared and pervasive condition of being with others, and the more its power was acknowledged, the more random, aimless violence seemed to take hold of people's experiences. Its power was in the small spaces between people and desires and was no longer in specific sites or remote places—like the hinterland imagined to be its primal source—where, for those who live in cities, it can be repressed in the collective unconscious as being restricted to its rightful place.

Mina

I do not know when the idea of the bombing was first proposed to Sami or how he weighed the risk to the lives of others against Mina's life and against his own desire. At some point life and death became two halves of a single, radical moment, and his sense of duty toward his sister overpowered him. To the extent that his goal was crazy, it was a madness that emerged not in relation to his previous judgments but in the instant of this enormous decision to act. Did Sami go mad or grow bold out of necessity? The split within him became harder to suppress and found him in different moments: It found him on that life-altering afternoon on his way to the hotel, in his general understanding of others, in court through the political difference between speech and writing, and above all, in the gap between his predicament and its representation as a particular kind of reality. Each of these moments was a marker of difference and of the importance of signs and their interplay in his life, they signified the loss of fixed meaning in his new reality. But each of these moments was also an opening, a crack or seam where reason, ethics, and madness came into contact. In the courtroom he crossed that divide by insisting on his broken speech, even though the judges heard it as the irrational proclivity for violence. He invoked "sister" even though Mina was not there, and he told us about the violence of the law and its inscription on his body. More generally he crossed the divide where the limit of what he could think and explain and accept, the life of his mind, touched the words and desires of others and pushed him toward a fateful bid to action.

I interpret Sami's despair as a response to his experience of loss and a powerful metaphor for an entire political and social order in upheaval. He lived in a dense and postmodern world of confusion in which he felt at a loss and in the center of events he could not contain or navigate on his own. He negotiated a tight, demoralized place where people had come to expect little from one another and where, depending on the situation, there might be no room for mistakes. His place became even tighter once he made the connection between Mina and the bombing in his mind. He said that he knew the bombing was his final recourse and that if he did not go through with it, his sister would die. He lived a solitary life, perhaps without much impact on others, but he was devoted to Mina.

The events leading up to Mina's absence were part of a small space of being in which thought and action were not necessarily linked through intention but part of a state of social and interpretive not knowing. For Sami, people and events were often illegible. And because circumstances moved fast and could quickly unravel, he expressed uncertainty about how to interpret and live with them all: "I did not always know how to think about the things happening around me," he said. There was a lot to think through. He was close to his mother, trusted her, and said that "heaven lies beneath the feet of your mother." He had an especially close bond with Mina. Now he had mental images of her suffering, they were separated, and there were unknown men in their lives and village. There was a singular man in her life he did not know about, and then there was the question of sectarian difference and the laws of custom regulating marriage—thus a marriage his mother and sister presumed he would not approve of—and he was mired in a volatile environment without much hope of gain.

Not only did he have no prospect of gain, no money, no work contracts, no commission, no connections, no bribes, and no combat experience, he did not own any weapons, did not speak English, and could not read or write. In sum, he lacked all the things that had come to define economic and political life in the province and across the country, where the instrumental value of an individual had become more important than ever. For years, after his village and the country transformed, he learned to keep "his head low," and in that linear, exclusive space Mina seemed to be the only person in his life. She embodied the tie of a dialectical bond that was indestructible and naive but authentic. For as long as he could remember, she had been by his side. Otherwise, he led a lonely life without many friends or people to lean on.

Mina's secret relationship with an older Shia man, whom I presume she talked to even more than she did to Sami, was known at least to their mother but not to him. I imagine that, unlike him, Mina was eager to be among people and talk about herself and her life, and perhaps when she spoke about the future, she seemed buoyant and full of desire. He did not ask her questions. But Mina, her mother, and the Shia man in her life decided to plan an elopement to Pakistan where, once she was far away from her village and everyone who knew her, they could easily visit an imam and be formally married. Her mother helped Mina arrange and carry out her plan with the shared understanding that after Mina's sudden departure, which to everyone else would seem like an inexplicable disappearance, the mother would tell anyone who asked that Mina had been kidnapped from the village center.

To be taken from a village, town, or city during that year when organized crime and violence had come to shape how people heard, watched, and spoke to one another was tantamount to having been killed. The likelihood of surviving an abduction was small under the best of circumstances, when the abductee had family connections and the promise of ransom. But in Kunar, as a woman from a poor family in a place where locals faced the violence of the insurgency and counterinsurgency in addition to an open-ended and nefarious network of connections to Kabul, Mina's situation would have been dire. Locals referred to things that were out of place or unexpected as *ajeeb* (strange, wondrous) and such things had become more common in daily life as well as more difficult to control or predict owing to various factors, including trade networks, illegal timber smuggling, the direction of the river and basin flow, political operatives, spies, "commission" workers, water and dam protectors, illegal mining, and criminals.[18]

Adversarial zones were cut out of older topographies, and cycles of retaliatory violence and revenge deterritorialized places and relations, turning information about people into a deadly and lucrative weapon. Streets and codes of honor were reterritorialized alongside chaos and power shifts. Local power brokers and tough men became a prominent social type. At the same time, a sense of caution about language and information unsettled people. Words mattered in ways that could not be foreseen and, because there were so many new possible sources of money, the betrayal of others could easily be worked into all sorts of plans. Sami tried to keep the chaos of this milieu controlled and shut out of his life, but once he made the connection in his mind between his family's misfortune and this new social reality, it began weighing on him: "I had no peace. I had no good thoughts. By God, I swear I was haunted night and day. I was drowning in thoughts of her suffering. There was no peace."

For Sami, Mina's absence was difficult. It was a political and national loss of a type he could never have imagined they would be swept up in: "Our adversity had become much larger; it was political and about the forces at war in our country. It was no longer about only us." Many of the failed suicide bombers had experienced the dissolution of family and social bonds and most had some experience of what they characterized as misfortune and pain (*ranj va moosibat*). These experiences were the condition for a new kind of social violence: bombings that, while sometimes political, touched on something more profoundly irreclaimable within the social.

The phenomenon of the bombings relied on a disavowal of the social but also took the social body as its object of attachment. Suspense, misfortune, unexpected delays, ambivalent ties, crowds, and the destruction of collective bodies all became part of the general experience of violence and, thus, the general understanding of "society." More than reflecting alienation from previous ways of knowing and being, which was true, there was a reckoning with the force of how to live anew with others. In Sami's case, misfortune took on a much more linear, direct relationship to the violence of his plan. At the same time, conditions in his village had generated a set of factors that made it difficult for him to comprehend the trajectory of events as he was led to understand them. The situation made it especially difficult to answer neighbors' and acquaintances' questions about why such a thing would happen to Sami's family. And why, of all people, to Mina?

Like terror and anxiety, misfortune involves the troubling sense of not knowing who one is in the eyes of others. It encourages the uncanny feeling that one has been singled out by adversity in a personal way, which results in a particular kind of anxiety that is as much about the future as it is the fear of an unwelcome recurrence from one's past. In this sense, misfortune is about the experience of exchange and singularity and the place of difference in our sense of general principles. Like a pure gift with no origin, the experience of an accident (or misfortune) comes from nowhere. It has no discernible cause and bears no trace of its movement or range.

Misfortune is also inseparable from the problem of interpretation (the question of why) and, thus, from the politics of naming and accusation. To this end, Siegel shows us that in cases involving accusations of witchcraft, what is initially believed to be an accident is later determined to be the act of a witch. In naming something that occurs "for no reason" as witchcraft, and in naming a "witch" responsible for it, the accident that "proceeds from no place namable is possibly recovered for the social."[19]

An event that is beyond our control is a difficult object of knowledge. Again, we can liken this to what Siegel describes as the persistence of what is not known, to the emergence of "non-meaning," and to the possibility of something foreign lying behind the work of signification.[20] It is not that there aren't any signs to read, in fact, they are abundant, but rather that the signs are discernable only by assuming that there is a larger, more inviolable power behind their emergence that cannot become an object of knowledge. In this important sense of being possible to reclaim, the unfortunate event becomes part of a more general truth that transcends any single occurrence. In the minds of those who experience it, the event transcends its own instance of manifestation to speak to something more pressing and inviolable.

PART 2: A MOTHER'S VOICE

Sami and his mother were illegible to each other but not complete strangers. As if in a tragic plot, they moved intensely and in doing so, both somewhat blindly transformed the meaning of actions in their lives without understanding the consequences. Each occupied a different relationship to the power of their own words. From the beginning, the mother spoke with a voice of authority that Sami considered true and inviolable. Her voice carried the force of the prior, of everything that he had known and taken for granted, and because it came first, he could turn to her for answers, and she could speak of the things he was not able to understand on his own.

When we claim to trust someone's words, we evoke the confidence that others speak for something we can believe and accept. Sami spoke in a plain manner that others perceived to be consistent with his illiteracy and straightforward view of the world that did not include metaphors or ambiguous meanings. For him, things are what they are. And as far as others were concerned, because his consciousness was unmediated by writing and reading and was incapable of a certain kind of deliberation, he understood the words of others in a matter-of-fact way.

It is impossible to speculate on what Sami was thinking when he decided to undertake the bombing or to fully grasp what he thought when his mother first told him Mina was missing. But I do not think his desperation to save Mina's life was heroic fantasy or part of a shared reality between brother and sister or mother and son. Instead, I think it emerged from his encounter with a form of fiction he could not read. His predicament is akin to the gap Barbara Johnson describes when judgment grounds itself not in the binary of good versus evil or the real versus its simulacrum but "in a suspension of the opposition between textuality and referentiality, just as politics can be seen as that which makes it impossible to draw the line between 'language' and 'life.'"[21] In Sami's story a line is drawn not only between mother and son but also between the fictive realm and event-making, the undecidable, intractable zone in which Gilles Deleuze situates events such that the "event" "is coextensive with becoming, and becoming is itself coextensive with language."[22]

My point is that Sami's mother's story enabled him to act, and his action was part of living with transformative forces he could not recognize let alone control on his own. He carried this rupture of signification, and the less he and others thought he could understand, the more he sought for the reality behind events. But the transformation of Sami into a man of frightening and bold action raises the question of what his mother's discourse is about. What does she foresee transpiring?

Mina went missing from Kunar in a summer when the insurgency was going strong. Both sides sustained heavy and unpredictable losses, and the frequency of violent encounters in Sami's village and region had made people wary. Across the country the military and political authority of the government was being contested. There were accusations of financial corruption against government officials ranging from high-level ministers to their staff to merchants and even clerics; meanwhile, insurgent and Afghan forces were embroiled in deadly firefights and ambush attacks across the major provinces.

In Kunar and elsewhere, foreign aid and development programs created a new class of beneficiaries and patronage networks with strong ties to Kabul, and the idea of prosperity, including social discourse about windfall gains, was sharply defined by notions of loyalty and sabotage. Loyalties and paranoia diverged with both dramatic and barely perceptible shifts in power. From courtrooms to corporate and government offices to people's homes and the front lines of battle, the prevalence of false information and intelligence gathering, including through torture, had turned the reality and fantasy of knowing something, especially about others—that is, knowing more than others do—into a new and deadly source of exchange value. Information, gossip, covert operations, mystic intuitions, conspiratorial theories, and dialogic relations became part of a formidable bind that was impossible to control. People spoke about the violence as impersonal, like a transcendent force, but also tenacious because it abruptly found them without sense or reason. Both cause and effect were more difficult to trust in. At the same time, notions of state sovereignty and order had largely come undone, and the precipitous mimesis of control by government and insurgent groups, who were sometimes separated by only a few miles of terrain, was part of a new tensile disorder.

After Mina's disappearance, the first couple of days passed without any information. Initially Sami's mother only told him she was "missing." He recalled that neighbors started to come to their house, at first to check on his and his mother's well-being, then later out of curiosity, to ask why Mina was inexplicably absent. Did Sami and his mother know who she was with? How could such a thing happen? Did they have more information? Mina was missing, but in many ways, it was the absence of interpretation and the social desire to fill that void, the desire to make it part of a narrative and for her absence to be subsumed into the unity of a plot, that confronted Sami and intensified his panic. The "outside" he had tried so hard to repress from his life found him not through the material violence he had witnessed but by way of a desire for an explanation. "People asked us all the time where Mina was and what had really happened," he said. "I could not take it. I never knew what to tell them or how to answer all the questions." A few days later, his mother told him Mina had been abducted by a group of men from the village. When he first heard this story, he was in shock that such an event could happen to his family. He recalled the moment: "My heart dropped. I did not know what to think."

Language is always a medium of communication and volatility. It enables our thoughts and consciousness and our making ourselves known to others, but it also exceeds those functions, making it impossible to say exactly what we mean or to know what, in turn, our words will mean to others. These are the fissures and, elsewhere, the aporetic opening that makes social life both violent and possible. That opening makes every representation dual: enabling and volatilizing communication, and thus making every element of reality a fiction just as every act of fiction bears some element of reality.[23] It was a partial reality that Mina was missing in the first place, but the absence of an explanation from her family and the villagers' collective desire to fill that void, to bear witness to the power of explanation and give her absence words, signs, fuller sense, and the image of direction, became an event just as consequential as her disappearance, if not more desperate and extreme. Where is Mina? Who is she with? Will she come home? What do we say to others? These are not universal questions, but they are general and urgent because others expect us to ask them of ourselves. They are determined by the kind of sense our language makes, not in a limited sense but in the broadest spirit of possibility. They relate to custom, honor, taboo, unspoken codes, and the social recognition of permissible forms of desire. Above all, the need to know what happened to Mina and close the gap between an event and its unexplained origin is part of the collective desire for communicability irrespective of cohesion. But Sami's misunderstanding tightened around him. He could only belatedly understand what had always been true or "there." In this sense, he was not only illiterate but also blind. This is not to say that had he or his mother "seen" things for what they were, then a different outcome would have transpired but rather that the inability to see extended to their relationship, to language, and thus to every possible representation they could believe in or act on.

Intuition, Knowing, Acting

In court, Sami spoke on his own behalf. Like many of the other defendants, he was confused by his thick manila case file, which the judges readily referenced, and sometimes he was met with silence rather than a dialogic reply from them. He recalled the difficult atmosphere in Kunar. He recollected details and a chronology of unexpected events that almost ended in death. He expressed fragments of thoughts and moments that seemed trivial at first but later revealed their full significance.

Something had been unleashed that touched on aspects of his life in a way he had not experienced before: "It is a very different time in our country" he said, "nothing resembles what used to be." At the same time, he wanted to protect what he had. And because he was asserting the primacy of a relationship he did not fully understand (Mina was, in fact, more of a stranger to him than perhaps anyone else), his mother's discourse became the sole source of a series of effects in him. Her voice contained the truth of something prior and well established and reassured him of what he could not grasp on his own. The only way for Sami to avoid death and killing was to not take his mother's words seriously and to give up the idea that she was the voice of truth. He could avoid death and killing by grounding his own judgment not in the discourse or tradition of the other but in its failure to relate to a new reality. But this he could not do: "I could not deny my mother's voice and words. She speaks the truth, and she is wise. To respect the words of our mother is something passed down in our religion and from my forefathers."

Sami had thought about the attack. I assume he was in touch with his handlers. And I assume he planned out the details and weighed the benefit to Mina before deciding to act. And yet, despite these rational deliberations, I also assume he was at the limit of what he could predict about what others were capable of based on his experience. Because he believed that Mina had been taken by force rather than leaving out of desire and that her absence was the outcome of the failure of the social fabric rather than its partial cohesion, he was led to pay attention to the social breakdown he had failed to see before. He became preoccupied with noticing things that were different and thus preoccupied with difference in general. This is an opening amid a series of closures that seem to have over-determined his life. Sami's awakening to the world required him to read his surroundings. He took for granted what his mother told him. He read people, signs, rumors, and occurrences with a new intensity in order to see how things differed from the quotidian context he had always known.[24] "Once I knew what happened in my own village, I began to pay attention to everything."

The more Sami came to see himself as more than just an illiterate man, the more the importance of being more than an "illiterate, plain" man impressed itself into his interpretation of events around him. He told the court he began to finally see things and to understand other people better. Because he understood clearly now, in a context when the entire scope of his subjective experience had become indeterminable, I believe the dialogue with his mother took on a new role and transformed an ambiguous situation into an actionable one. In deciding to act with the insurgency to end his sister's suffering, he was both consciously seeking his own death and unconsciously repeating the kind of terror and violence he feared and hated most. His judgment inscribes his action within an order of deferral he cannot accept and beyond the order of law or rational thought. He transcends the law of collective norms and even the opposition of good versus evil. This is not to suggest that remaining in the realm of language, especially listening and talking but not acting upon what one hears, or existing in a state of ambivalence, is the same as avoiding death and violence nor to say that acting is destructive while speaking is not; instead, it makes clear that in this case the role of dialogue was deadly precisely because language was already a violent action in his world and its dialectical relationship to further action was not something that could be contained in words alone.

I want to return to the idea that Sami is simple, forthright, and literal-minded, in short, that "he is what he is." In fact, his self-understanding is dynamic (he refers to himself as *having been* simple) compared to the static, unchanging way others read him. Sami's predicament is not only how to keep a world of confusion and political violence at bay but also how to live with those who presume he is still unambiguous to himself and others in the way he has been. In the courthouse this predicament manifests as the problem of judgment and how to understand the place of reason in the absence of writing. What kind of defendant is Sami? What kind of criminal? What is the consequence of releasing him into society? Would he commit violence again? Would he do so only for Mina's sake? For the judges there were two distinct aspects to this risk: Some people (usually literate ones) possess good judgment that is close to truth, to meaning, and to the processes of reason, while others (usually illiterate) possess bad judgment that reflects irrational thoughts and violent desires. Thus, to understand what is at stake in Sami's trial, it is crucial to situate the juridical opposition between guilt and innocence not as a matter of terror versus law or guilt versus innocence but as part of the difference between two ways of encountering language and the type of judgment or reason each presumes.

Confusion, or the Failure of Representation

From whatever angle we consider Sami's ordeal, the problem of interpretation and language, including the presumption that, compared to illiteracy, literacy entails a more cohesive, deliberative understanding of the world, had thoroughly invaded his life. It extended to the farthest reaches of what he could expect and what others in turn, and at great cost, expected of him. For his mother and for the legal system and the social networks he was immersed in (without belonging to), the power to read and write had become synonymous with the capacity to discern and understand general forces at work. Literacy had become the same as predicting the relationship between one's actions and their consequences and being able to introduce "circumstance and distinction where there had only been conformity and belonging"; in other words, the ability to recognize the workings of a political and symbolic order.[25]

The question of whether a crime was committed against the Afghan state is inseparable from the assumption that illiterate individuals are beyond the reach of the law and are driven by compulsion. Sami's attempted suicide-murder to save Mina's life at the cost of his own is part of a moving series in which the conditions of discourse, truth, and action have become confused. But it is also part of the power of storytelling and the place of fiction in our daily and political lives and in confronting the law.

Sami was caught between deception and the belief that his mother's discourse was free of deception and still pure. What was impossible for Sami to achieve in the symbolic domain—he had no wife, no child, and I assume not many friends—was transformed into the singular bond of flesh for which he was willing to die and kill others. The last tear of signification found him not through illiteracy but through a sense of duty toward Mina who, being irreplaceable, was more significant than anyone else, even though she had started a new life without telling him. He read the situation in search of what, amid the fungibility of life around him, was still priceless and worthy of love.

All of this shows us that the place of subjectivity in language is never one of simple opposition or conformity. Sami was always attuned to the power of difference even if his illiteracy cast him in the eyes of others as blind to its place in language and deferral, and thus as unable to avoid the violence of literalism. He felt and looked for what was different and singular while other people—including his mother and perhaps earlier Mina, who did not appear in court a single time on his behalf—presumed the singular had been effaced by their circumstances and more importantly, insofar as Sami was concerned, by his inability to see beyond the manifest content of the things. But there is another uncertainty over what in the end Sami represents and how to understand the kind of madness that begins in the absence of the letter and becomes an immeasurable duty that goes beyond one's own life and name.

Sami's story reveals how desire and political action emerge through the intersubjective process Jacques Lacan describes "as the major determination the subject receives from the itinerary of a signifier" and how, in turn, that movement determines the place of the subject in the symbolic order.[26] For Sami there was no meaning in his life without Mina. She was crucial to his sense of self and the ethical duty he carried that took precedence over rational precept or collective life. In relation to her he fulfilled, in a way that rivals Antigone, "a pure concept of duty" and the decision to act "beyond the realm of rational discourse and the collective norms of human satisfaction it implies."[27] And yet there was no Mina to be seen. I do not know for certain if she knew about Sami's ordeal, but the judges spoke as if his family was aware. Were they? As the proceedings went on, no statement, recording, or any form of corroboration came from her that could be used in his defense. She was present only in name and as an ideal type; she was there through her desire and absence but not through devotion to Sami.

She was absent in another sense, too. She was present to him by virtue of being estranged from herself. She was his sister only as long as she was not in love. When she fell in love, she felt she could no longer be a sister or daughter, and she eloped. She was present through the trace of this double absence, and it revealed her place in another discontinuous chain of desire and subjectivity. But the limit to being for the other is also a condition of possibility for an ethics beyond the self or collective understanding. Thus, whether we understand her "absence" as the culmination of her radical desire or as the tactical precondition for violent political action in her name, it is also part of a more profound metaphor for the moving place of relations in this story and, therefore, a metaphor for the place of signification in our lives. No matter how hard Sami might have tried to do things differently, the meaning of the loss of control could be understood only through a trace structure he did not see. It transpired between everyone involved, especially between him and his mother, and it changed the place of absence in their lives from what was missing to that which was overdetermined and was too close to handle.

The movement of signification determines the place of the subject in a political and symbolic order and in relation to the question of what the other wants from us. Sami's story is about how narrative and desire move in the same orbit, and like in fiction, how that orbit encompasses different signs and meanings we rely on but cannot control. It illuminates how phenomena and events can only be understood retrospectively and through how they are "related to the symbolic chain that binds and orients them."[28] In other words, nothing about this kind of predicament and intersubjective necessity, not its words or actions or the larger mise-en-scène, can be considered apart from the place of language between subjects and apart from their respective desires.

What would we do if we found ourselves in Sami's place? In his mother's place? In Mina's place? To me, this dilemma recalls the movement of subjectivity and desire in Edgar Allan Poe's "The Purloined Letter," where a secret letter addressed to a queen without the king's knowledge, the contents of which the reader also does not know, shapes desire, being, and the perception of power between all the subjects in the story. I think of this tale because Mina's absence also unfolds in scenes that Sami can and cannot read. The initial scene of discovering she is gone and the confusion over what happened, followed by the collective scene of neighbors and relatives coming and asking whether she would return, and finally his mother's story.

These function as three scenes but also as a metaphor for the role of signification in Sami's crumbling lifeworld and its power to bring the pressure of insurgent violence to bear on his body and life. When his mother tells him Mina has been abducted from the village by a group of men, she reads Sami as someone who is unable to read beyond the face value of words and discourse; he recalled this experience, and perhaps that very moment, as "listening to his mother's voice." Perhaps she thought Sami would interpret their misfortune as something best left in the hands of God. Instead, he understood her story as another sign of the increasing politicization of experience and social life he could no longer bear.

Mina's absence is part of a social desire for explanation without the possibility of understanding. It is both an absence and the presence of collective anxiety about a range of supplementary meanings that could not be controlled: What does it mean to go missing, to leave, to be found, or to be found and no longer be the same person? She was free and undefined as long as she was gone. If she were found, that would raise numerous questions about who she could be and for whom. The trace is "the mark of the absence of a presence, an always already absent present, of the lack at the origin that is the condition of thought and experience."[29] In a similar way, given that Mina was never self-same or transparent to others, nor absent from their minds, her absence is not a lack but a metaphor for the deferral of meaning at the center of the story and a crucial *point de capiton* in Sami's trajectory.[30] Following her absence, the family name, Sami's memories, and his relations with others all became unstable relative to the way they had been: a dishonorable name, false memories, insidious relationships, and so on. In this sense, her absence and presence were not opposite realities but were interconnected throughout his experience of her being missing from the place where he had always expected to find her.

Movement and Plot

What moves or takes hold of us and our desires? The reader of the story and the judges of Sami's predicament (the judges, his neighbors, his mother, and us) move through signs and representations that are never what they seem or are not to be found in one place. How does the difference between a possible interpretation and a phenomenon (the "event") bear on the power of narrative and understanding but also on Sami's decision to act?

I read Sami's misunderstanding in two dimensions of experience. The first is the tangible, everyday reality of political unrest and violence in

Kunar, which disrupted daily life and left people feeling deeply insecure. This is what I interpret as the dimension of Mina's absence that Sami and his neighbors understand as her being "missing" from her rightful place with her family. But there is another linguistic aspect to her absence, which is the narrative reality of Mina being taken. This becomes a story about a plot and then, more consequentially, about her being irrevocably gone through a twist of fate.

A narrative is part of a sustained but finite structure: Every plot has a beginning, middle, and ending and a hermeneutic of meaning that unfolds over time, with the end being foreshadowed in the beginning and with breakthrough moments of sense. Writing about this logic of deferral, Peter Brooks describes the place of the reader within its temporal structure as embedded in the "anticipation of retrospection as our chief tool in making sense of narrative, the master trope of its strange logic."[31]

To think of Sami's story and the narrative his mother told him as stories with a fixed duration that move through the principles of displacement and coherence, through metonymy and metaphor, is to begin to come to grips with its near-tragic ending and with the intersubjective reading that moved the plot forward without ever rising to consciousness but that was retrospectively revealed through his understanding that others saw in him the embodiment of an illiterate dunce. That "reading" of Sami as plain and stupid is woven into the play and into the deferral of meaning as well as the moments when things fall into place, the moments when the power of metaphoric unity serves as the quilting point of comprehension and action.

The sense or feeling of a hypothetical "Yes, of course!" or "Yes, that's what I must do!" is gained through narrative, when metaphoric binding overwhelms the play of meaning to reach a final, motherly, and sovereign point. Sami reaches a unity of meaning (we can think of this as an endpoint rather than a chain of signification) through recasting her intuition as direct understanding and by taking her words as deadly serious.

Sami tells us he was lonely. He worried about the future of his small village, kept his head down, had a sense of duty toward his family and, above all, he loved Mina. He explained all of this, along with the violence of interrogation and prison life, in scattered but revealing speech. But in describing how he navigated the series of events leading up to the planned hotel bombing, Sami sometimes fell silent and at other times expressed the difficulty of putting into words the misfortune of his life: "I do not know what to say sometimes, but a lot happened to me." "How should I say this . . . ?," "I will try to say this the best way I know how." "Oh, I cannot say what I mean!"

Sami's speech is full of the signs of language. They reveal his fear and understanding that the words and manner of his speech can determine the outcome of his trial. I think he speaks to tell us he is uncertain of how to speak, and his discourse about the place of language reveals what he knows and how, in turn, he will be understood by others. He is overdetermined by language. But he is also driven by desire and the call of the other that is beyond collective norms or translation. In his seminar on Antigone, Lacan shows us that the scope and intensity of a tragic story expand through the force of desire. For Antigone this is the expression of a death drive through her singular will to honor her brother, Polynices. In this effort she transgresses the law of the city and submits to the higher law of the dead. This higher law necessitates a more powerful moral intervention than what is proscribed by the civic or symbolic order; the ethical duty to the dead requires a singular devotion to caring for and honoring and being with those who can no longer speak on their own behalf; thus, Antigone must bury Polynices, whose burial and mourning Creon has prohibited, despite the limits of sovereignty and customary law.[32]

Sami's choice was beyond rational limits, but it also transcended the customary oppositions that defined social life and collective thought around him. His choice was about duty and an insistence on distinguishing himself from a sea of sameness in which betrayal had become routine, and nothing mattered. In this dystopian world, he insisted that Mina was different. The questions of who he became for others and what they in turn meant to him were caught in the gap between speculation and knowing that was opened by language. This gap arose in part due to his mother's initial story of abduction, but in a more complicated sense, it was due to the idea of Mina's presence and absence being obscurely connected to different ideas, symbols, and actions. Every narrative, and therefore every process of becoming for and learning to be with others, is part of a complicated interplay between metonymic and metaphorical processes. And where the former displaces, puts together, and at times marks a gesture toward contiguity through related symbols and incidental juxtaposition, the latter bestows sense and order and, as Brooks puts it, carries out the "metaphoric work of eventual totalization" that "determines the meaning and status of the metonymic work of sequence—though it must also be claimed that the metonymies of the middle produced, gave birth to, the final metaphor."[33] In this sense, I understand Sami's mother's intuition and ability to comprehend without conscious deliberation to be the final point of cohesion that turned a series of discontinuous events into a story that could only mean one thing.

Metaphoric Moment

As the meaning behind her absence became clear and an object of knowledge, so did Sami's desire for intervention become a reply to the call of the Other. He entered what Lacan describes as the metaphoric pole of a "signifying quest" that is otherwise interminable and without unity and which did not, as he described, give him any answers or hope prior to his decision to act. His mother's intuition carried the power of certainty. It presupposed all the confusion he was working through and bestowed a meaning and coherence that would otherwise be lost in the world of speech and doubt. Sami described this moment when the disparate meaninglessness of his suspicions began to cohere as being strange like a dream. He entered an oneiric world that finally structured the displacement he experienced through the deferral of meaning. In this sense, he was caught between persons but also caught in a narrative structure that did not reveal its significance, that moved in the space Roland Barthes describes as "dilatory" and gained coherence through his mother's presentiment and in the moment when everything suddenly fell into place.[34] Sami followed this narrative to its limit and discovered the beginning of action. Yet, he was still traversing what others had done or known or said; he was covering the ground already trod by Mina and his mother and that was repeated in the space of narrative as the place in which he would come to be and understand how he could act.

As a political allegory, Sami's ordeal, which resulted in a ten-year sentence in prison, is irreducible to the place of terror in Afghan society or the consciousness of truth and lie. It is about the itinerant place of the symbolic in our psychic life and in the distorted, unpredictable relations that emerge between knowing and speaking, dying, and learning how to trust and doubt. In other words, it exemplifies everything that makes political and subjective life impossible to predict and that makes the object of desire a moving target we can never be sure we will reach. For Sami the things he did not know but trusted to be true were not severed from rational thought so much as they were bound to his perception of the place of intuition; or to put it differently, the discourse of *not just any other but his mother*. Sami, who did not understand that this could nonetheless be untrue, and who clearly lived to repress both violence and untruth in general, was no less a reader of his mother and his surroundings than they were of him and his illiterate plainness.

CHAPTER TWO

Rumors of Love

[Berganza:] I understand everything you say, Cipión. . . . I have heard on many different occasions about our great virtues . . . and signs of our being close to demonstrating that we have some kind of understanding capable of speech and reflection.

[Cipión:] What I have heard lauded and praised is our remarkable memory, our gratitude, and great fidelity, so that we are often painted as symbols of friendship; and you'll have seen, if you have looked, that on alabaster tombs with figures of those buried there, when they are husband and wife, between the two, at their feet, the figure of a dog is placed as a sign that in life their friendship and fidelity were inviolable.

—MIGUEL DE CERVANTES, "The Novel of the Colloquy of the Dogs"

This was the air in which the glance of a boy fell for the first time on a passing girl, while he talked all the more zealously to his friend. And such were his efforts to betray himself neither by his eyes nor his voice that he saw nothing of her.

—WALTER BENJAMIN, "A Berlin Chronicle"

Your honor, these days you cannot speak with someone who does not want to speak with you.

—SOHRAB (spoken at his trial)

PART 1: "I SHOULD HAVE KNOWN"

Sohrab is a young police officer from Police District 8 in West Kabul, a mostly working-class area that is densely inhabited and is a crucial route between Kabul and provinces in the east of Afghanistan where the insurgency was peaking in 2013, the year of his trial. He has what is best described as a bewildered drive for love. When he fell in love, sometime in 2011, it was like a gift. He said he felt as if he had "just been born." But by the summer of the next year, without any indication or warning (at least not upon first reflection, because there were some signs along the way) Sohrab was charged with the abduction of his legal wife. He only learned of those crimes on the night of his wedding party at his sister's house, when he was accused in what he described as a few astounding minutes. He said that the accusation against him was part of a series of moves, like pieces on a chessboard, that he could not have foreseen and that stymied him from being happy in life.

The sense that an eclipse of meaning had generated a series of moves and encounters, leading to accusation and encompassing the loss of love and happiness, marks the dilemma of this chapter and the attempt to understand the complex gift of love amid the breakdown of social exchange. In tracing its power, both in dialogue with others and as a feature of life in Kabul, I situate love, accusation, and absence as constituting the recurring problem of how, or whether, it is possible to know the other and to express that knowing in dialogue. This is the quandary Sohrab expresses to the court, even as he repeatedly relies on the refrain that he should have known better than to believe transformative, lasting love was possible. How do we experience loss in language? How does this bear on the experience of love and accusation, and on the discourse of the other as very close, formative even, but not grounded in reality? In the second part of the chapter, entitled "See My Desire," these questions and the loss Sohrab describes in the language of what he *should have known* is braided into the accusation against him, an accusation made in the form of a written statement to the court by Razia (aka Soraya), his legal wife. That accusation defers its meaning to the representative order of images, to photographic capture and its unexpected emergence outside of the spoken and written word. In dialogue with the story and case against Sami, this chapter seeks to trace the partial meanings, incoherences, and place of gain and loss as mediated through the role of language in collective life and the discourse of the other, which is at times spoken, at other times written, and sometimes caught by the photographic flash.

. . . .

On his first day in court in central Kabul, Sohrab entered the room and stood before the judges with a tired, forlorn demeanor but was direct in his answers.

JUDGE: Do we have our defendant here?

SOHRAB: I understand how this works. I am a man of the law myself. It has always been an honor to represent the law.

JUDGE: Oh, really? I take it you are Abdul Hamid then? No. That is your father's name. Well, is your father's name Abdul Hamid?

SOHRAB: Abdul Hamid. Yes.

JUDGE: Good we are getting somewhere. I understand that you were a cop, is that right?

SOHRAB: Yes.

JUDGE: And where exactly did you go out on duty?

SOHRAB It isn't always the same place. We go on patrol in various neighborhoods. We go where there is an issue or possible danger and when we are needed, and sometimes we are on patrol across the city. Because of the recent violence and uncertainty, our patrols have changed, and we go where we think there is a risk to the public.

JUDGE: And how do you understand your duty as a police officer? You are the face of the law in the city.

SOHRAB: That is how I understand it, Your Honor. I am the face of the law in a city with many troubles and many people. But I represent the law; I protect people from harm and violence, and I try my best to see that justice finds those who are most deserving and who suffer because of crime and evil.

JUDGE: I see. Well, you yourself have now been accused of a very serious crime. How long have you known the woman who is accusing you?

[Sohrab suddenly looks pained. He answers in a more earnest tone.]

SOHRAB: Soraya worked at the television station where my nephew also works. It was my nephew who eventually arranged for us to speak on the telephone. We established contact through the phone. I was in touch with her directly every day. Soraya told me about her abusive mother who prohibited her from going to college and kept her at home for domestic duties. Your Honor, she told me she was like a slave in that household. That she was mistreated and suicidal and that she had tried to commit suicide several times before.[1]

JUDGE: How long did you know her prior to that?

SOHRAB: I knew her for about one year before we married. It was for at least one year.

JUDGE: I see. So you knew her for one year and then you married, as you say. And who works at the television station? Your cousin?

SOHRAB: He is my younger nephew.

JUDGE: OK. And a relative of the woman works there as well?

SOHRAB: No.

JUDGE: How did you get in touch with her? Your nephew was the connection?

SOHRAB: On the phone. My nephew is only fifteen. He told me to get in touch with her directly, so I got her number and I called her. She works at the station with him, and he knew her through work. That is why I asked him to ask her for her number, and she gave it to him.

JUDGE: And you just called her like that?

SOHRAB: Well, yes. I made the first contact. She did not give it to me directly, but she knew, after speaking to my nephew about it, that it [her phone number] was intended for me, so in that sense she was expecting me to call. Your Honor, these days you cannot speak with someone who does not want to speak with you. It is only when that person also desires it that it is possible to have a conversation and to continue speaking. We spoke many times.

JUDGE: OK. Look: let's get to the point. When you took her from her house, was anyone else with you or were you all alone?

SOHRAB: No. I was alone. And when I left my own house, I was alone. Nobody saw me.

JUDGE: Was anyone else present in the house with her?

SOHRAB: It was just her and her sister, Your Honor.

JUDGE: Just her and her sister. Alone. I see. And what was in the car?

SOHRAB: Well, it was a rental car. I cannot afford a new car. There was nothing inside of it.

JUDGE: A rental car? Was it a hatchback (*saracha*)?[2]

SOHRAB: Yes, yes, a hatchback, a rental hatchback. She told me she was in love with me, that she wanted to be with me, and I wanted to send my family to her house to formally ask for her hand, but she said she would be beaten by her family because I am Sunni. She said they would ask her: "Where in the city did you find this Sunni man?" So, she promised she would elope with me. On the phone that afternoon she said, "I am dressed but my sister is in the front yard doing laundry. When she goes inside, I will run out!" We had her cousin call and divert her sister, and she finally came out. We ran away. She spent one night in my house, the first night, and then the following day we were married. She did not accept the officiation of a Sunni cleric, but she got up and performed ablutions, came back and recited verses, and that's it, we were married.

JUDGE: That was your entire marriage ceremony? No dowry, no parental consent, nothing?

SOHRAB: That was it. We were married, and a few days later, my sister had a dinner party for us—we were all there: my parents, my siblings, laughing, having a good time. And suddenly, members of the Afghan National Police and the National Directorate of Security stormed the house, armed, and arrested me for kidnapping.

JUDGE: So let me get the facts straight. Except for her sister, this woman told you that nobody was home, not her mom nor her father and brother. She admits to you that she is more or less alone in a house in Kabul. In fact, she tells you more than this right? She admits to you that her entire family was in Dubai or somewhere, right? So, in fact, she also happens to be all alone in the country.

SOHRAB: It was different than that. How can I put it? She did not speak in those kinds of words, and she did not mean "I am alone in the country now." Yes, she did tell me her family was abroad in an Arab country. I do not know which specific one; you see, at that time the detail was not very important to me, but I believe they were in Dubai for a wedding.

JUDGE: In any event, they were someplace foreign, and she was all alone. Correct? Where exactly they were or why the family left the country without her is not on trial here. You are on trial.

SOHRAB: Honorable Judge, I understand.

JUDGE: Good. But didn't you understand or anticipate that you would create a major problem for yourself if you took her from her house while nobody else was there? Do you understand this? You took a young woman from her home in broad daylight without permission or even the knowledge of her family. And you are a police officer? If this is your quality of judgment, what can we expect of the actions of ordinary people? How can we expect other people to be law-abiding?

SOHRAB: But Your Honor, surely you can understand that is not the entire story. It is not a matter of suddenly going to her house one day and taking her. Or of going to her house to take her because she happened to be alone. That would be very stupid. That would be abduction. I know this, I am not very educated or involved in studying the law, but I do know that much.

JUDGE: What is the true story, then?

SOHRAB: The story is something else entirely! I feel like whatever I say will fail me. Honorable Judge, it was completely different from that. We spoke on the telephone and in person for many months and for hours at a time. We knew one another, we understood each other deeply, and she told me many times that she loved me, that she loved me more than all others. I felt exactly the same way about her! I had never experienced that kind of feeling before, and it changed everything in my life. It let me believe in the future, and for the first time I felt I was alive, like I was born again. She said she loved me. That was everything. I could not believe what happened.

JUDGE: So, you are telling me that she was not happy to be with her own family?

SOHRAB: Well, there was another sad reality behind that for her. In her own family she was much more of a slave than a family member. She did not feel loved, and she described herself as more of a serving maid than a true daughter. Pushing out a tea trolley for guests or making black tea and then green tea, that sort of a life, you see. She dreamed of much more than this, and she wanted to feel free and able to be her true self. For as long as she could remember, she said she was mistreated by her family.

You see, it was not that she lacked things; she had many things. As a matter of fact, they had whatever they needed, but she did not have love. Honorable Judge, I should not reveal such intimate things, but she was so mistreated in her family that she was done with life and God's gift.

She had forsaken everything and attempted several times to take her life before we met. She told me that, and my heart broke for her.

JUDGE: OK. OK. So, you are telling me that if someone is mistreated or even feeling suicidal or like they cannot live in a certain way or because they feel depressed that you will take on the burden of giving them a new life and that you will take on the risk of whisking them away from their home, family, from everything they have known? Are you telling me that you rescued her from her own life?

SOHRAB: I was devastated by her story, and I loved her. I helped her. I helped her run away from her mother's house and we eloped. I had a car and waited patiently outside her house as she devised a way to distract her sister. I did not mean to say that I was rescuing her or that I can rescue people. Who am I to rescue someone else? This is not about that. And it is not about taking someone away from their home just because I can. That is a terrible thing: to show up at someone's house uninvited or unwanted. Your Honor, the simple fact is that we were in love. And she wanted to leave her house. She wanted to leave with me. She wanted to marry me and live with me. That is not the same thing as taking someone from their house for the sake of taking them away. We planned to spend the rest of our lives together. We wanted to start our lives together, or at least that is what I believed. I should have known better.

JUDGE: We will see what the other side of this tale is, and we will examine all the evidence, and that will enable us to discern truth from lie and reality from fiction. I expect to hear a lot from you in these sessions to explain all of this.

SOHRAB: I will. I am an honest person. Everything will show you that I am telling you the truth.

. . . .

When Sohrab fell in love, he described the feeling as waking up to the world. His sense of self transcended previous boundaries and he was happy. He experienced a fundamental openness to the world, which included seeing things he had previously been blind to, reckoning with the place of others and, because every other is also a radical other, coming to understand what he described as "the true meaning of life as God intended it to be." He said in the Holy Quran God promises that for every person there is a mate and companion on this earth.[3]

In this way, he had reached an all-encompassing point, and any attempt to think of "life" and "happiness" or even "society" without love was now out of the question for him. He spoke as if his prior experience of life was a mundane, half-real approximation of a much deeper possibility that evaded him until that fateful year when he reclaimed authentic purpose. Thinking about its power he said, "There is no real true meaning or life without love," and although these things had existed before, his experience of the social world and his previous encounters with others were mere glimpses of what was possible, "it was another life," he mused.

His experiences formed a bridge between the appearance and essence of life. It made sense of his distant memories, and the more proximate hurdles he seemed to clear; he had a new sense of purpose: "For the first time in life I felt I truly understood why my life was the way it was. Things became clear for me."

In his mind's eye his life had become the intense history of an *ibar*, a sign or hint contained in events and in the world of experience around him that revealed its significance in retrospect.[4] Being in touch with the *ibar*, he could assess the difference from his previous life. There was no place for him to live except in quintessence and with the true spirit of things; anything less than this purity raised the question he posed to us when he pondered the dramatic loss of love and freedom: "I sometimes wonder if it is better not to have been born at all."

. . . .

For Sohrab, to ask if it is better not to have been born is a way of questioning his understanding of things and people around him. He is expressing doubts about whether true knowledge, including self-knowledge, has been supplanted by an inadequate substitute, a partial mode or way of thinking that cannot grasp the essence of things and renders what he knows inferior and perhaps even useless in the face of change. I believe this is what he evokes when he states things like "I should have known," "If I knew then what I know now," and most tellingly, because it suggests other outcomes, "I would have acted very differently if I had known." These are the moments of voicing a recognition that if he had been in possession of certain knowledge and a more unified self, he would have taken a different path. Instead, he said everything became difficult afterward. To not understand an original sign or event in the way he invokes meant other signifiers also dissipated from view and put him on a path of misunderstanding. Not knowing moved him along an axis of confusion: In the face of love and confusion in the city and confused over the diminishing power of interpretation and action his problem was not only being in love with someone he did not *know* but also entering an epistemic order in which both language and events were devoid of the kind of referential ground that could help him read his surroundings and the words of others to find a clear direction.

Sohrab did not encounter paradox and nonsense as radical or freeing.[5] Everything around him was uncertain: the Afghan government's precarious sovereignty outside major cities; ministerial and institutional corruption; urban demarcations; and social, military, paramilitary, and insurgent violence. Contrary to the idea of freedom through a nomadic distribution of the senses, we see nonconforming lines of flight and assemblages that make knowing both impossible and oppressive, which is the opposite of what Gilles Deleuze hypostatized as the emergence of a radical, freer kind of being. What Sohrab sought was the common sense shared and affirmed by others but instead he faced a juncture where representations, symptoms, and metaphoric knots retreated from his horizon of thought and action. There was only the intensity of desire outside of symbolic exchange, a desire that was its own object bordering on non-desire, or what Jacques Lacan describes as encountering "das ideal Ich" (the ideal or specular I) that recognizes its absolute being in an image on the cusp of entering into the symbolic domain but not yet crossing over.[6] It is neither here nor there.

....

Sohrab was not involved in politics or corrupt schemes, nor was he interested in the local and national power struggles that had come to define symbolic economies and law in Kabul. He described looking at people he knew or worked with, not out of envy, but with a sense of bewilderment because of all the incredible changes in the city, its economy, and their lives. He didn't aspire to have the same, and he understood that some of these boons were unsustainable, but he did long to change his own life and find happiness.

Sohrab is handsome and tall, with intelligent eyes and a full head of hair. Calm and sometimes reticent he was often on the verge of tears before the judges or when at a loss for the right words. Sohrab was still a young child when his family escaped Kabul after the communist People's Democratic Party of Afghanistan (PDPA) launched a wave of repression against its ideological opponents. His family was not politically active or associated with either the PDPA or the Islamist opposition, but the brutal campaign of mass arrests and executions across the country, and particularly in

Kabul, made them fear for their lives. But violent discrimination and harsh conditions in Iran caused them to return to Afghanistan just three years later, in 1981, during the first year of the Iran-Iraq War (1980–88).

When Sohrab returned to Kabul, the city was at the center of a widening circle of distrust. Violence and the risk of arrest or death were omnipresent for any number of reasons: being attracted to politics in the city or involved in its institutions, moving in the wrong social or religious circle, praying at the wrong mosque, or daring to voice intellectual or religious opposition to the new regime. A new political and social paradigm emerged under a series of three PDPA leaders: First came "The Great Leader of the April Revolution," Noor Mohammad Taraki, who was assassinated in 1979 by men under the direction of one his comrades, Hafizullah Amin, the chairman of the Revolutionary Council. Amin served briefly as head of state from September 1979 to December 1979, when he was assassinated by KGB special forces, and then was succeeded by President Babrak Karmal (1979–86). The violent purges centered around the notion of purification, the idea that to be a modern political party ready for a modern global order, the PDPA needed to become clean and hardened, devoid of any trace of difference and opposition so that the revolution could push forward through mass arrests and executions, including in the infamous Pol-e-Charkhi Prison, where Sohrab was now imprisoned along with Sami and others.

....

Sohrab had lived in Kabul his entire adult life, in the same rundown, busy district simply called District 8. In 1981, after returning from Iran, his family settled in a small middle-class neighborhood called Karte Nau (the New Quarter). He eventually joined the city's police force and witnessed the dramatic changes that swept over Kabul in a tide of social change and violence that seemed impossible to control and which he and, in sidebar conversations, the judges, denounced as part of a generalized and dark obsession with money. The city expanded alongside that violence, a violence that cut across economic and political life but also fragmented more distant flows of people and interests, shaping new behaviors and ways of dealing with people that some Kabulis describe as part of "the house of evil" (*khaneh e zulm*).

Karte Nau is a dense neighborhood of apartment complexes and bustling streets, featuring wide thoroughfares and one of the busiest markets in Kabul. It is a mixed residential and commercial area popular with daily wage laborers. Surrounding it are residential areas, with even lower-income residents who often work as day laborers and grapple with inadequate water supplies and resources.

The neighborhood lies on flat ground south of Maranjan Hill, with easy access to the Kabul-Jalalabad Highway and the Bagrami Industrial Complex.[7] Initially built in the 1950s as part of the city's eastward expansion plan from the old center of the city toward Logar and the east, in the 1990s it turned into a key battleground between different Mujahideen factions fighting Soviet and Afghan military forces. More recently, after the fall of the government in August 2021 and the Taliban's subsequent takeover of the city, Karte Nau has become the site of at least one Islamic State (ISIS) militant hideout in a residential area.[8] Like in surrounding neighborhoods, increasing crime gradually transformed the experience of daily life, with house burglaries, robberies, and actual or threatened kidnappings for ransom becoming more common and deadlier. In the neighboring Bagrami District, local merchants, factory owners, and residents were subjected to the encroachment of organized crime as well as land grabbing allegedly at the behest of influential members of the Afghan parliament, some of whom had their own armed militias.[9]

For Sohrab, his community and the entirety of Police District 8 morphed into a desolate place. He felt he had to escape: "The feeling inside me that I had to get out became very strong. I could not ignore it." Order and fear worked most intensely in widening circles outside the center of the city and its modern arrangement and lines of military and juridical exception, an exception that reveals the extralegal not as preserving the law but as the constant transgression of the very possibility of the rule of law.[10] Kabul became a place where paramilitary, national, insurgent, and mercenary groups all encroached on public spaces, asserting their dominance over the streets in an attempt to enclose power in smaller and more manageable spaces and to make the idea of escaping one's era, rather than dwelling in it, the same as getting away from a place. Authenticity in urban space was more possible in memory than in contemporary experience. It became difficult for residents to bind themselves to a place, and the idea of crossing, whether of class and sectarian lines or across streets, was no longer real or forward-going but "rather, an obstinate and voluptuous hovering on the brink, a hesitation that has its most cogent motive in the circumstance that beyond this frontier lies nothingness."[11]

I imagine that for Sohrab there was no unbreakable bond in District 8. He did not have a place to embrace in the present, neither in the image of the alley nor in the metropolis. Instead, he felt "lost" and "uncertain," caught up in the life of the city and burdened by work. Yet he still believed in fate and was ready for love. When the judges asked about his position in society, he described himself as the embodiment of the law within the city, but he just as quickly acknowledged that being a representative of the law was difficult because, like everyone else, he was entangled in a complex and shifting realm amid unstoppable waves of crime and corruption. This realm encompassed not only violent challenges to the notion of representative government but also the very idea of representation itself, and being the face of the law was discontinuous with this shared, often lawless reality. Crime had become more difficult to control. But he wanted to contribute to his society in a small way, or as he put it, "be of some service to the ordinary people." He talked a lot about place and city life and events that could not be contained. He conveyed the experience of a place undergoing urban change and potential renewal, which I had also observed in new roads, parks, a recreational reservoir (this reservoir would be a crucial detail in the accusation against him), restaurants, cafés, and public spaces available to residents. But none of it was master planned or guaranteed to work, and its new appearance generated a feeling of modern permutation and clutter.

This idea of a unified and more structured city fed by urban revival and municipal plans, development aid, and foreign capital was in large part reflective of a desire for the effective centralization of government power. As its ideal counterpart, Kabulis hoped for a new, more cosmopolitan way of life in new neighborhoods, quarters, and districts. And this dream of development was connected to a regional and international sphere, to new places of consumption and new forms of desire that were sometimes embodied in images of elsewhere (Dubai, Abu Dhabi, Istanbul, "Europa," and "Amreeka") and at other times embodied in more ordinary possessions: smartphones, cars, laptops, clothes in the style of "Istanbul Street Wear," accessories, and modern furnishings.

For residents who did not travel these were the objects that caught their attention and created a new tempo for social life and consumption. The new social life was about commodities but also a speed and connectivity that was not mechanical or electric but peopled and pushed forward by desire; the tempo of accumulating new things and generating images of wealth that were nested in the images of wealth that poured in from "the foreign places" people could look at but not go to. These changes were not so much geopolitical but rather about people's collective desire for the elsewhere internalized at home, any elsewhere would do, and in this way, any foreign place felt closer.[12] This tempo began to fill space, fit in more directly, and answer a need. It made the city more open, faster paced, and erratic but also part of something much larger and more worldly.

The new fitting in and expansion of commodities happened alongside a sense of disorder in Kabul where, for many people and especially those in the poorer, more isolated districts far from the malls and city centers, the tenuous illusion of social order had already fallen apart. Sohrab and many other Kabulis referred to a time of "chaos" and "madness." In the media, news of a (then) imminent US/NATO military withdrawal was circulating widely, and the Afghan military was keen on showing a doubtful public that it had the personnel and firepower to regain control of territories lost to "the enemy," to "the opposition."[13]

Earlier, at the turn of the twentieth century, the British attempt at colonial rule and subjugation was met with Afghan resistance in cities and the hinterland in equal measure. At the same time a new culture that was more modern, steelier, more connected and confident, and that looked toward Russia and Japan more than Europe was emerging. As was happening elsewhere in Asia, including in Turkey and Iran, "The colony, perhaps because more visibly sick than the metropolis, sensed more acutely that the modernity of the age should, and did, look hard for a purist and escapist solution."[14]

There was a lot to run from. Conflict, sabotage, new media technology, espionage ranging from botanical to railway prospecting missions, and the presence of colonial officials and emissaries in Kabul raised the question of how to be a nation on the global scene and what it meant to have contact with other countries, or "imperial nation-states,"[15] and how, if at all, an escape could be possible. But modernization was not yet, as it was in the Indies, a clear matter of a new order and a purer, dedicated aesthetic such that "parallel to the pure-energy, pure-technology, pure esthetics modern and avant-garde ideas of habitation in the West—the 'geometric cities' or 'linear cities,' as they were sometimes defined—there was, in the Indies, a distinct and increasing emphasis on putting matters, sort of, in line too."[16]

. . . .

Many urban residents saw a utopian future, urbanization, power, order, money, technology, and the fantasy of those developments moving into the hinterland to displace tradition, orality, foraging, and husbandry as the only possible way for the country to survive political and social disintegration. In the meantime, the violence of the insurgency, expropriation, large-scale fraud (ranging from drug and weapons smuggling to sex work and ministerial corruption), a struggling class of workers and dissidents, and most of all, the upheaval of old ways of inhabiting the city pressurized everyday life.

The aesthetic of development was visible across town. Modern and avant-garde styles were borrowed from the "modern world," mainly Dubai and Istanbul, and a certain dialectic of renewal was incorporated alongside the ruins of more than forty years of conflict. Color, mirrored windows, older Soviet apartment blocks, office buildings, and a new one-hundred-store shopping mall with elevators and escalators became part of a new culture of desire. In some neighborhoods—such as Wazir Akbar Khan and Taimani or Shahr e Nau, the most prestigious parts of the city—the entrances to restaurants and offices were sometimes so tucked away that it seemed the new was there not to be seen but inferred like a spectral background.

As Fredric Jameson describes, in late capitalism this new "spatial logic of the simulacrum" has a "momentous effect on what used to be historical time" and on nostalgia and histories of political violence.[17] The mall, like several others across the city and like the expensive new restaurants and social clubs, were at once ideal images of a modern urban experience and empty simulacra of space intended to displace and refract the outmoded city around it. They were not places of consumption per se, or even places where people could find their bearings or meet one another. They were more important, enlarged, and worldlier than that: like a "total space, a complete world, a kind of miniature city" that approximates, in the social realm, "a new collective practice, a new mode in which individuals move and congregate, something like the practice of a new and historically original kind of hypercrowd."[18]

. . . .

For many Kabulis lacking access to money or people in power, daily life became uncertain and more volatile. Social relationships outside and within families resulted in unforeseen consequences. People turned on one another or betrayed family members for property or money, left their hometowns to escape debts, or were caught in intensifying conflicts that ended in retaliation and even murder. When circumstances folded in on people, it was not the "why" that mattered but the "what might happen next?" or "what should I do now?" or the "I should have known" that Sohrab invokes as the epistemic gap between the experience of gain and loss in love. People were engulfed in future conditional thoughts that morphed from mere concerns into deep-seated anxieties, discussing and in some senses responding to the event or crisis *that would be*. For the young men I came to know, this torrent made it difficult to envision a future or to imagine that their despair could dissipate in time. These kinds of feelings and actions became the basis of an intensification and the more abstract force some called "kismet." Kismet was not kind, but it was inimitable and politically important. It was the rarefied answer to a series of dilemmas that had worsened, were hard to contain, and felt increasingly anticipatory. And kismet was everywhere: on the street, in family matters, and in questions of national, global survival. All of these were under its general direction, and ideas of change and reaction now bore the weight of an enigmatic order that was coupled with people's willingness to do whatever it took to get by.

People like Sohrab felt this boldness on the loose. It moved fast and hardened people, but it also made them feel invincible and part of the global sphere. The world was fast, bold, and hard too. Place, desires, and the social body changed in a way he could not anticipate nor fully fathom but which he nonetheless lived with and even admired. "These days many people travel, they come and go to Dubai and Turkey, and they are bringing change to the city, and you see it all around you, but it is also difficult to know who people are when they change." The more he traveled within the city, the less he recognized it and the less he felt he had anything to tell us that we did not already know: "What can I tell you that you don't know already? The situation in Kabul is bad," he said. He existed in this tenuous place, and he imagined how people would see him: "When people see me, I wonder what they think or will think of me when they know about this story. I wonder if they will see me only as a criminal." He did not see the violence of deceit until after the fact. It was precisely what he could not know until it was too late, and even then, only when it was reiterated in the experience of one violent affirmation after the other, first at his wedding party, when his wife suddenly became a stranger to him; then after his arrest, when she disappeared from his life and Kabul; and finally when she did not reappear but instead formally accused him in the form of a disembodied written statement.

How was he to imagine the gaze of the other? These were the things that transformed him into a doubting subject. At the same time, he knew that he understood things, many things about the way the world worked. But despite that achievement, it was impossible to balance what he knew against everything he thought he could not understand or that he would try to fathom in vain, because others had probably understood it before him. The frustration of thought and explication was palpable, and he would start and stop and give up sometimes and say, "But what can I say, there is nothing I can say now." In this way, standing in front of the world and all it might contain he was, like Sami, speechless and unable to tell us anything new. Except he did.

. . . .

I remember thinking that if he had lived in another part of town, things could have turned out differently for him. If he had learned English in a private school or worked for an international organization, he might have ended up with a position in government, in a national corporation, or in the local media. He might have traveled the country and made connections. These were the changes that he witnessed in others, usually young men, some of whom he knew in passing and used to talk to more regularly but now he mostly observed from a distance as their lives transformed; their lives were less poor and more exciting. "There are many people who are quickly moving ahead and finding wealth and even some young folks I know and used to talk to who now have good jobs. I don't see them very much anymore. They have good prospects, but I always had more modest ambitions. I wanted to live an honest life."

It was not that Sohrab did not desire change in his own life. He did, but the changes he observed in other people's lives were too radical and fast for him and made him nervous because he could not predict where they would all end up. He spoke about all of this with a certain ennui and the antihero feeling he called feeling "world weary" (*behzar az dunya*). He was a lot like Sami before his mother's words radically transformed him. There was no shared condition for a cosmopolitan experience, which some assumed would happen if change could persist long and fast enough; instead, the boundaries he relied on to discern between the reality and the appearance of things had become confused: "The inside and outside of things and people are very different, one realizes," he said.

In this sense, everything that transpired in his world and made him beleaguered seemed also to have happened without much struggle. It was the ancient difference between essences and appearances and he, like others, was not able to discern the difference on his own. Doing so would require social interpretation. I think he believed that as well, but he only said: "This is just how life is." He was quietly swept up in an intensity that was drawn-out, formative, and inextricable from the social violence that was all around him but that he was nonetheless unable to discern, let alone predict its scope. That's OK too. He didn't protest its ingress. Then, when he met Soraya, the love of his life, he had an even more powerful, indomitable defense. He was in love and for Sohrab love was diametrically opposed to this wave of confusion and change, it was in the life of love, not in the life of the mind or money, that he believed he could finally find ground to stand on, a referential and livable ground from which he could make sound judgments, find good words to speak, and discover a way of being that could not be taken from him the way everything else seemed to come and go.

No matter how much he imagined things would be different for him after he found love, the deferral of violence, and especially the power of rumor and accusation to remake reality, found him at every turn. Its power subverted his thoughts and actions: "It felt like whenever I tried to do the right thing or wherever I turned. there was deception. Sometimes I wonder if it is better not to have been born at all."

He did not defend his actions. He admitted that he acted beyond rational, acceptable behavior and custom but remarked that those norms were no longer things he could abide if he were to stay true to his feelings and the true self who was in love. Compared to his previous self, he was different in a way that overwhelmed his judgment but that made him happy because it also freed him from everything he sought to escape. He carried this feeling with him until he could no longer ignore the fact that his life had radically changed. "I suddenly realized that everything had changed, and we had to marry and spend our lives together." "There was no honorable or honest way for me to live other than to marry her." But then his troubles began to multiply, and he no longer understood them or knew what to call them, so he referred to them as his given fate and remarked that everything in his life suddenly became "very strange and unbelievable."

Becoming Strange

Prior to meeting or coming in contact with "Soraya," Sohrab had heard about her from others in the social circles he was familiar with in certain neighborhoods in Kabul. He believed what he heard. Young, single Kabulis often spoke about one another to friends and generated a feeling of excitement about so-and-so or so-and-so's (*filani*) son or daughter from a certain neighborhood, before any kind of dating or contact took place. That contact almost always initially occurred over the phone followed by a meeting in one of the city's many tucked-away café-gardens where only those who know they exist go to meet. He heard from people that Soraya was beautiful and successful; she was university educated, worked for a major television channel, and was from a respected family. It was even possible that she would be on television herself and might become a national media personality one day. As he put it, she was "the kind of woman who could be on channel 3 news on TV."

I imagine that as Sohrab listened to people talk about Soraya, their descriptions were in stark contrast to the way he described his own life as a police officer. The experience of hearing about her, first in passing and then more directly, led him to believe she was unique, and as he said, "The more I heard about her, the more I wanted to know her." He said he thought about her, and it was hard to put all his emotions into words because he had a feeling for which he "didn't have words."

He had been on countless patrols all around town and was privy to information about the dangerous nexus between urban crime and life. Like most Kabulis, he knew which areas were targeted by criminals, gangsters, and insurgents and how the flow of persons, weapons, and cars determined the path of material violence and its topography of bodies and destruction. But when he heard people talk about Soraya, he said he felt a sense of being alive in the city and world.

After months of hearing about her, he said he had to meet her. The first meeting was arranged with the help of his young nephew, Hasan. Hasan had been working at the same television station as Soraya. Because he had been there for some time, Hasan and Soraya were friends and talked openly. Sohrab implored Hasan to ask Soraya for her phone number. Hasan initially told him he felt awkward about doing so because it was impolite, but in the end, to Sohrab's surprise, Soraya willingly gave out her phone number, knowing it was for Hasan's young, single uncle.

Sohrab felt bold enough to call her, and to his surprise she answered. He recalled he was nervous and "I did not know what to say. I was very quiet," so he proposed they meet in person at the Kabul Zoo on the bank of the river, close to the traffic police directorate by the large Deh Mazang traffic circle that connects the center of the city to West Kabul. I imagine he had a vision of freedom and openness being possible at the zoo, which was enclosed and isolated from the rest of city life, even if the zoo and the city can never be kept apart from each other or from political and retaliatory violence. The most famous animal in the Kabul Zoo was undoubtedly Marjan the lion (*marjan* means "coral" in Persian). Marjan was born in 1976 in West Germany and gifted by the Cologne Zoo in 1978 during the year of the bloody PDPA revolution and subsequent era of communist rule.

Marjan was blinded by a hand grenade tossed in her cage in the 1990s by a Taliban fighter avenging his brother's death; Marjan ate the man after he climbed into her cage as a demonstration of his courage.

Yet, I think for Sohrab, the Kabul Zoo was more of a garden. It was a place where nature and culture touched each other to make possible something he did not seek out in the city but hoped for on its primal margin. Many young Kabulis met one another this way. The scenario always involved someone coming through a guarded gate but not an ordinary front door or into an open courtyard but not a room or house or in the presence of other people. The pattern was to meet outside first, then if enough trust was built, to move inside to be seen together by others. All of this was to avoid talk and rumors in town.

As a police officer he knew that place and accusation can go hand in hand when people find themselves in the wrong place at the wrong time. I think he opted for the zoo because he did not want to worry about what it would mean to be heard or seen with a woman on the street or about what street to walk on or avoid, how close he could pass to a mosque or a police checkpoint, a side alley, and so on. Perhaps, like so many others, he experienced the city as a place to get to know and get away from, like when Walter Benjamin recalls his nursemaid introducing him to the city of Berlin and its expanses through Tiergarten Park and the zoo, where he later finds refuge from the rest of the city and is transported by music, animals, and the gaze of the other:

> Never again has music possessed so dehumanized and shameless a quality as that of the two brass bands that tempered the flood of people surging torpidly along "Scandal Avenue" between the café restaurants of the Zoo. Today I perceive what gave this flow its elemental force. For the city dweller there was no higher school of flirtation than this, surrounded by the sandy precincts of gnus and zebras, the bare trees and clefts where vultures and condors nested, the stinking enclosures of wolves, and the hatcheries of pelicans and herons. The calls and screeches of these animals mingled with the noise of drums and percussion. This was the air in which the glance of a boy fell for the first time on a passing girl, while he talked all the more zealously to his friend. And such were his efforts to betray himself neither by his eyes nor his voice that he saw nothing of her.[19]

Just a few months earlier, in January 2013, the Deh Mazang traffic circle next to the zoo, which had an Afghan National Security Forces (ANSF) post, came under concerted attack. After an initial car bomb detonated, five heavily armed men entered the traffic police headquarters and a nine-hour gunbattle ensued. Movement, traffic, and weapons collided in a way that was not new; in fact, these kinds of targets were frequently subject to car bombings. However, attacks like this (which were on the rise that year) changed the idea of what it meant to move through the city, especially from its center to the outskirts and then back again to the center, where the markets, roads, and traffic circles were the best and busiest (and thus attractive targets).[20]

The wave of violence had taken on a new intensity and pace. The car bomb method was becoming popular in attacks on cafés, shops, government offices, and mosques; either as one large explosion at the front gate or door of a building or as a detonation followed by gunmen entering and killing their targets in prolonged gunbattles. On some level, entering a guarded gate or main entrance of a building to meet someone meant risking one's life.

Responses to these kinds of attacks had previously fallen within the purview of NATO forces, but by 2013 the transition to Afghan security forces taking responsibility for the entire country was well underway, and local forces were tasked with providing security across the country and conducting counterinsurgency efforts in the city.[21] The security and combat transition (including to the Afghan National Police) was a watershed moment in the experience of national sovereignty; it represented to people like Sohrab, who were a crucial part of this transfer, a larger, pivotal shift in power from external and regional actors to Afghans themselves. Most of the young men who were a part of the enlarged security apparatus came from impoverished neighborhoods in Kabul where street violence and crime were common. For them, the transition signified not only a change in physical presence on the ground, and especially in Kabul's central neighborhoods, but in the collective understanding of self-representation.

The traffic circle appears in Sohrab's narrative as a mnemonic detail that helps him recall their first meeting and the location of the Kabul Zoo within the flow of movement to and from the center of Kabul. But it is a detail that speaks to the collision of insurgency, bodies, and urban sites dense with activity and traffic, and it was an unexpected and perhaps repressed aspect of Sohrab's own experience of life in the city as a police officer. In remembering and naming the traffic circle, he gestures to the tense topographic and ideological battle that made the city impossible to traverse safely for security personnel and civilians alike. It reveals in narrative form what Allen Feldman calls a "relation of antagonism" grounded in a political rationality that rivals the state, but unlike the state's "closed sphere of cognition, exchange, and symbiotic representation,"[22] it is carved out of the space of the city and its dense flows of people; it is a form of political and material violence that in part seeks to make the city a site of blockage and enclosure rather than nomadic flow or assemblage.

Many Kabulis felt strong aversion or fear toward certain parts of town. Anxiety about potential danger or direct exposure to violence had become common, and the likelihood of danger in certain areas gave them an atmospheric quality that superseded any individual event. In some of those areas, Sohrab confessed he felt out of his league as a police officer. Behind the city's managed chaos, there was a world of economic development and sometimes organized crime, and billions of dollars were associated with these activities, which ranged from back-alley crime to meetings in luxury hotels, multinational corporations and international travel.

Immersed in a city of impenetrable centers and bypasses that ring around the city without ever quite touching it or feeling free and open to movement produces the sense that one is only encircling a lack; moving around but never encountering the real of a place and feeling like there is a concealed interior, another possible life, beyond its surface. Other elements—like the old Soviet-built, state-owned Silo bread factory; the newer wedding halls; and the dried-up Kabul River—give the city its shape in a discourse of historical memory. It becomes place as a monument to the passage of time and a stubborn encapsulation of collective memory because "to live and die through this space, as well as merely to pass by this space, it may become (it may be reduced to) 'an act of remembrance.'"[23] A popular joke about the Kabul River goes like this: "What does a frog in the Kabul River do at prayer time? He starts by doing his *tayammum*."[24]

There were rumors that year that the weapons found in Kabul and used in attacks across the city were being brought in from the countryside, and that the real danger was in rural, less contained parts of the country where resentment and scarcity made people more inclined to cooperate with the insurgents. The rural population had become less predictable. This was not necessarily true, was not the path the insurgency took, and was not even a major reason why some people felt inclined to cooperate with the insurgents. Usually, they cooperated because they were blackmailed or afraid of what would happen if they did not. And when they refused, awful things did happen; young men were beheaded as an example to the rest, and lives were made smaller and intensely difficult.

City life was volatilized by the idea of what was lying in wait on the outside. Living in Kabul was about participating in life only with those one trusted and when it was possible. The city was at the center of historical memory and a certain order of experience and around it in unknown, expanding circles a sense of vague contingency spread until it touched on the radical alterity of the violent man from the hinterland who raged from a distance that was also close. Movement between rural and urban areas and between small, sometimes obscure villages and Kabul had dramatically increased and made it impossible to imagine that order and governance or cleanliness could flow from the center. Instead, people noticed the filth, grime, dust storms, urine, and debris that came into the city from somewhere else, the thick smell of another place, time, or way of life, that found people through new channels of intensity and flow.

I often wonder if on the day he met Soraya in the zoo Sohrab was excited about being in town not on patrol but as part of living more freely when subjectivity and place are able to join in a new way. As a police officer he was sent out to patrol or help cordon off certain areas and access points. Up to that point he had primarily experienced the city as a series of problems and knots.[25] Now he found passages that shaped desire and movement and made up a new dream of urban life. Sohrab and Soraya met in the Kabul Zoo, and he said he experienced a feeling he could not quite put into words, even though he did: "It was, it was . . . well, how should I put this in words that will make it clear to you? I suppose it all felt like a dream." He recalled with a smile the excitement he felt when she initially introduced herself simply as "Soraya from Pol e Sorkh."[26] In collective life, as Walter Benjamin observed, we have peculiar "dream houses" that include "arcades, winter gardens, panoramas, factories, wax museums, casinos, railroad stations," and to this list we must also add the city zoo.[27]

Over the Telephone

Sohrab situates himself in a longer, diachronic narrative of change that includes a new sense of how to be in the world. Love was the operation of difference, it was the event within a larger movement of sameness he was living out, even though nothing was the same in Kabul. In that process the phone became a place in lieu of the city, where there were too many people and only one zoo. It was a private channel hidden from the eye and gaze of others, and from what Lacan describes as "the split in which the drive is manifested at the level of the scopic field," no longer simply his own private space, but a scene structured by the gaze, the object through which, as Lacan notes, the drive emerges.[28] The telephone was part of the fantasy of a self beyond the collective order. Sohrab said he and Soraya spoke almost daily when he was not on a work mission, and that they developed an intense love.

The Afghan National Police had become critical to the government's security apparatus. The expansion of "public order" they were tasked with meant that officers were increasingly sent to provinces, where they had little experience with or knowledge of local life, and where they were either killed or tasked with killing those suspected of being terrorists. These "missions" were part of the Afghan government's faltering response to insurgent, foreign, and criminal activity in various provinces. It resulted in counterattacks and gun and grenade battles in Kabul, during, for example, the 2011 and 2018 sieges of the Intercontinental Hotel, and the responses to the attacks on the Deh Mazang traffic circle, the election commission headquarters, Kabul's Supreme Court, foreign guesthouses, and military camps. Such battles were common, but in the media and in local discourse (the talk that spread in their aftermath), they were never considered missions because a "mission" meant fighting outside the city in remote places where the government had little or no authority and where the symbolic exchange of provocation and response—a counterattack for an attack, like-for-like—was no longer legible as such.[29]

In Kabul, the English word *mission*, a mid-sixteenth-century word that denotes the Holy Spirit being sent into the world (from the Latin word *mittere*, "to send"), had come into usage, particularly among young men, security officers, translators, mineral prospectors, and soldiers. Those familiar with the term, often through personal connections to individuals who had undertaken missions, tended to align themselves with the government and Afghan security forces rather than the insurgency or foreign powers such as Saudi Arabia and Pakistan, commonly associated with "backing them" (the insurgency). I think for Sohrab the notion of going on a mission represented the antithesis of being in Karte Nau and having phone conversations with Soraya. The phone became a space where the emergence of something beyond the dichotomy of "us" versus "them" "national" versus "backed by foreigners" was possible. It represented something altogether different and separate from the city.

Over the phone Soraya disclosed to him that she was being abused at home. This surprised Sohrab because her family was well educated, and he reflected on how "you can never truly know what others are like." He was especially shocked that the abuse occurred at the hands of her mother, for reasons he could "not understand properly over the phone." She sometimes prohibited Soraya from going to school or being out in the city other than for work and treated her, as Soraya put it to him, "just like a slave in a *sahib*'s [master's] house."

There were other things he could not anticipate. During one conversation she told him her real name was Razia not Soraya, as she pretended. And she did not come from just any family in the Pol e Sorkh neighborhood but from one of the wealthiest Shia families in the country.

Sohrab's family followed Sunni Islam. He would not be prohibited from marrying a Shia woman, but Soraya's family, from what we know from her statement and Sohrab's story, would strongly resist her marriage to a Sunni man. What was possible, or at least a more ambivalent stance, for Sohrab was foreclosed for Soraya, and the issue of their union became a matter of transgression, a fallout, and a secret that couldn't really be kept. But Soraya was not merely from a minority community, because she was also Razia and very wealthy. Her name signified dissolution of subjectivity, class, and sectarian identity as he presumed to know it. These differences did not change Sohrab's feelings, but he could not quite put them into words either: "I was in shock. I did not know what to say, but I felt the same feeling for her."

Few Afghans felt like the *sahib* of their house; property disputes among neighbors and within families were deadly, and court battles over the dispossession of people or murder over a deed or the taking of too much land (even a couple of meters) on one side of a fence or wall or garden or farm had become among the most common cases heard in Kabul's courthouses. Consequently, people lived in their homes with the anxiety that another deed or document could be produced against them in a court system open to bribery, which could mean the end of their homeownership and domicile and possibly the end of their life or the inception of their willingness to take another person's life. There were other problems, too, including rumors about sleeper cells and hidden weapons caches in different neighborhoods in Kabul. It was hard to know which areas or houses were suspect or who was blackmailing whom or if any of the rumors were even true.

People felt surrounded by "both sides," "all sides," and foreign powers.[30] They were part of a larger geopolitical context they could not influence. They talked about the government being compromised and paid off by foreigners. They talked about political and infrastructure projects that were just a cover for corruption, or about China gobbling up the country's mineral resources. They were anxious about the battle between "East" and "West," between the United States and Russia and between Saudi Arabia and Iran or India and Pakistan and the factions they each backed in pursuing their own economic and political interests.

Those interests (some of which the Afghan National Police were tasked with taking down) ranged from ensuring a situation of managed chaos that weapon dealers, private security groups, contractors, and subcontractors could benefit from to destabilizing the Afghan government to help the insurgency gain mineral-rich territory in the south and east; smuggling networks of arms, timber, and gems; facilitating the drug trade; gaining access to crucial water supplies, which has been a political conflict between Afghanistan and Iran since the 1973 Helmand River Treaty; and competing over exploratory rights to mine Afghanistan's copper, iron, gold, and marble resources. It was rumored that these interests required certain movements, assets on the ground, and a culture of fear and silence, and that if the right amount of money and violence were added together, as a single assemblage, those interests would be impossible to dismantle. All of this was part of the fear of hidden forces coming to the surface, including sleeper cells carrying out attacks that sometimes focused on a single target and at other times were part of a more concerted effort to simultaneously attack Afghan security forces in different places or to destroy the main defense or backup for one security unit before moving on to attack the next post or the next police station, traffic circle, and so on.

In the city, Sohrab was part of the noise and disease. His job had become more difficult. He knew that criminals were operating in the country, he knew about the grisly eruption of street violence and bombings, including in neighborhoods he regularly patrolled or visited. The phone became a lifeline for him. He and Razia spoke daily, and he fell in love with her and the quotidian communication between them. He spoke several times about this phase of their relationship, the importance to him of contact and communication with another person, and this new way of being in the world that was safeguarded by the dialogic channel of the telephone. The experience bordered on feeling "like a single being not two," which made their universe of voice "rise over the multitude of sounds and noises, another even wilder and wider jungle: sounds of nature, sounds of machines and technology." The distinction between one and two, mine and yours, passion and technology gave way to "a zone of undecidability, of a between-the-two, an intermediacy, which will be, as we shall see, one of the paramount features of the voice."[31]

Their conversations were the dividing line between voice and noise. The noise of animals, old cars and wheelbarrow carts, street vendors, and money changers; the whistle of traffic officers and police; the throbbing of helicopters in the sky and construction work; the car sirens of the National Directorate of Security; the songs played in restaurants and cafés and inside taxis; the sound of gunfire and explosions; and the calls to prayer were not and could not be considered in the same metaphysical sense as a single voice. They signified a different kind of communication, one that, despite signifying the world around him, could not for him touch on the power of one and not two but still other.

The Plan

Sohrab found the opening in language that made him feel like he found happiness. He said he was in love with Razia. The more he spoke to her, the more he had to say to her and, I imagine, the more talking helped him cope with the rest of the time in his day. But voice and the meaning it conveys only ever "implies a subjectivity which 'expresses itself' . . . if the voice is thus the quasi-natural bearer of the production of meaning, it also proves to be strangely recalcitrant to it. If we speak to 'make sense,' to signify, to convey something, then the voice is the material support of bringing about meaning, yet it does not contribute to it itself. It is, rather, something like the vanishing mediator . . . it makes the utterance possible, but it disappears in it, it goes up in smoke in the meaning being produced."[32]

The truth of subjectivity and voice disappear in the same flash, through the "vanishing mediator" that Sohrab could not possibly see. During his most memorable and profound conversations with Razia, they confessed their love to each other and decided to marry; he recalled how happy it made him feel, even though he immediately felt a sense of responsibility to make their relationship official. He wanted to marry her according to custom because "in custom of our forefathers there is a lot of wisdom," he said. He insisted that he would send his parents to her home to formally ask for her hand, but she refused, claiming that her Shia family would beat her for marrying a Sunni man and worse, that they would demand to know "where in the city did you find this man?" The couple agreed to elope and planned for him to pick her up at her family house in Pol e Sorkh. He recalled the day of the plan again. She said something along the lines of this:

> SOHRAB [voicing his recollection]: She said, "Today is the day. My mother is out of the country. She is somewhere in 'Arabistan' for a

wedding, and my sister will be doing all the laundry in the front yard this afternoon. As soon as she goes out to the yard, I will come to the back of the house and meet you."

JUDGE: And what did you say in response to this proposition?

SOHRAB: What could I say, Honorable Judge? Of course, I asked her: "Are you sure?" She said yes and I told her not to worry further and that I would meet her outside her house at the agreed time.

He said he was nervous, but he drove ahead on the road toward Pol e Sorkh.

SOHRAB: I just drove and kept my eyes on the road and looked straight ahead and drove.

Sohrab put all his faith in the details of the plan. In the small things that could open something impossibly large and new. To start, Razia's cousin, Zahra, who was present as a chaperone during their first meeting at the zoo, agreed she would call to distract Razia's sister, drawing her from the front lawn where she hangs laundry back into the house. This would allow Razia to escape through the back door and into Sohrab's white hatchback.

SOHRAB: I was waiting and becoming very nervous. I waited for what felt like hours in the car. My hands were shaking, and then she suddenly burst out of the house. It all happened so quickly it is like a blur in my mind. But I know we left instantly. I drove us out of there and only breathed when we entered my neighborhood and went to my parent's house. She spent that night in our house. But, Your Honor, it was as our guest not as my wife. Her status was that of a guest. . . . What I mean is that after that first night, when everything was still frantic and we felt full of panic and happiness and fear, after that night, I immediately went to the mosque and brought the Mullah Imam from Karte Nau to our house. He performed our marriage ceremony on the spot.

But something happened that I cannot shake off. I don't know if it means anything or even if it is important enough to recall. It did not feel like a good sign at the time. When the Mullah Imam came from the mosque to perform the ceremony, she unexpectedly became defensive about the differences between Sunni and Shia ceremonies. We did not know what to say or do. We were taken aback, but in any case, she went and performed her ablutions and then we read a few verses from the Quran and the ceremony [*nikka*] was finalized. She was my wife. I had a wife. My happiness was unlike anything I had ever known, and we were very happy together, we were very happy for the first month.

My mother and father and sister were also very happy for us, and because our ceremony was so hurried and small, my sister wanted to make it up to us by hosting a dinner party. That is where this incident took place. I was at my sister's house, enjoying my own wedding party and, without warning, several police officers burst into the house and arrested me right there and then. It is difficult to explain the shock of this moment. I thought I would soon have a family and a home, and suddenly instead of that dream, I was arrested and now I am in prison living out a daily nightmare. This should have never happened.

JUDGE: I want to revisit something. Her home life. Tell me what was it like. You already said she complained to you of being mistreated in her home. Specifically, by her mother. She complained to you on several occasions that her mother kept her at home against her will. Is that correct? Do you still stand by that?

SOHRAB: Yes. Your Honor, I am ashamed and sorry to be revealing these deeply personal things she confided to me. But I have no choice. The violence of her home life is something she confided to me many times. It broke my heart. She would tell me things like that, that her mother abused her, that she often left the country to go to "Arabistan" and left the sisters alone in the house. She told me she was like a servant, only there to perform chores but not loved, not taken care of. She was not valued by her family, and this made her very depressed. She even became suicidal.

JUDGE: And you still insist this is why you decided to partake in this ill-conceived plan to help her escape from the house?

SOHRAB: Your Honor, at the time we did not see it in those terms. I imagined a very different future for us. I wanted her to have a different life, one of love and respect and mutual care. I wanted to commit my life to her and to show her the love she deserves to have. I wanted us to have a home. I wanted that home to be very different from the one she grew up in. Now I wish I could forget it all.

Toward the end of the trial Sohrab said, "If only I could forget it all," "This should never have happened," and "I should have known." He was disappointed in himself and in Razia. His love and desire, rather than sustaining a new relationship to the world around him, as he had hoped it would, became a source of confusion and pain. This is what he was struggling to comprehend while making it legible in court as the opposite of criminal intent. He defended himself against the charges of abduction but also attempted to convey the loss of interpretive power and to make clear how that loss bore on his ordeal. He suggested that he should have known better, or at least understood that falling in love was not entirely good or bad but complex and uncontrollable, like all the other significant events in his life: the violence of the 1979 Soviet invasion, his childhood migration to Iran, the family's return to Kabul, his experience of District 8, his life in Karte Nau, and his employment as a police officer in Kabul. Thereby, he spoke about a judgment he should have reached but failed to. He spoke to the idea that the mode of thought most resonant with his life experience and most appropriate to understanding dramatic change was not available to him. The violence of thought, or better yet the un-thought, was inherent in the possibility of being in love in the first place.

How do we understand his narrative? The place of rumor and ac-cusation? His hindsight of not understanding in the first place? What is being deferred? The disconnect between his intuition, thoughts, and action is a key factor that shapes his bad fate. This is part of the irony of his embodying the law and being accused of one of the most serious crimes possible, a crime that is particularly charged in the collective per-ception of social turmoil, in a milieu that includes rampant abduction and killing, and that many people argue should be punishable by death. At the same time, the accusation against him is part of an introspective process that prompts him to confront missed opportunities in thought. He struggles with the accusation and his own failure to interpret mean-ingful signs, which led to his misguided judgment. Putting the marriage plan into motion resulted in more irrational behavior. In other words, he did not know what he was doing because he was not himself, and in be-coming other he acted through unconscious belief, which even if he had known better at the time, would not lose its force because his judgments were always deferred. Speaking on his own behalf in court was in part an attempt to come to grips with and try to situate himself as a unified self. He also said: "All I wanted is for her to understand me for who I am."

. . . .

An *ibar* (a sign, a hint, or a small passage) is not only a crossing in space or between orders of time but a translation that occurs between people and the simple truth of what he describes as being seen and understood by the other. For him, the goal of love was about replacing the doubting subject (who is uncertain, blind, alienated, unseen, unheard) with a subject who can see the truth of the other and be seen. It was a path toward dislodging the psychic violence of ambivalence with something free and bold and more fulfilling. And yet, it was only after the love ended that he experienced a profound shift and realized the need to be more aware of his environment. As was the case for Sami in the aftermath of Mina's disappearance, it became increasingly important for Sohrab to understand things that were and were not yet objects of knowledge for him.

The subject of knowledge is always subverted by the relations and events that seem to come from elsewhere, when one least expects or feels ready for them. Why me? How could this happen? These are the kinds of questions we ask ourselves amid misfortune or when we receive a gift or find love; in other words, when kismet is kind or cruel. During his trial Sohrab repeated phrases like "she said she loved me" and "I could not believe what happened" several times, as markers of interpretive anguish and his testimony to a transformative love that was somewhere between metamorphosis (because he said love transformed him) and violence (because, as he also put it, he "lost everything"). He conveys this alternation between having gained and having lost everything as his bad kismet and something he should have seen coming. This proximity to but loss of a singular love is too much in the sense that his feelings are not about what is missing (that is, not only about Soraya, his lost happiness, or his lack of trust in others) but about an uncontrollable alternation that is too close and overdetermining. When Sohrab asserts he wants to understand what he missed and to take better stock of his surroundings, he means he wants to reestablish trust in the intuitive knowledge love suspended but also learn to see that which is too close, is too much, and emerges when lack lacks.[33]

Sohrab wanted to draw upon understanding rather than a blind faith in others. And the more he described his loss, the more he reflected on his perceptions of other people, the importance of watching his language or not being too open-hearted, and even not trusting the intercession of extraordinary powers like love and "kismet." He also described his life as governed by a powerful logic of withholding. The happiness he wanted found him when he did not expect it but also at a point when he could not understand its implications. This was the point when love, talk, marriage, escape, accusation, and crime all shifted in relation to one another and to what he thought were his life prospects.

Many young men either sympathized with the insurgency or wanted to be a part of the Afghan government's enlarged security and military apparatus. But the more I got to know them, the more they opened up about their desperate wish to find the love of their life. They were also anxious about their ability to interpret phenomena. Many of them said things like, "It's impossible to know what is really going on"; "We only see what is in front of the curtain"; "I know love will fix everything"; or "When I find love, my life will start." One young man, who worked at a Pizza Hut inside a small shipping container in Camp Eggers in the Green Zone, told me about the young woman he loved. He had seen her around town, followed her, gotten to know her, and fallen deeply in love. His father prohibited him from marrying her because she spoke and taught English, but without love, he said he wanted either to commit suicide or fight the terrorists like "Jack Bauer 24."

I think Sohrab experienced a similar sense of enormity when he met Soraya. At the same time, his belief in a life-transforming love created a limit to his experience and the condition for its disruption, one he was still trying to fathom as he testified on his own behalf. By *limit* I mean the loss of his love object, and by *disruption* I refer to the force of desire that works, moves, and plots in the direction of fulfillment, much like a narrative scheme, but that also stymies his every move. Those beliefs, which were with him throughout the experience and embedded in his narrative, were expressed in similar terms as others: "We were meant to be together." "My life had just begun and now it is all over."

Part testimony and part regret, these statements express his vision of a totality at large and beyond his control, but they are also uncertain fragments of speech, uttered at different moments during his trial, sometimes to a judge, sometimes to everyone in the room, but always symptomatic of the loss of access to a stable set of meanings that might otherwise be within reach. In this way, the experience of recurrence, disruption, trailing off, invoking vague generalities, or waiting for a revelation that does not occur are ways in which we cannot gain distance from the very thing that alienates us in language; they are moments when the lack of language lacks.[34] He leans on these moments to gesture toward what eludes him but also compels him to believe, and these beliefs, located somewhere between having it all and losing everything, became an existential triangle with Soraya/Razia as a mobile figure between its points. Together, these belief-thoughts constitute a foundation, and in the absence of other sources of certainty, they are the dividing line from which he can look toward the future and speak of a self that might be legible to others and to the law. And yet, they generate a feeling that his life is overdetermined and therefore not quite part of the symbolic domain in which language and exchange could make some of those wishes come true. They are powerful beliefs but not objects of knowledge or forms of experience. And they do not lose their power precisely because they are "fundamentally situated in relation to the object—which is not the object of knowledge."[35] So where was he to turn? How can we think about the relationship between the over- and underdetermined for him? What is the relationship between not knowing and knowing too much?

The Accusation

Sohrab's story shows us that the form an accusation takes is inseparable from what we believe the other wants from us. It is an expression of anxiety as the sensation of the desire of the other and therefore a symptom of uncertainty and ambivalence within closeness. But this becomes more complicated if we follow Lacan because the question of desire when taken up first through the mediation of language (that is, the trajectory of the signifier) and then in response to the other (a double movement epitomized by Lacan's graph of desire) is a movement that produces the question *Chè vuoi?* (What do you want?) but no response; it is part movement and part a fiction that reveals the fiction of the other and of a symbolic order without guarantee or certainty. In other words, as a matter of collective life, the silence of the other is not just a refusal of what the subject desires (the "no" of prohibition) but a deeper silence of the shared symbolic order (now) revealed to have no Other backing it, and therefore exposed as both a stock of possible signification and its lack.[36] What did Sohrab want and what was he accused of? What did Razia communicate in the form of a dangerous, even deadly, accusation? And what does the accusation have to do with excess and with what Sohrab initially perceived to be his good fortune in difficult times? If the city with its densities and knots is the context for love, how does it become part of accusation?

That winter there was near-daily snowfall. It blanketed the landscape in white and quieted the city and pace of life despite causing widespread suffering. It drew out a tough inner force in people that made them (to borrow from Marshall Berman and Ivan Karamazov) "keep on keeping on." Labor, fortitude, and both modernist and antimodernist actions felt more like actions of a collective people adapting to the flux and pressure to "seize control of the city's elemental matter and make it their own" such that "the 'heroism of modern life' that Baudelaire longed to see will be born from his primal scene in the street . . . born again and again out of the street's inner contradictions. It may burst into life at any moment, often when it is least expected."[37]

At all hours military tanks rumbled alongside trucks fully loaded with cargo transporting goods to and from nearby provinces and making commodities the lifeblood between places. In Kabul there was still an alarming scarcity of basic goods, including things like firewood and fuel, but the slowing violence of the insurgency (which picked up again in the spring) became more bearable and a more nuanced, dialectical matter in public discourse and reflection. People's frustrations and desires seemed acutely tuned to the landscape. The cold weather, the rising cost of electricity and fuel, and the difficulty of obtaining firewood caused anxiety, suffering, and eventually the deaths of people from illnesses like pneumonia or carbon monoxide poisoning from makeshift heaters.[38] All of these issues became part of the discourse on the government's inability to manage crisis or energy supplies, and news of death was typically followed by talk and rumor: Was it really an unfortunate accident or was it foul play within the family? Was it a political hit? What is the government doing with the city's electricity? Can a homemade heater really kill you? A quick death is a good death.

For years large-scale infrastructure projects had integrated certain parts of the city at the expense of other, poorer districts and fueled a cycle of political violence in which powerful local and minority leaders had access to parliament and its patronage networks, or owned some of those projects, or "villa" communities, that were frequently targeted. Modern housing and smooth, all-weather asphalt roads became a signifier of the concentration of wealth and political power and were inseparable from the idea of access to the heart of power, the corruption of contracts, and corporate bidding that was crucial to profiteering and construction.

In the well-to-do neighborhood of Pol e Sorkh (where Razia lived with her family) wide roads divide traffic and make it easy to access the center of the city and the markets.[39] The city's social and political landscape shifted in the months leading up to Sohrab's trial. The rise of attacks on minority political leaders, including one in Pol e Sorkh on the prominent Hazara politician Mohammad Mohaqiq (who was a member of parliament and the leader of the opposition party Hezb-e Wahdat Islami Mardum-e Afghanistan, or People's Islamic Unity Party of Afghanistan) was another sign of the city's divisions along sectarian and ethnic lines.[40] In 2012 there were three separate assassination attempts on Mohammad Mohaqiq, ranging from a roadside bomb to an assailant breaking into the Wahdat News Agency (owned by Mohaqiq). By 2013, because of the transfer of responsibility for security to the Afghan National Army and National Police, the relentless string of political violence cast an ominous uncertainty over the city and called into question whether political opposition to the government would remain possible under the new security framework. In Pol e Sorkh, a neighborhood popular with the Hazara community, the reverberations of these attacks magnified the sense of turmoil and possible consequences of traveling in the city or being caught in traffic, on the side of a road, or in the blast range of a roadside bomb. The attacks also communicated the shifting front line of ethnic and sectarian violence and the capacity of the opposition (which was largely Sunni and Pashtun) to enter Shia neighborhoods and target leading figures. The destruction of security perimeters, buildings, and new roads—even in the Wazir Akbar Khan neighborhood occupied by US and NATO troops and several embassies—were material and symbolic acts that confirmed to Kabulis the volatility of urban development and political patronage and revealed the larger territorial and deterritorializing practices they signified. The common experience of construction followed by destruction became part of people's discourse on the place of death and killing, constituting what Allen Feldman describes in the context of Northern Ireland as a "metaphysics of contiguity" found in both place and in storytelling, including in descriptions of sectarian and ethnic violence.[41]

Unpredictable events gave way to narrative representations of "what happened" and a symbolic order that drew upon material referents and violence to "recuperate its own necessity."[42] Yet, rather than standing outside the experiential world, the symbolic order gave the domain of events a causal ground it did not otherwise possess and, thus, the necessary links between place, event, and sense-making. Of course, the symbolic order is never reducible to the effects it makes possible. The violence dislocated space from the city and neighborhood from neighborhood so that attacks and disorder in any given police district or ghetto or city block featured as anarchic rather than contiguous and made sense only in a narrative frame rather than in the indomitable "real" that stood apart from symbolic assimilation.[43] Urban violence and, especially, the unpredictable nature of roadside violence (the planting of roadside bombs as well as the use of explosives and car bombs on streets and in front of important buildings) inscribe a material order of destruction made up of cars, steel, concrete, HESCO barriers, police checkpoints, building access points, and makeshift barricades into a discourse in which a deeper metonymic connection emerges. There is a profound link between talk surrounding the violent acts—Where did it happen? In whose neighborhood? Who was responsible? For what end?—and the exclusion experienced by certain segments of the population during the city's metamorphosis.

. . . .

Sohrab was charged with the kidnapping of Razia, the only daughter of Mohammad, a wealthy and a well-known entrepreneur from Pol e Sorkh who was part of the big business scene in Kabul and across the country. According to Razia's statement, Mohammad was deceased. Razia's brother, a young man named Ali, filed the charges against Sohrab on behalf of his mother and sister.

Ali alleged Razia was kidnapped by "unknown persons" (a description that recalls the abductors in Sami's mother's narrative about Mina) in exchange for gold and money, and that his sister was held for ransom in a dilapidated house in Qargha, a popular, newly revived lakeside district less than an hour outside of Kabul. To those of us in the courtroom, Razia was an enigma: a woman about whom people spoke, for whom they planned and sacrificed, and who was at the center of the case and narrative even as she defied understanding. This was true for Sohrab more than anyone else, and he said he "could never understand who she really is." Her case was different from the many others I had seen in which women routinely took the stand to represent themselves in court in a spectrum of disputes ranging from inheritance struggles to divorce to the accusation of incest between mother and son. Razia's middle-aged lawyer did not explain her absence. He was wearing a suit and adjusted his tie when he rose to speak. Without responding to any part of Sohrab's testimony, he addressed the court in a courteous, matter-of-fact way: "I am Ahmad Reza, the attorney representing Razia and her family. I have a sworn statement from her as her representative, which I would like to read before the court and esteemed judges. The written statement reads as follows:"

In the name of Allah, the most merciful the most beneficial. I live in the Pol e Sorkh neighborhood of Kabul and was very busy with my studies at university. My father died, and I have only my mother, one uncle, and siblings. While I was engaged in my studies, a strange man, unknown to me, somehow obtained my phone number and got in touch with me. He began stalking me on my way to school and threatened me explicitly. He said if I uttered a word of this to anyone, he would put up my photos all over town, plaster them everywhere, or he would kill me. About a month later, while I was walking to my aunt's house, I was confronted by Sohrab. He kidnapped me. He forcibly threw me into a car, and he held me down. He held a poisoned handkerchief against my mouth, and I lost consciousness.

He took me to a flat single-level house, and when I regained consciousness, he told me we are in the Karte Nau neighborhood of Kabul. And at other times he would tell me we are in Pol-e-Charkhi prison. I tried to escape but could not, because he would always catch me in the act. Then, one day, he brought a mullah to the house. He told me to sign on a line of a marriage document. I said, "But how can I sign when my mother and uncle are not present to bear witness?" So, they took my two thumbs and put my thumbprints on the document instead. They made it happen anyway. . . . I tried to resist him, but I could not free myself from his grip. Eventually, the national police arrived and freed me.

On the afternoon her testimony was read aloud to the court, everyone was taken aback by its disorienting content. Sohrab was completely silent and looked forlorn; the judges were silent too, and the chief judge closed his eyes and then opened them to say:

We have heard a great deal today. Like all of you here today, I am at a loss for words and judgment. But what I also want to ask is, What has become of our society and what has become of our people's lives? It is our duty and obligation to render a judgment, but that duty is made more difficult when it is so hard to see the truth or to tell between accusations that are as wildly different from each other as the persons involved in this case.

The voice we hear about from Sohrab and that he heard numerous times over the telephone line, a line he claimed was a link between their hearts, was silent in the courtroom. There was no progression from voice to subjectivity to the truth of their relationship or to the "blind spot" of meaning.[44] The written accusation is an indictment of Sohrab and the world of images; it occupies the space between a desire for an unadulterated reality, one that might transcend all forms of representation, and the transformative potency wielded by narrative representation to dislocate or replace that reality. To show us, in other words, who she *really is*.

Dissemination

An abduction is both the act of taking someone by force or deception and the emergence of absence where someone should be present. But for Razia, her absence is not only the result of external violence and coercion, including a poisoned handkerchief and being locked in a safe house by the lake, but also part of the enigma of the photographic form. Her going missing is inseparable from the photographs that remain unseen and the lack of a material referent, and thus her abduction is another profound testament to her absence but it also possesses the power of constituting the alleged initial violence of blackmail that was followed up by the abduction.

How do we understand this double void? Razia was terrified of the photographic form (but not video images, which is an irony that I will return to), terrified of a world in which photographic evidence and dissemination would become not the excrescence of the real (which the photographic fetish purports to achieve through a stubborn insistence on a referential moment) but its total and violent displacement such that in living memory, she could only ever be whatever the image depicted of her *as real*. The photographs in question, which she alleges Sohrab took while stalking her around town (which the judges could not consider as part of the evidence in the case because they were never produced in court) floated like signifiers without referents, except that they had the power to stand apart from other metonymic or imaginary sequences she was part of (for example, all the other photographs of her that existed with her family, the self-image she evoked in her statement, and so on) and to make real a particular image of her in the collective gaze.

In part, this is a problem of form.[45] A photograph fixates on a given moment or occurrence; for example, the poignant or compelling private detail Roland Barthes calls the *punctum,* and more generally the play of absence and presence depicted by the peculiar death of the photographic subject (who is after the "click" and moment of photographic capture less alive than before but whose photograph also becomes more poignant after death). Thus, the photograph is a temporal fixation with what "was" rather than with the time that is passing by.[46]

This metamorphosis into a fetish-object occurs when a cut in the real, the "click" of the camera, becomes a moment of capture (or another "abduction" to refer to Soraya's account of events). "The photographic *take* is immediate and definitive, like death and like the constitution of the fetish in the unconscious, fixed by a glance in childhood, unchanged and always active later. Photography is a cut inside the referent, it cuts off a piece of it, a fragment, a part object, for a long immobile travel of no return."[47] The point I want to make here is that the photograph, especially when it is involuntarily disseminated for others to see, holds up a peculiar mirror to the idea of being and having been seen; it is, to quote Christian Metz, who in turn cites Dubois, a one-way mirror of the unique reality of being "dead for having been seen" and thus a radical alterity that cannot be assimilated within a preexisting grammar of being or presence.[48] It is a cut in the real, to be sure, but more so in the fantasy of the subject—divided not only between conscious and unconscious life but also between the interior fold of time captured in the photographic frame and the moment that was but can no longer be after the "click," when it is legible only as what "was" there.[49]

This speaks to Razia's concern about her image before the law, and more tellingly, to the nature of the accusation at hand. The accusation, she implies, becomes more urgent as the photographs recede from view but as the power of their dissemination intensifies, something her statement focuses on as much as the experience of being abducted and that she recognizes as unstoppable. What does she see, and fear will be seen by others, in the photographs Sohrab allegedly threatened to post across Kabul? What kind of excess is this? We know from Frantz Fanon and Jacques Lacan that the mirror is an object of alienation as much as it is unbearably close; a tooclose closeness captured in the loss of jouissance and the feeling that it is not a lack one encircles but a lack that is lacking.[50] More generally, the moment of fetishistic fixation is the halt of a glance Freud reveals as the cutoff point when the fear of lack (an unexpected absence) becomes too much to bear.[51] It is a glance that stops short of loss and, in stopping, also generates something that was not there before. Thus, as Metz points out, every fetish exists in two chains of meaning: a metonymic chain in which it is contiguous (and indicative) of lack and a metaphoric chain in which it becomes the equivalent of something else, when it becomes more than it was before (the glance that becomes a *Glanz* or the projection of social envy that becomes the fear of the evil eye, for example), in short when absence is crossed by presence. At the junction between anxiety and power, the fetish always combines "this double and contradictory function," and the amulet or charm or part-object that wards off the unknown can do so only by gesturing toward its power.[52]

In a temporal sense, the Razia of the photographic image becomes what she "was" because the instant of capture is irrevocable but also, in anticipating the gaze of the other, as she does and fears, the image continues to exist in the future perfect of what she "will have been" once it is seen by others: the public, the judges, and the law.[53] There is the Razia that has already been captured and the one that will be the outcome of the collective gaze. And yet, the Other in Razia's statement is not merely Sohrab or the force of the law. It is symbolic in nature and symptomatic of a cultural moment when the interpretation of social and linguistic difference was difficult if not impossible. The photographs—which were never adduced in court but only alluded to in the statement, a statement that functions as an "off frame" moment in which another image of Razia is constructed—possess a signifying force powerful enough to alter the reality of who she professes to be. The photos do not show us anything, but they lay out the path of absence, the loss of control, and the unwanted proximity of the desire of the other.

Accusation and Symptom

If we take Lacan on the question of the Other as a difficult but provisional starting point that necessitates a certain charting or "graph" (a spatial thinking) and thus a trajectory of desire that takes seriously the principle of movement and of missing the mark, then the question of what Sohrab wanted and expected from a love that made him feel like he had finally been "born" becomes doubly urgent to ask. On one hand, in the exchange of love how could he expect more than he could give? What kind of excess is this? On the other, why did he fail to hit the mark entirely? In the realm of photography, where Sohrab and Razia meet a second and more elusive time, lack (the absence of love or of the image) is transformed into the sense of overproximity to oneself, the image, and the Other. Perhaps a better way to phrase this is to say Sohrab was "dead for having been born again." Because he was born again due to having gained love, he gained much more than he ever bargained for: a gift of love. But this required Razia, who never admitted in her statement to being in love with him, to be "dead for having been seen" or dead for having become more to him than she could ever accept and thus dead for having received more than she could give.

What is missing in the trial is not only Razia or the photographs but an answer to the question of how to relate to others, how to desire, predict, understand, and control; in other words, how to close the gap and aporia that impede our complete understanding of the other but that are also crucial to desire and violence. In photography, this interplay is best described as the crossing of absence and presence that is part of a photograph's referential context insofar as this is also the omission of whatever is outside the frame: the outside we can infer but never see or know.[54] What was she doing before and after the photos were taken? Did she look at them and smile? Was she embarrassed? We cannot know.

The unseen photos of Razia are crucial to her abduction and crucial, if we read between the lines, to what she suggests might be the reason for her initial apparent willingness to go along with Sohrab, specifically, her state of duress and unreason over the prospect of photographic reproduction and scandal.[55] To imagine the elusive photos as specific scenes in which she was caught—and after which she faced certain consequences, meanings, people, and even a sectarian marriage she did not want—is to understand the predicament of the signifier that "gathers the language together, the promised or threatened language, promising all the way to the point of threatening."[56] What gathers around the photos is the possibility of their endless signification but also a social order in which the principle of exchange (for example, the performance of a proper, legible Shia ceremony to which she would otherwise consent) is overtaken by the threat of the proliferation of signs and thus belongs neither to desire nor custom and not even to the index as the mark of her presence (that is, her thumbprints) but to this larger threat.

Perhaps in refusing to appear in court and submitting a disembodied written statement Razia gestures to the division between who she is and who she might be perceived as, not just as the consequence of an image or fingerprint but also owing to the division internal to language that makes it impossible to speak or write in the manner we wish but holds open that possibility and the traversal of one by the other. Perhaps she writes better than she speaks, or she speaks better, too well even, in comparison to the ambivalence in her writing. If she appears in person, will she speak the way she writes and be who she conveys she is in her statement? We can't know, but it is not an accident that the first two sentences of the statement invoke speaking in the name of Allah (in the name of God, logos and divine truth) and her own studious nature, her commitment, in other words, to learning the word. That is her desire.

Language, like trauma, is always structured by what it seeks to repress.[57] And in a telling way, Razia's statement functions as the false image of self-presence and unequivocal meaning. The more closely we read the statement, the more its meanings diverge. The subversion of any single meaning unfolds through three discrete moments of Razia's testimony—the violence of the abduction, the ritual and legal performance of sectarian marriage, and the dissemination of the photographs—each of which bears its own narrative of representational violence. Each one is a symptom of the limitation of a single or coherent meaning.

At this point, to borrow from Barbara Johnson, instead of simply believing or doubting, we can do the work of pulling out the "warring forces of signification within the text itself."[58] This work shows not only the different forms of representational violence Razia narrates (photographic, gendered, sectarian, and legal and contractual) but also how the narrative cannot settle on a single meaning or depiction of what happened nor on the domination of one experience (abduction) over the other (being photographed). Of course, the point is not to conflate discrepancy with falsehood but to reveal the principle of necessity through which everything she writes and intends to convey is intrinsically related to everything she cannot repress or discern. I think one issue in particular stands out: the problem of indexicality. This is exemplified by her willingness to provide "thumbprints" to her abductor but contingent upon the imam's sectarian affiliation. This slip, where the index's position in her narrative and the progression of violence from abduction to photography to contractual exchange converge, reveals the symptomatic return from the future, a consequence neither Razia nor Sohrab could foresee but that constitutes the force of social difference at the origin and end of their relationship, and of the political sphere in 2014, when the Taliban initiated a campaign of amputating fingers that were ink stained on election day.

Recall that one of the reasons why Sohrab was so infatuated with the woman "who could one day be on channel 3" was because she seemed so different from him. That woman worthy of being captured in videographic form for the nation to see was in fact seen by the judges in a cellphone video she was unaware of. These are not the images she refers to in her statement, but rather a video of her wedding party which, according to the judges, shows her in a carefree state—dancing and laughing with Sohrab at the party—evidence that ultimately exonerated Sohrab. This is another indexical slip that is a symptom of the challenge of social and sectarian difference amid the breakdown of exchange. As a symptom it reveals the challenge of encountering a form of difference that cannot be interpreted or allowed to remain ambiguous but is instead given unequivocal meaning through the accusation against Sohrab. Yet, at the same time, despite being as close to the root of what went wrong between them as we can hope to understand, this indexical slip is not part of what she meant to say. Through its emergence at the points in her narrative when intention, sense, and story converge to say something other than what she intends (the moments when there is no predictable relationship between "saying" and "meaning" and "doing" and no anecdotal stability), it reveals that she is not in the place she claims to think, write, testify, or speak from.[59]

It matters that the trace of difference emerges wherever we seek or impose meaning. For Lacan, thinking that we are "thinking" is a fiction that obscures the more volatile process of becoming through signification, an insight we can see in the unraveling of Razia's statement and in her thinking that this statement would guarantee Sohrab's conviction. Conversely, for Sohrab, the fiction lies in expecting a final, complete understanding, a fantasy that masks the ongoing transformation and disjointed exchange between two series, one giving and the other receiving, which communicate through difference but never achieve perfect alignment.[60] They do not settle down. Caught in this gap, Razia could never communicate enough to achieve her desired end, nor could Sohrab receive more than he ever expected to have. Does (or did) she love him? Was she abducted or did she willingly disappear from her place? Do the photos exist? Does he still love her? Common sense would answer no, she never loved him; perhaps she eloped and then changed her mind, leading to the accusation; no, he no longer loves her. How could he? Yet the idea that a trace structure exists in the unconscious reveals that subjectivity and common sense are split along a double axis amid the dispersion of signs: Perhaps she loved him but felt ambivalent about the social difference between them; she was always missing from what she fantasized as being her rightful place; the photos are deferred across a material-imaginary divide that cannot become the object of a shared gaze; he still loves her and wants to be with her; and he is afraid she does not love him enough, or perhaps she loves him too much.

The matter of love always speaks to questions of life and death. The difference between conviction and his acquittal is the dispersion of meaning in Razia's testimony and the court's possession of the video (not a photograph) of them dancing and drinking at the house party during the period she described as her imprisonment either in Pol-e-Charkhi or the Qargha safehouse. The other uncanny opening still is not what the video depicts, or what the judges decide, but that there is no continuity between what we profess, write, read, and experience. Statements like, "I felt I had been born again" or "I was keeping my head low" and violence and accusation reveal the crossing of presence with absence and the place of lack in desire and symbolic life. It is also what accusation seeks to name and restore.

PART II   ON CIRCUITOUS PATHWAYS

The place of translation in contemporary Afghan society and historical memory is a strange one: It entails a demand for the validation of social and political "truth" in translational encounters and the simultaneous disavowal of the discourse of the other as nonsensical and devoid of reason. In tracing this paradox, the second part of this book marks a conceptual turn toward translation both as a trope for social difference in modern Afghan history and as a form of engagement that traverses self, other, urban, rural, and the perception of reason and its absence in social life. As we will read, in Zia's and Matin's narratives (in chapters 4 and 5, respectively), a sense of national defeat is largely a problem of the hinterland, where speech and discourse are overcome by the emptiness of local life and where, unlike in Kabul, language cannot signify how the world works. And yet, despite their monolingual fantasy of working toward a singular point of articulation and catharsis, translation goes elsewhere toward fragmented meanings, including in catastrophic moments of collapse, and in other moments that become the scene of the translator's extraordinary survival.

In looking for what haunts translation, I begin chapter 3 with a historical aperçu in which the political real, a referential ground beyond fragmented meaning, is stymied by the radiophonic play of undecidable, floating signifiers that, in turn, become a source of imperial anxiety. From here I move to a consideration of the contemporary place of mishearing in the context of a counterinsurgency mission. Again, the question arises: How are certain voices and modes of speech heard, and what can be said in dialogue overdetermined by the exigencies of war and counterinsurgency? In examining the place of translation as an encounter with difference in social life, I show that it is inseparable from the material violence of war; legacies of counterinsurgency, which include the fantasy that insurgent groups are inspired through language; and, in the European imperial imaginary, the status of the frontier in Afghanistan.

The colonial fantasy of a political real belied by Afghan discourse is, I illustrate, crucial both to the place of language in Afghan modernism and to the contemporary problem of speech and mishearing that is inseparable from the violence of translation in counterinsurgency campaigns. This recurring dilemma, which I return to in chapters 4 and 5 through the experiences of Zia and Matin, two wartime translators from Kabul, is grounded in a much longer history of Afghanistan as a hinterland in the global imaginary of the East and as a scene and source of linguistic violence in various imperial and discursive formations. Thus, in tracing the historical, conceptual, and ethnographic place of translation in encounters between places, lifeworlds, and persons, I seek to understand a temporal structure of deferral and return in which the fantasy of translational power bears on encounters with difference, subjective life (in, for example, the encounter with the stranger, or "barbarian") and the translator's fantasy of a purist and modern revival in contemporary Kabul.

CHAPTER THREE

The Alternation of World and Word

It is not easy to convey the truth in a country in which
so many of the inhabitants are as illiterate as they are
credulous.
—WILLIAM KERR FRASER-TYTLER, Confidential Despatch
to the Secretary of State for Foreign Affairs, April 19, 1940

On June 26, 1943, the London tabloid *Evening Standard* published an
article, "Secret Axis Radio," on the presence of a covert wireless station
in western Afghanistan, fifty miles from the ancient city of Herat. Herat
had captured the imagination of Ptolemy, Herodotus, Timur Lane, Geng-
his Khan, Alexander the Great (who left behind a stunning citadel), and
Rumi, who likened the city to an oyster's pearl. Now, in 1943, the greater
Herat region was the alleged site of a radio station broadcasting a clandes-
tine voice that spoke in two directions, one toward Europe and the other in
solidarity with Asia. The Hungarian announcer, ostensibly financed by the
Berlin Academy of Science, was an expert on Afghan tribes and dialects.
The *Evening Standard* article suggested that the twin voices broadcast mes-
sages that appeared meaningless, such as "Tea will be ready at dinner time
tonight," but that the ghostly prattle was a deceptive cover for the coded
exchange of Hungarian military information for Axis aircraft flying between Berlin and Tokyo.[1]

This accusation was preposterous, yet it reflected a broader and intense
preoccupation with Afghanistan's place in the imperial global order and
more specifically with the role of oral and radio propaganda. Consider this
paragraph from a telegram sent on May 8, 1940, by William Kerr Fraser-
Tytler, Britain's envoy to Afghanistan, to Major W. R. Hay, deputy secretary to the government of India in the External Affairs Department in
Simla: "German propaganda is widespread and mendacious. Apart from

the radio it consists in the dissemination of oral propaganda by Germans employed in Afghanistan in the secret distribution of pamphlets such as 'Polish atrocities against the German minority in Poland' and in the issue of a daily German bulletin which consists almost entirely of false or highly exaggerated reports of current events. I have taken every opportunity to warn the Afghans against the dangers of oral propaganda, and have protested strongly whenever pamphlets of the type described above have come to my notice."[2] More dangerously, in the British imperial imagination, Afghanistan was "a country which lends itself particularly well to German intrigue against Great Britain; for it borders on the North West Frontier of India; and to stir up trouble amongst the turbulent tribes of the borderland is an easy matter."[3]

The mysterious voice over the radio is not the voice of truth or disclosure but of its other and of rupture from within. It is an opening in a field of political maneuvers and, in the colonial world, a form of alterity neither present nor absent, excessive and too close for comfort but also reflecting the dangerously native, acousmatic gap between continents, empires, and reason under threat of lawlessness and the warring other. The voice is on the ulterior side of logos, a voice of semantic doubles and "nonsense" which is part of an entire order of voicing and speech that moves through what Jacques Derrida calls a "zone of passing turbulence in public or political language."[4] In the contemporary moment, these voices constitute what I call the "discourse of another other"; they bear the mark of radical alterity with devastating consequences in translational encounters in places my Kabuli interlocuters referred to simply as *atraf*, "the hinterland" or "the countryside." How do speech and voicing become a problem of political life and translation? How are they part of a dangerous opening and limit to connecting with the global sphere? How does speech determine forms of access and violence, ranging from interrogation to sacrifice and death?

ALTERNATING WORDS

In "On Alternating Sounds" (1889) Franz Boas warns anthropologists about the predilection to hear *from* different languages. The experience of "sound blindness," he argues, is not about the inability to grasp subtle differences between phonetic sounds—for example, the kind of mishearing that collapses polysyllabic words into monosyllabic ones—but rather relates to how we classify new phenomena. For Boas difference is perceived through similar sounds being categorized differently according to one's native language. Thus, while there is no such thing as "sound blindness," there are alternating apperceptions of sounds that come to us from different languages. Boas makes another subtle but crucial argument about why this happens. While phonetic elements are generally categorized according to the sounds of the hearer's language, the interval and duration between sensations also play important roles in perception. He notes that if there is a long interval between sensations (colors, sounds, and so on) we are likely to *psychically* mistake them as the same, whereas when they adjoin, misrecognition is due to the *physiological* incapacity to perceive phonological difference. Thus, in the first case mishearing after a long interval suggests apperceptive prejudice, but in the latter case it indicates an incapacity in hearing caused by a rapid shift. One could say that, rather than a bias or mistake, it is an accident originating from outside the listener.

In part, this is a commonsensical claim. After all, parsing a succession of sounds or notes is what we do when we hear speech or a musical composition; doing so requires reading the difference and delay between phonetic signs in order to impose meaning. For Boas, the issue is how quickly signs follow one another and the length of the gap between them such that blindness to difference is symptomatic rather than structural to linguistic difference. But sound blindness is also related to the possession or lack of our "own" language, and therefore to the violence of monolingualism. The alterity captured by the radio voice is one we will encounter in other moments, ranging from broken and fraught dialogue in scenes of interrogation to the exchange of words and gifts; these are moments of voicing and speech but also part of experiencing the discourse of others as an uncanny power that displaces the political reality with dissimulation or absurdity. How does this displacement emerge within the discourse and practice of counterinsurgency? How does it emerge relative to one's own relationship to language and in the encounter with the stranger, barbarian, or outsider? And crucially, how is it a problem of translation?

THE TASK OF THE ANGEL

In Walter Benjamin's "Theses on the Philosophy of History" the angel of history looks at an accumulation of catastrophic effects irreducible to any single chain of events. It is a storm that "irresistibly propels him into the future to which his back is turned, while the pile of debris before him grows skyward. This storm is what we call progress."[5] This is the force of historical materialism and its complex cultural politics, but the sight of the wreck, as Paul de Man suggests, cannot be understood without a recognition of the presence of its counterpart: the figure of the translator. Wherever there is meaning and catastrophe, there are also the traces of language in motion and of the supplemental, fragmented relationships between languages; this movement constitutes the meaning of history for Benjamin:

> Now it is this motion, this errancy of language which never reaches the mark, which is always displaced in relation to what it meant to reach, it is this errancy of language, this illusion of a life that is only an afterlife, that Benjamin calls history. As such, history is not human, because it pertains strictly to the order of language; it is not natural, for the same reason; it is not phenomenal, in the sense that no cognition, no knowledge about man, can be deprived from a history which as such is purely a linguistic complication; and it is not really temporal either, because the structure that animates it is not a temporal structure.[6]

My intention here is not to make a claim about historical time or the place of historiography in the distribution of memory and crisis. Instead, I think this "errancy of language" demands a critical examination of translation, not solely as a practice of mediation but as a metaphor for the trace of time in language; thus, we must think beyond commensuration to analyze moments of disjunction and the retroactive meaning we find in critical inquiry.[7] At the same time, for Benjamin, translation brings to the surface something latent that is not expressed in a language's mode of intention.[8] Translation reveals the kinship of languages not through the emergence of likeness (for example, resemblance to an original text or meaning) but in the mode of intention that exists in every language and allows it to become other (a stranger, foreigner) and greater than itself.[9]

Whenever we intend to say something, the intervention of a foreign signifying chain makes communication more difficult and imbues our words with a meaning or possibility we do not intend. For Benjamin, the German word *Brot* and the French word *pain* intend the same object (bread) but the way in which German and French *intend that object is not the same*.[10] This is why the word *Brot* means something different to a German speaker than *pain* does to a French speaker. The way in which *Brot* (*Brot, Brot und Bier, Brötchen*) intends or suggests or culls in German could even interfere with or disturb the intention (the movement of signs) someone might seek from the word *pain* (*pain, pâtisserie, pain et vin, pain au lait, pain au chocolat*). Similarly, the Persian word *naan* means baked bread but also food and sustenance more generally; for example, the Afghan saying *naan e roz wa shab e khod e nadareh* (to not even have one's daily bread) connotes lacking sustenance and the capacity to sustain life. The point is that the foreign signifying chain alters one's mode of intention and reveals the play of intention between languages that allows meaning to emerge not as an autonomous feature of any single language but as "pure language from the harmony of all the various modes of intention."[11]

Yet, translation also creates strangeness and the possibility of chaos and death. It is part of an aporia that shapes political and ethical trajectories: On one hand, the transcendence and the afterlife of language are such that they are irreducible to any single language (or linguistic realm); on the other, the interlinguistic domain is marked by ambivalence, interpretation, and violence. Rather than bridging a set of meanings, translation can just as easily blur them and subvert what Ibn Khaldûn refers to as "group feeling," making it possible to inflict violence on those who were previously kindred or legible to us.[12] In these moments, the translator must also reckon with incommunicability and the rare "total linguistic barrier," which Primo Levi evokes as the difference between life and the domain of war.[13]

"TWO RAKAT"

This complexity requires us to think about translation not as a practice or mystical experience but as a "theoretical metaphor through which to think about difference."[14] During the insurgency, the concern with oral culture in Afghanistan was a crucial factor in the ironic and sometimes deadly misunderstandings that unfolded in rural villages that surrounded major cities like Kabul, Herat, and Kandahar and that were invoked as the violent or romanticized other of the urban. Translators from Kabul told me stories of civilians coerced to betray their fellow villagers and divulge vital information regarding the whereabouts of hiding insurgents.[15] Village elders or leaders sometimes responded to these overtures and to bribes framed in the language of the gift. At times, they spread disinformation, having been previously paid off by the Taliban to stymie information-gathering endeavors and point the forces not in the direction of *this* village, where the Taliban had a presence, but *that* one, where they suspected their enemies were hiding.

This and that, here and there are caught up in the tactics of intelligence gathering but also in the ethnic and linguistic structures of difference crucial to political violence and counterinsurgency. Consider the following story a young translator from Kabul told me about the experience of his friend, another translator. In this narrative of a narrative of translation, a moment of mishearing occurred precisely when the mode of intention became dangerous in the gap between languages. The friend was working with a search mission led by a group of American soldiers in a rural village in Helmand Province and approached the house of an elderly Afghan man in the middle of the night. The Persian-speaking Afghan translator asked if they could question him about possible insurgent activity in this village and the man replied in Pashto that he would go with them for questioning "after two *rakat.*"

The *rakat*, from the Arabic word *rakah* (movement), is an iteration of prescribed movements and supplications within the Islamic act of prayer known as *salah* or *namaaz*. It is never just a response to canonical injunction. Instead, praying two *rakats* indicates that the supplicant is asking for blessing or protection, for example, when feeling endangered or sending blessings to the dead. The translator told the soldiers that he thought the man had just admitted to having "two rockets" in his home. I do not know the outcome of this mishearing. It is plausible that after a search of his home the man was exonerated. It is equally plausible that he found himself in an increasingly tortuous web of interrogation, detention, and possible deportation to Guantánamo, his family left behind without knowledge of his whereabouts, like so many who still await "the imprisoned."[16]

We listen for what sounds like common sense, for the taken-for-granted that rises to the top of a stream of words. Thus, both mishearing and sense-making are part of what Gilles Deleuze deconstructs as the dogmatic form of common sense and thought valorized by traditional philosophy.[17] In this instance mishearing the word may be attributable to the translator's difficulty understanding Pashto (Persian and Pashto are not mutually intelligible). The misunderstanding is also part of the hierarchy of difference in intervals between instances of speech that are overdetermined by representational and material violence: The gap between "after two *rakat*" and the translation "he has two rockets" is a duration determined not by the mode of intention but primarily by the exigencies of reconnaissance and combat. If for Louis Althusser the moment of interpellation is one of subjectification, then in the practice of interrogation the subject of address confronts the demand to say precisely what the interrogator expects and wants to hear. The violence of such an address is that the representation of difference (for example, insisting on one's innocence or providing alternative information) becomes equivalent to inviting a violent response. The subject cannot not reply in the right way.[18]

The Afghan-Soviet War of 1979–89 transformed Afghanistan into one of the world's largest weapons markets and introduced the rocket and Kalashnikov assault rifle as the weapons of choice for the American-backed Mujahideen who were fighting the invading Soviet Army. As Afghanistan became increasingly enmeshed in the Cold War and drawn into global circuits of weapons exchange, the "type 63" 107-millimeter rocket, first produced in China in 1963 under Mao Ze Dung in order to free the People's Liberation Army from its dependency on Soviet weaponry and imports, became a privileged weapon. During the Afghan-Soviet War, it was primarily used in rural areas, then later during the Afghan Civil War of 1989–94, it was regularly launched in cities and especially in Kabul.[19]

Rockets are a testament to much more than the continued use of Cold War munitions and a global weapons market that invests proxy conflicts with a duration they would not otherwise have. The word *rocket* stems from the Italian word *rocca*, which derives from the German word *rocko* (distaff) and ultimately from the root word *rug* (woven or spun fabric). This etymological root, like the prayer rug the elderly Afghan man intended to pray two *rakat* on, contains not only the awful irony of the mishearing but also the rotating mechanism by which the rocket is a deadly and mobile weapon of choice that was used pervasively and became ingrained as a fixture of the physical and social landscape as well as the linguistic imaginary. The mishearing of *rocket* for *rakat* reflects a world of idiomatic and metaphoric expressions, of unique adjectives like *rocketee* (an Afghan nickname for an adept rocket handler) and nouns like *rocket* that circulate as floating signifiers.

Like the weapon it denotes, the word *rocket* comes from elsewhere. Not only is there no Persian or Pashto equivalent for the term, but there is also no domestically produced rocket despite its widespread use.[20] The 107-millimeter rocket is encased in a twelve-tube launcher; its cylindrical form is designed for the quick and steady infliction of firepower, and when propelled, it spins more than 366 times per second. It is this spinning (which underlies the origin of the word and its various etymological roots) that causes the rocket to project outward regardless of where it is launched from: the dirt, a car jack, a person's shoulder, or a makeshift ramp. If a *rocca* spins yarn into textile, the spinning of the rocket produces the fantasy of a linear trajectory that guides the rocket to its intended target. The metal slots welded onto rockets, through which fabric is slung so that men can carry the rockets on their backs from town to city to village, are a testament to this belief in the disassembled rocket's continued linear efficacy.[21]

The transformation of bulky rocket launcher systems into mobile rockets launched using everyday items turned rockets into ubiquitous but not very accurate weapons. In densely populated urban areas, especially in Kabul during the Civil War, they were launched from different neighborhoods and veered drastically off course. They hit schools, homes, cars, and pedestrians and littered cities with rocket remains that children still mistake for toys and that farmers reweld into agricultural tools. In the 1980s, Nadia's five-year-old son died suddenly while playing on the grass in front of a house in Kabul. She recalled the event in a succinct, plainspoken way, claiming that the grass outside killed him. It "snatched" him from her that afternoon because it had toxic rocket powder residue on it. It happened "just like that" she said.[22]

The rocket assumed a privileged position as cause and adjective. Well-known and well-trained guerrilla fighters were called *rocketees*, explosions were ascribed to rockets regardless of their various causes, and death assumed an intimate relationship not only to rockets but also to the toxic residue and shrapnel they left behind.[23] Kabulis learned to listen to the blasts of rockets and to discern from their residual echoes the intended targets and trajectories, spinning narratives about what happened, where, and why out of the sounds they heard. Initial bangs and echoes turned into language and speculation, into rumor and assertions of cause. Stories about rockets proliferated, becoming a source of local knowledge and later of expertise for those who lived through violent decades, invoked in the 2010s to make sense of the various booms of car bombs, grenades, and suicide bombers.

TOTAL WAR

It wasn't until World War I, when European cities were first subjected to large-scale destruction, that aerial bombing became a question of moral sensibility. Prior to that, reckless attacks mostly determined the fate of besieged colonies, the places Mahmud Tarzī describes as caught in a web of colonial expansion and a "conflagration of fire and smoke." In South Asia, the bombings were primarily directed first at the northwest frontier of India, then during the third Anglo-Afghan War of 1919, against the cities of Kabul and Jalalabad. Other bombings were carried out in Iran, Trans-Jordan, and Iraq where "in principle, the inhabitants were supposed to be warned before a raid . . . houses, animals, and soldiers were supposed to be targets, and not the elderly, women or children," but in reality "things didn't always go that way."[24] From a different perspective, the fire-bombings of German cities by the Royal Air Force were an "undisguised" and "pure war," a type of war, W. G. Sebald writes, that turns victims not into means toward an end but, like in the irrationality of torture, "both the means and the end in themselves."[25]

Theorizing this situation in 1915, Freud wrote that the ordinary prohibitions of war respected for the sake of future peace had been forsaken and that this loss had shattered the illusion that European cultural and scientific achievement represented psychic progress or the instinctual restraint required not to subject civilians, livestock, property, and the wounded to violence.[26] The heart of Freud's argument is about psychic ambivalence and a fundamentally altered modern attitude toward death. In contradistinction to the primeval ethic, this new attitude rejected the possibility of haunting or an ethics of guilt based on fear; and as a result, enabled the rise of mass destruction and killing.[27]

In the US war in Afghanistan and in the global counterinsurgency agenda, the indiscriminate killing of civilians and targeting of paramilitary or nonmilitary fighting groups assumed another dimension whereby the cohesion achieved through hierarchical command was imagined to inhere in linguistic life as a source of inspiration and unity. This was coupled with the discourse that insurgents embedded themselves within the civilian population, taking cover in densely populated areas and necessitating civilian causalities, a discourse that rests on deeply racialized fantasies about the nature of the Muslim mob, feared as much because of racial difference as its purported disregard for private property,[28] its mobility, and its ability to embed itself in the natural and urban landscape, emanating from tunnels, caves, and the like. In both the archival record of the Anglo-Afghan Wars and in the more recent discourse of counterinsurgency, anxiety around the figure of the insurgent has been crucial to a larger fear of rebellious movements and to the subsequent paradigm of "targeting" the enemy.[29] Moreover, the contemporary concern that Cold War–era weapons stockpiles are outmoded in the digital information age, where so-called cutting-edge precision weapons are increasingly the norm, shapes a strategic "smart weapons" discourse that gives the US military a competitive advantage and forces its adversaries to rely on new organizational idioms, making them harder to target by conventional aerial bombing.[30]

The fantasy of being able to know and see all elements of battle in a phantasmatic whole is part of a larger transition from multilateral deterrence during the Cold War to preemptive attacks and endless war against elusive terrorist networks purportedly bound by the ideological role of narrative language. Crucially, in the US military imagination, the idea that language and storytelling bind members of a terrorist group together through shared ideals and beliefs buttresses the notion that the "network" is horizontal and extends in time and space through the work of language as the medium of relations that should be, ideally, the content of visual technology or, if that fails, of translational labor. Thus, the medium of storied language does the work performed by hierarchical relations of authority and submission in traditional military formations. Network members (insurgents) are bound by the power of stories that disseminate from doctrinal leaders and forge libidinal ties between group members. At the same time, translational labor is tasked with mediating, capturing, and neutralizing that which visual and other non-kinetic technologies cannot capture or parse.

The idea that the network possesses a psychic and linguistic force that holds the group together turns it into an "irreducible virtuality" that becomes difficult to dismantle, far less target. Here we can make an important distinction: This military and political logic incorporates what Jean Baudrillard calls the logic of the hyperreal, and thus the pure repetition and aesthetic force of simulation.[31] In part, the political logic is rooted in a structural shift Baudrillard describes as the radicalization (or "total liberty") of the sign-function, which he extends to a new culture of violence in the relaying of battlefield images characterized by the "structural unreality" of the image. What, after all, is one looking at? But the logic also reflects a narcissistic political ideology in which the function of war is war on the other's symbolic capacity.[32] It is this sense of a war waged on difference and the idea of an enemy (on the opposition of enemy and friend), that Baudrillard understands both as the end of conventional war and the basis for the provocative claim that the First Gulf War did not take place.[33]

What is important about this transformation in modern warfare is that counterinsurgency relies on the fetishistic misrecognition of speaking as immediate inspiration, a discourse which takes linguistic expression as the dissemination of violence through oral networks of exchange in which ideological truth and violent action are one. Speak, exhort, command, and it shall be done. In Afghanistan, it also illustrates the complex geopolitical history of frontier relations that characterizes the imperial discourse on social form and paranoia about foreign voices, mobs, and the general force of linguistic and ideological difference. Thus, while these moments are separated by techno-military (and media) cultures that stretch across a century, they reflect the signal anxiety that arises in contexts of ideological difference (in this case, the fear of Islamism and pan-Islamism), an anxiety that is shaped by the dread of imminent threat and results in the desire to contain the other's speech and lessen its political force.

. . . .

Two orders of translation are crucial to modern *and modernist* Afghan history: (1) the idea of Afghanistan as a coeval, cosmopolitan site of knowledge and (2) the imperial perception of it as an ungovernable place where modernity is endlessly deferred and thus as the ultimate frontier for empire to traverse. In each of these encounters, one a modernist encounter with the world, and the other a modern colonial anxiety over frontiers, the status of discourse and language rises to the surface of a series of entanglements that shape (1) historical anxiety about the Eastern frontier as a site of radical alterity, (2) the modernist silhouette of an Afghanistan-to-come, and (3) the concern with dialect and speech in areas outside of Kabul where translation was the most fraught with danger and was often deadly. But first, whose speech becomes the dissimulation of logos and presence? And whose idea of translation do we think with? How are concepts embedded in place, and what is the place of conceptual difference?

As we have seen, the desire to neutralize political difference is inseparable from the kinds of cultural excess and impulse satisfaction thought to permeate oral lifeworlds—the spartan places imagined as immune to the force of written law and constantly generating more war. Thus, the subject-targets of a reconnaissance mission can only position themselves as entities who harbor thoughts of imminent violence and spread a discourse of danger and absurdity or who speak to consent to their own violation.[34] Who, after all, would immediately reply with "I have two rockets"? More tellingly, who would presume that on waking someone up in the middle of the night, this is the first thing the person would say to them? These complexities abound in the contemporary moment and shape myriad forms of misunderstanding that occur not only in translation but also in urban life, in love, and within families. But the violence of translation is different from these other manifestations because it is the ideological heir of an earlier, global moment when imperial politics was inseparable from a concern with the place of oral culture in the frontier and the fear that where written propaganda is of little use, political momentum and rebellion can be as straightforward as harnessing the most resonant and passionate forms of speech.[35] For example, during the Anglo-Afghan Wars (in 1839, 1878, and 1919) British anxiety over the movement and activities of Afghan tribes along the British-Indian border was based on the phonocentric fantasy that truth and speech are hallmarks of modern subjectivity but that this is inverted on the frontier as the problem of dissimulation and counterfeit voices. Wartime political anxiety, including during World War I and World War II, was experienced through the prism of nomadism and tribal rebellion, but it was always connected to a linguistic and political vision where speech and logos cannot be unified within the other.

Modern communication began on the wire when cable telegraphy was offered to Afghanistan as a gift after the third Anglo-Afghan War, in part as gesture of goodwill but ultimately to stymie Bolshevik propaganda through media technology. Then, as now, media technology was a bridge to the less-than-known (but not entirely unknown) frontier and to the discourse of the other, deemed to be subversive and dangerous and, therefore, in the waning decades of imperial rule in the subcontinent, more crucial than ever to decipher and understand. Throughout this era of colonial paranoia, a time of modernist ambition, the status of an oral lifeworld in Afghanistan transformed from the imagined prior ground on which different technological orders were introduced (to mitigate the problem of illiteracy and tribal uprising) to a technology of persuasion and propaganda and "whispering campaigns" on behalf of British rule in India. This project encompassed listening in on Afghan radio broadcasts; dissemination of oral propaganda, particularly in regions populated by tribes along the border with British India; indoctrination; and sabotage of communication technologies.

One version of this colonial paranoia is the fear of the voice over the radio, suspected of transmitting military information to Axis powers, a voice that is part of an era of technological mediation in Kabul and opens new ground for the empire's fear of political subterfuge. The belief that communication technologies (including cable and wireless telegraphy, radio, telephone, and cinema) could facilitate immediacy and access (specifically, the connective powers that might enable political suasion) was counterposed with the problem of uncontrolled transmissions and the presumption of rampant whispering campaigns that could be harnessed against the British Empire. In this context, owing to the uncontrollable nature of mechanical reproduction, the transition to oral propaganda was deemed especially urgent. Consider the following communications I found in the British Museum archives in London in a bulging file on wartime British propaganda in Afghanistan. The first is a telegram from the British government's External Affairs Department to the Secretary of State for India in Simla:

> We have set up an agency suitable for a whispering campaign in and across the frontier. General line should be to put out (? incidents) illustrating practical meaning of unwise Nazi rule to a villager in a subject country and how British victory will ensure safety of Islamic Afghanistan, the (? tribes) trade and general progress . . . such stories would be related by agents in village guest houses, tea shops and on journeys and supported by guide notes which would take account constantly of movement of public opinion in Afghanistan.[36]

And this letter from the British legation in Kabul, which reads in part:

> The most important aspect is, in my opinion, the immediate and effective dissemination of news in and through the tribal areas. I consider it essential to have ready a system for this purpose which can be put into immediate operation along the whole frontier. I think it is quite certain that the outbreak of war would be the signal for a virulent anti-British campaign on the part of all enemy subjects in various parts of Afghanistan . . . a vigorous counter offensive is essential, particularly in the tribal areas whence the greatest menace will come, and steps should now be taken to work out a system of propaganda so that the machinery will be ready to set in motion at once. . It would be advisable to make preparations for such broadcasts now, from Delhi or Lahore, both of which stations can be fairly well heard in Kabul, Kandahar and Herat and probably also in Jalalabad, though there are at present no receiving sets at the latter place. It would be advantageous to start a daily Persian broadcast of news without delay, but such news would of course have to be carefully edited, and to consist mainly of world affairs and matters of general interest.[37]

A whispering campaign is the systemic dissemination of rumors and political tactics rooted in the power of the object-voice. This is precisely the voice Mladen Dolar describes as the remainder of a phonocentric reduction, a voice that is not the voice of logos and truth but that refuses to disappear or be silenced. It circulates with force, turning political difference into the basis of an oral offensive in a place where written propaganda was deemed useless. And, as we will see, these voices and campaigns emerge when the experience of modernity cannot be translated into an object of desire nor denied as a political force that disrupts categories of understanding and collective life.

In the aftermath of a period of isolation and conflict, in the first decades of the twentieth century, the population in Kabul was buoyed by the desire for new, exciting forms of global contact and address, including the idea that telegraphic, telephonic, and radio communication could transform Kabul into a modern, ordered city, in control of its hinterland and part of a new and electrified era in which international connectivity was the basis for political and symbolic recognition. It was not about techne but technological thinking and what Marshall McLuhan calls a "social hormone" that influences the milieu and idea of governance and transforms the sense of contemporary consciousness.

But this desire for exchange was met with a series of complex maneuverings, including the sabotage of Afghan communication systems or deliberate maintenance shortfalls that kept the systems precariously near failure but with just enough power to keep the dream going. Global and electronic communication was disrupted and silenced and sometimes broken but nonetheless it remained part of the consciousness of modernity. Electronic communication was embedded in a cosmopolitan, coeval sense of politics, national identity, and progress. Yet, this was also the moment of openness that transformed the possible encounter with the foreign—and thus, with ideological difference—into a matter of collective anxiety. Through the telegraph, telephone, radio, and eventually cinema houses, the Afghan desire to be in the contemporary moment, to have something to say to the world (to speak back, so to speak) was volatilized by the same radical opening of technology that now appeared unstoppable on the global political stage. Consider this dispatch on the transmission of BBC Russian programs in Kabul from the British minister in Kabul, Giles Squire, to Ernest Bevin, M.P. and Secretary of State for Foreign Affairs in London:

> Listeners here report that the announcer's Russian is good and clear and they appreciate that the matter of these broadcasts is factual and accurate. They feel however that they might go a great deal further in representing and emphasising the British point of view. . . . Too much emphasis is in fact often given to the Russian point of view with the result that the broadcasts on occasion appear to be a somewhat pale form of red propaganda. I am told, for instance, that Russian speeches at the Paris Peace Conference and in the Security Council have been quoted in extenso and without comment

while the replies are often only given in brief and without sufficient emphasis on the points of view in which they differ from the Russian point of view. . . . It is vital that everyone, including the Russians themselves, should understand that we stand for the greatest possible freedom for everybody as opposed to the tyrannical "dictatorship of the proletariat" or rather of their self-appointed leaders.[38]

This was no longer simply a question of technological reach, but also of tonal calibration and ideological power. Even as wireless broadcasts connected distant publics, they gave rise to new uncertainties about voice, allegiance, and interpretive control. What emerged in these global circuits was not just contact but distortion, a struggle over which voices would be heard, how they would be framed, and whose vision of the world they would transmit in an era of volatilized communication. As much as these technologies were about connections between continents, capital cities, and imperial aims, they also condensed cultural anxiety about the other into new media and a new consciousness of the hidden dangers of global address and exchange; that is, the unmanageable politics of representation understood as the coeval desire to "be with" and "to talk to" others alongside a fear of the unknown.

What kind of encounter was this? And insofar as voice, speech, and public discourse became a threat, what was the danger? In Afghanistan the British Empire faced an oral lifeworld deemed unsuitable to its governing order. It was encountered, heard, overheard, and feared as the Janus-faced other—in other words, not a voice that could be incorporated in service of colonial rule and its bureaucratic and technological extensions, not a logocentric opening, but a voice immune to truth-seeking, truth-saying, and truthful doing.[39] Native and ideological discourse revealed the impossibility of logos and coherence and raised the specter of dissimulation and political unrest made all but certain because those very voices, on the radio, in the hinterland, on the phone, and among restless border tribes, could not be contained by written propaganda or juridical discourse; thus, they could only be countered with the additional false voices of whispering campaigns.

This history is crucial to contemporary anxiety surrounding the place of dialect and speech in the Afghan countryside, where linguistic difference is conflated with the specter of irrational violence and where, again, we witness the crossing of a phonocentric fantasy (as lack) with territorial and economic ambition, including in new forms of paid labor as translators.

While this is particularly true in the early and mid-twentieth century, during the era of technological connectivity, the fixation with Afghan lawlessness and political speech is part of the more general nexus of industrial war and the Orientalist construction of an "Eastern frontier" as a dangerous site of contact and proximity; a discourse that transformed Afghanistan into the frontier for the United Kingdom, British India, and the Soviet Union, where it was crucial to the cultural boundaries of the "Russian Orient," in which Afghanistan occupies an emblematic role best described in the Freudian idiom as the scene of violent repetition compulsion.[40]

In the global imperial imagination of this era, Afghanistan became a site of tribal and political power in the Asiatic world, becoming a place of ideological danger and excess but also the frontier where modernity was endlessly deferred.[41] This anxiety was, in turn, part of a more concerted Allied effort in the interwar years to secure Afghanistan as a place of resistance to Russian and Axis influence. As a result, political speech, the radio dispatch, the voice, and the porosity of media technology all became crucial forms of global connectivity and new sources of danger.

And yet, there is still another fear: the fear and deep ambivalence over the place of ideological and cultural difference in the modern era that manifests as the problem of technology or political suasion but is principally about the encounter with untranslatable difference. Thus, the more electronic communication technologies outperformed the political and symbolic effectiveness of oral and written propaganda, the more anxiety was generated about interpreting the differences between oral, literate, and techno-mediated societies. In this context—stretched across the divide between self and other, order and excess—colonial projects were suspended in the mutual constitution of empire, nation, and frontier but also in projects of linguistic nationalism which inspired political and cultural movements that were deeply modernist *and* committed to anticolonial solidarity within the broader colonial world. How does this history of the frontier and the status of Afghan discourse as its porous and deceptive manifestation bear on Afghan modernism? What is the place of translation in that imaginary? What is the place of historical ruins? What does the angel of history, crucial to time and translation, look at when looking from the frontier?

. . . .

In the twentieth century new cultural and political movements expressed new forms of literary-aesthetic production that were national (what Fredric

Jameson describes as the allegory of the nation and its subjects of modernity) but also caught in the irrational global dissemination of industrialized mass violence across the colonial and Asiatic world. In Kabul the preoccupation with literary-aesthetic production became deeply entwined with the experience of modernity and the place of translation as a metaphorical reflection of modernity's transformative force. More than an allegory, this literary-aesthetic production was a discourse and project with an aesthetic purpose and a literary and political commitment to Afghanistan's global and modernist aspiration. It sought to translate the inner dialectic of modernity, of progress and ruin, into a collective experience of a national and epistemic revival that contested the foundation of what it means to have rational knowledge and be in the world with others; it was a modernity that was always universal and borrowed, undeniably global but not "locked in a life-and death struggle with first world cultural imperialism" and inspired by the very ideological entanglements that constituted its other(s).[42]

These dialectic entanglements, including those between empire and frontier, are crucial to the idea of literary commitment and the translation of modernity into an understanding of history that eschews the empirical order of historical events (with disaster being *one aspect* of historical relations but not its constitutive drive), replacing it with the importance of reassessing knowledge and the question of *what it means to know and be in the world*. For Afghan modernists like Mahmud Tarzī, the translation of experience and ideas—including the encounter between Afghanistan and empire(s)—was the gateway to a more transcendental and protean opening. He understood this opening as the topology of the modern and its structure of possibilities, which offers positions and epistemes that can be variously occupied in the form of a symbolic order that exceeds the hegemony of any single place, trope, or philosophical tradition.

Tarzī expressed this notion through a series of contradictory political commitments in the pages of *Siraj al Akhbar* (The torch of news), the journal he founded and edited, and in his other writings. Upon returning to Kabul after two decades of exile in Istanbul and Damascus, he emphasized the undesirable consequences of national isolationism in his writings and in *Siraj al Akhbar*. He published foreign and domestic news and poetry, and translated various publications and novels from English, Turkish, Urdu, and Arabic into Persian. And yet, his writings are irreducible to issues of cultural exchange or to an analysis of global imperialism as experienced in the colonies. He wrote passionately about his era as a time for technological acquisition, global aspiration, and pan-Asian solidarity, as well as for poetry and novelistic prose. In turn, these diverse aspirations influenced the literary and political discourses he communicated in *Siraj al Akhbar* and the complicated relationship between nationalism and internationalism within the Afghan modernist movement.[43] In the end what mattered to the Afghan modernists and their political project was the importance of difference in thought and the capacity to imagine and reimagine the world from its margins, a scope that cannot be reduced to the fantasy of an "alternative modernity" in the Asiatic or Islamic world but was an impassioned and continuous disruption of established frameworks on political, epistemic, and even technological grounds.[44]

In this worldview, concepts, including those of modernity and its translation into political and intellectual experience, do not come from distinct worlds but are porous, cracked, and used and rethought in the service of a "worldling practice."[45] In this sense, as a call for the using and undoing of ideas to achieve epistemic renewal, the literary production of *Siraj al Akhbar* also constituted a critical intervention into how nations, people, national "spirits," and ways of knowing are bounded and relational but retain the political capacity to resist, including resisting the violence of colonialism and that which has not yet taken place; in other words, to refuse subjugation in the way Pierre Clastres describes as the aporetic capacity to resist without having known or experienced the thing being resisted.[46]

How we translate modernity has implications for our understanding of translation more broadly. In this discourse modernity is no single, unified thing that can be mimetically approximated, translated, or rejected on grounds of ideological or aesthetic difference. The concept is already partial and fragmented, and its phenomenological and cultural manifestations reflect those fissures. For Tarzī, insofar as he gives modernity any coherence, it is a topological scene: It is another space, a scene of ruins but also of momentum and the encounter with difference.[47] It is another elsewhere and a set of detours in language. Irreducible to political difference or the formation of a discursive tradition, the quality of being modern is always suspended in the possibilities of representing difference at the level of conceptual form and its corollary of a different collective unconscious.[48] Modernism is not a discourse of anthropological difference but a political vision of metamorphosis on a global scale; an itinerant, emergent process in which political discourse and print media are a crucial and uncontrollable part of global cosmopolitanism but where the idea of cosmopolitanism is itself fragmented by the necessity of thinking about its undoing. Thus, while he praises new technology, seamless railway connections, the telephone, telegraph, and the possibilities of electrical connectivity across the globe—and went so far as to contrast them to the stationary, oral lifeworld and the "camel, that slow-gaited creature"—to read Tarzī as a figure who champions the circulation of texts and ideas, and who specifies that possibility in an act of translation or the spaces opened by the work of global capital or new forms of connectivity, is to efface the nature of his ambivalence. He feared that without the intervention of an ethical and cultural labor of reassessing the place of modern knowledge in the world, destruction would overwhelm populations, particularly in Asia and Africa. And he was concerned with the rapid expansion of nineteenth- and twentieth-century industrial capitalism, envisioning in that progress a much deeper omen of the possibility of catastrophic violence across the world. Thus, his writings urge Afghans to consider the relationship between knowledge (including science) and unconscious phenomena, and to reflect on the differences between ways of knowing and what it means to know. Perhaps most powerfully, the hope Tarzī's writings express is that the transformation in collective thought (how and why we know what we know, and to what ends) can mitigate the destruction of capitalist modernity and total war on the global stage.[49]

To see a unified canon or hierarchy in aesthetic life in lieu of this fragmentation and porosity is another form of sound blindness. It relies on the fantasy of a totalizing allegory that situates writers in singular places of determination from which translation is difficult not because of the power of polysemy or the logic of textuality but because of the barrier of experience and history. Thus, for Jameson, literary production in the "third world," which writes beyond or despite the Western canon, "can be conceived as anthropologically independent or autonomous," and owing to its particularity, is best understood as a national allegory that tells the story of the nation as it is caught in a cultural struggle with the structural violence of capitalist modernity. For Jameson, literature bears witness to the structural violence of capitalism signified by modernization and especially by the split between the personal and political that renders unconscious, subjective life incommensurable to the abstractions of political order, something third world texts reject in the form of an allegory of the nation. Thus, unlike modernist literature's radical split between the poetic and political (private and public) third world literature is infused with libidinal investment and is alien to the Western reader (or translator) precisely because of this different "ratio of the political to the personal."[50]

But how would we locate such a ratio in Tarzī's writings and in the collectively authored pages of *Siraj al Akhbar*, which contain an allegory of the nation in decline but only insofar as that decline is reflected in the Islamic world and, more generally, as the barbarous world Europe constructed as the distorted reflection of itself in other places? This is what he evokes through the metaphor of a butterfly, emerging from its chrysalis and heading for ruin but also ruining the world of the other, even if in historical terms Afghanistan avoided direct colonial rule. As Wali Ahmadi asserts, "Afghanistan can indeed be read as an allegory, an allegory, however that is 'national'—because it imagines and narrates the national community/society of modernity—but is also, in a strict sense, profoundly political . . . and presents a substantial ground of distinction between the officially sanctioned delineation of the nation (as a conventional allegory) prescribed by the dominant state . . . and the imagination of the nation as a deeply political allegory as part of an overall critical/oppositional project."[51]

Mahmud Tarzī and the "Young Afghans," the group of writers and intellectuals he led, traced the outline of an Afghanistan to come but were shaped by a world of multiple and cross-cutting determinants that influenced their relationship to literary-aesthetic production.[52] This complicates the categorization of their writing as an attempt either to reclaim native authenticity or to promote the mimetic adoption of Western ideological, material, and subjective templates. Instead, the relationship of literary commitment to history and translation is entwined in the twofold experience of modernity I've tried to limn: first, the history of violence and alienation (and, following Clastres, its refusal), particularly as it manifests in the violence of industrial war and extractive capitalism; and second, the possibility of epistemic revival and of translating the idea of modernity into something new and undetermined so that the global dissemination of violence could become the ground of multiplicities and rethinking(s), including a rethinking of the place of political projects of opposition.

Thus, to the extent that one can read an allegory in the Afghan modernist project, it is not reducible to the story of the nation. It is a chronicle of the change and irresolvable tension between nationalism and internationalism as one version of a dynamic engagement with modern change that implies, as its flipside, relinquishing the idea that modernity can have a transcendental signified. Like a floating signifier it is perpetually in movement, open to translation and creative, imaginative adoption. For Tarzī and the modernists, the idea and lived experience of modernity carries this inherent dynamism; it does not culminate in a Eurocentric or Asiatic or alternative ideal; it unfolds in the absence of an all-encompassing signified; and thus, in the movement of detours and symbolic life that make collective thought and life imaginable even amid profound global upheaval.[53] That life, in turn, is never reducible to acts of substituting one modernity for another; rather, as a circuitous process, it speaks to Gayatri Spivak's insight that a critical endeavor must begin by supplementing "the category of substitution by the category of desire."[54]

For Tarzī the ascendance of post-Enlightenment rationality has the unexpected but evocative counterpart of catalyzing new sites of philosophical inquiry that are not antimodern but are *modern-questioning* inasmuch as they are the corollary of structural transformation. Modernity, in the early years of the twentieth century, could transpire in the periphery as a confrontation with the instruments of violence or as a revolution in thinking that is more like the amalgamation of dream images than a dominant symbol. What matters, when this encounter is at the heart of a political and epistemological project (that is sometimes but not always revolutionary) is not to reduce it to the discourse of an alternative modernity or to the experiential-literary divide that Jameson presents as the difference between lifeworlds. In essence, there is no analogous relation between the style of literary tradition and the form of subjugation or lifeworld it represents.

. . . .

This returns us to the issue of translation in collective life. The perpetual displacement of any single or dominant symbol to which the concept of modernity can be anchored reflects the gap between what we intend to mean (including in literary discourse) and what is understood through the "mode of intention." Modernity and translation, like translation and temporal disjunction, share the same aporia; they are part of the same "errancy" we find in language that makes it impossible to know whether we have hit the mark of our intended meaning. Perhaps this is why for Walter Benjamin there is no way of intervening in the ruins of modernity; there is only a structure of witnessing that is already linguistic because the effect of the storm of progress is the same as being in language without ever reaching our aim. And what could that aim possibly be? How can one find fulfillment in the play of signifiers, in modern upheaval, or in a structure of delay that stretches across the collective experience of knowing and being? The thing, the sign or dream image, the event, or the literature that interrupts a universal idea is not its alternative other(s) but its own internal difference. This is the difference that makes a difference when people navigate moments of collective life that are fundamentally structured by aporia and indeterminacy, where every attempt at resolution unfolds as uncertain improvisation and shapes the encounter with estrangement or intimacy. It is irreducible to the work of culture and ideological assimilation or to the perpetual deferral of its coherence, which is precisely what Benjamin understands as the problem of translation and "History."[55]

Again, the vision of the angel cannot be understood without first passing through the task of the translator.[56] The direction of this vision is part of a translation between the gaze (future oriented) and the ironic task of translation that "can only be free if it reveals the instability of the original, and if it reveals that instability as the linguistic tension between trope and meaning."[57] In other words, an imperfect or partial translation does not mean that the original was whole or that historical remembrance requires a total or clear vision.[58] Splitting, looking both ways, and fragmenting are part of the promise of translation, and they manifest as the *mise en abyme* of uncontrollable meanings that language produces but does not hold still or clarify once and for all.[59] In this sense, the vision and experience of modernity can never hide the seam that runs through it and makes it other and different in the precise moment when we suspect things might come together as one. This is as true for life on the street, in the city, and in networks of transportation or communication as it is for the linguistic imaginary of the nation-state. Marshall Berman remarked that the modernism and antimodernism of the 1960s reflected the intensity of a shared experience that was fundamentally historical in its orientation but also traced the silhouette of the future: "All these visions and revisions of modernity were active orientations toward history, attempts to connect the turbulent present and a future, to help men and women all over the contemporary world to make themselves at home in this world."[60] The discourse of modernity reflects a temporal feeling of being itinerant, a state of being in between like Georg Simmel's figure of the stranger who is not "here" but not elsewhere either; in short, this sentiment could either turn toward nostalgia for the past or push forward with the conviction that new ideas are the mirror image of what lies ahead.[61]

Translation is deeply entwined with Benjamin's understanding of the history of modernity and the deeper, structural problem of translating cultural and historical contexts as they evolve over time into a representational category of linguistic meaning. Thus, it is not merely a linguistic act of exchange but also a metaphorical reflection of modernity's transformative forces, which are themselves another metaphor for the disjunction inherent in meaning (a disjunction that is in language, symbolism, interlinguistic relations, and all our totalizing tropes). In translation, like in history, meaning is always retrospective and reveals fragments and ruins rather than a totality.[62] In a similar vein, for Tarzī, the small, fleeting difference between the era he limns as a butterfly heading for ruin and the modern future he desires for Afghanistan makes the role of translation doubly important: Translation is crucial as a linguistic act (the publishing of foreign and domestic news, poetry, and translation of various novels into Persian) but is also part of historical reflection and of transformative changes that necessitate the translation of cultural and historical contexts and also reveal endless internal differences.[63]

We have already seen the tension in language between the sign and symbol (*rakat*) and the thing being symbolized (rocket), as well as the place of translation in political life. But in a broad, polysemic sense, translation possesses a historical force (for example, the translation of a modernist drive into Persian, one of the two official languages in Afghanistan) and enables new forms of social violence and accusation when the aporia of meaning internal to language becomes a problem of interlinguistic relations and a crisis of representation that doubly exposes Afghans to military violence. As we will see in the experiences of Matin and Zia, this crisis of representation ranges across ethnographic sites but always returns us to the problem of appearances (being other than one claims) and of speech as a technology of wartime access. Thus, even though translation is predicated on the exchange of meaning as a means of avoiding direct combat, the subjects of military campaigns experience it as a profound harbinger of tragedy and death. Translation suggests that the work of culture is largely about the possibility of living with the aporia of both language and a war machine that refuses to distinguish between civilian and insurgent populations, turning the former into the medium for accessing the latter.[64]

CHAPTER FOUR

Discourses of Another Other

What can I do when my own face and voice betray me?
—ZIA (translator from Kabul)

And this active participation of every utterance in living
heteroglossia determines the linguistic profile and style
of the utterance.
—M. M. BAKHTIN, "Discourse in the Novel"

When I first met Zia, a twenty-five-year-old translator from Kabul who was embedded with foreign military units, he expressed a fear of the hinterland and its residents, who could "just like that," he snapped his fingers, come to Kabul and point him out as "the translator." He had a nightmare in which this happened: An impassioned, disheveled rural man seeking revenge against translators who worked with foreign forces came to town and recognized him close-up. In both his waking life and his dreams, Zia is afraid of the day when his face and voice betray him, like a premature perversion of the Quranic prophecy that on the Day of Judgment bodies testify for and against themselves. His anxiety evokes the figure of the stranger who appears faraway but is close by. It also evokes a spatial and conceptual frontier he reckons with amid the breakdown of symbolic relations when interpretation and translation are inseparable from the place of the other, from deferred meanings and a political narrative that constructs Kabul as a tenuous center facing its own volatile frontier. This nightmare of a city and subjectivity under threat disrupt the fantasy of wholeness and presence that, in waking life, becomes the basis for a series of representational practices that inscribe Zia and his speech as the opposite of his discourse, which emphasizes the other's proclivity for movement, invasion, theft, excess, and irrationality.

In this chapter I examine the idea of translation as a porous, shifting form of relation which is braided into new forms of social violence that attack people through the spoken word. Translation doubles as a drama and an encounter with difference that is not understood, such that relationality is not possible without violent sense-making that has the power to force others to make better, more acceptable and *truer* sense.[1] And yet, translation is not perceived as social violence but rather as a measure taken to prevent the eruption of violence in Kabul, a city that, according to my interlocuters, should ideally be kept pure of the people they describe as rural barbarians.

For Zia and his friend Matin, who is also from Kabul, mediating on behalf of others requires them to speak for a population they deem to be dangerous but still undefined in the cultural imaginary. In this sense, they are on an interpretive frontier and their task emerges in the encounter with scenes of life and narration they understand as a primal source of social difference. At the same time, as they push farther into their missions, translation becomes impossible, including on the front lines of war where language appears to serve as a lifeline for representative capacity but is actually determined by forces of displacement and ambiguity, and by the detours of the other's discourse that range from explosive to deceptive to insistent on the possibility of a gift.

Zia and Matin enter a realm of dependence on the social body, codes, fissures, and entrapments of language, which render them unable to articulate the real. As part of their commodified expertise, they navigate a crack between self and other, urban and rural, innocence and danger, a space where the detours of signification provide relief from the literalism that otherwise condemns people, almost to the point of death. They perform their work in a geographic and imagined scene where a modern revolution of life was desired but not achieved, as evidenced by the rural others' idle and senseless talk, mispronunciations, and colloquial expressions, all of which reveal to the translators an absence of thought. Yet, even as they make all these claims, a more ambiguous set of meanings makes it possible for them to say more than that.

DREAMS AND BAD OBJECTS

Zia's nightmare about the repressed violence of the Afghan hinterland and its population finding him in Kabul reflects his anxiety about the figure of the stranger. But it also reveals the spatial and conceptual frontier between urban versus rural and reason versus its absence, a dividing line that he seeks to identify and control through translation. He embarks on a series of representational encounters, what Michel de Certeau describes as listening to a "*speaking* body more than a *visible* one," that inscribe him and his discourse as the opposite of the play of signifiers, excess, dissimulation, and erratic movement he discerns in others.[2] His experiences of translation are caught in a crisis of representation that emerges through the stranger as an object of both fear and desire, turning language encounters into predicaments that unfold in space but also through certain voices and rhetorical lifeworlds deemed *ajeeb* (strange).[3] Moreover, the place of the other and the forms of difference he hopes can be repressed through symbolic relations and the mediation of the Afghan state reveal the force of monolingualism in the political imagination of the future. Zia and Matin are both Persian speakers but primarily encounter Pashto-speaking populations on their translation missions. Afghan Persian (Farsi, also called Dari) and Pashto are the two national languages of Afghanistan, although Persian has enjoyed the status of being the country's lingua franca and historically the preferred language of government administration, national media, and literary production.[4] For Zia, the ideal future of Afghanistan is Persian-speaking only. Thus, monolingualism is the limit of translation, which seems strange to say since translation is assumed to entail linguistic relations and the ability to cross between and understand two languages. Yet, monolingualism is precisely what we will encounter again and again as translation becomes symptomatic of the crisis of meaning and reveals the ambivalent nature of the frontier as both a space and a contemporary phenomenon embodied in certain forms of speech.

....

In Afghanistan, this symbolic crisis of meaning has changed the understanding of collective life, politics, and above all, what it means to live with the figure of the stranger. The *beganeh*—a stranger, often non-kin, and at times perceived as duplicitous, and unfamiliar—is (in some Kabuli imaginaries) elusive, itinerant and marked by an unclear dialect or uncertain origin. In this context, the work of paid translation entails two functions it cannot reconcile. On one hand, it endeavors to decode the subject who eludes full comprehension because of a partial command of language. It hinges on this subjectivity whose demystification is an insurmountable challenge. On the other, it turns the destruction of that subject into the price to be paid for access to the symbolic realm and a social body slated for preservation (that is, the world the translator imagines as literate, settled, and urban). These contradictions perpetuate each other: The belief in translation is upheld by the social body that translation also seeks to dissolve, while the loss of social order in Kabul is predicated on the belief that the other is always too close by and ready to disrupt the good urban life.

In seeking to translate a form of language imposed on him by political circumstance, Zia accepts and pushes forward an old imperial fantasy of the other as the phantasmic source of speech destined for erasure. To this extent, he views speaking Pashto as a form of difference he cannot live with in the modern world. Zia pursues a vision of language that is a space of pure control. Its purity cannot be challenged by the Janus-faced image of the other's language, an image that is sometimes spectral and sometimes in his face but always too close and intractable. It is never fully ontologized like his own. Thus, the problems of the other and of monolingualism emerge in tandem. He speaks to people to mediate the emergence of social difference, but his speech is confined to seeking its own reflection in the other's discourse and is outside the realm of political relationality. Zia's speech enacts its own distribution of reason and unreason in the spaces he bears witness to as sites of primordial distinction between the still-bearable, still-livable, and still-modern present and the unknowable future that returns from the past-of-elsewhere.

During the period when Zia was on various military missions, the situation in Kabul and the provinces was out of control. Fault lines in politics and battle fronts reshaped the social world as a phantomlike and deadly division between the living and those suddenly closer to being marked for death. Uncertainty, guilt, and revenge seeking were in the air, especially in rural towns where scores were quickly settled without the intervention of the Afghan state. Ordinary people were suspected of harboring dangerous affiliations or having access to secret sources of money or ties with insurgents. Liquid cash (mainly dollars) flooded the national and informal economies, giving the appearance of excess. In the countryside, the ingress of foreign capital combined with the destruction of traditional agriculture, large-scale bombing campaigns, and violence surrounding the black market fostered the cultivation of opium crops; of deadly exchanges in hostages for ransom, drugs, precious and semiprecious gems, timber, weapons; and of the sourcing of suicide bombers from a growing pool of unemployed young men.

In Kabul, the sense of danger was invoked as the phantom of a rural insurgency closing in on the city. People feared the destruction of their urban world and cosmopolitan outlook. As social bonds dissolved, they feared above all else the inescapable, arbitrary distrust of the other. Such fears proliferated alongside the growing complexity of city life, developmental projects, the rise of armed groups, and the emergence of surveillance and biometric technologies. The situation was different from but also an extension of the older network of political and military-urban violence sustained through intelligence-gathering campaigns and the division of the social body along ideological lines in the 1970s and 1980s, during the Afghan-Soviet War followed by the Afghan Civil War. Anxiety about the other and the stranger became the topic of social discourse and a metonym for the general experience of social disintegration and war.[5] People grappled with the nearly inescapable reality that unpredictable acts of violence could befall them, a characteristic of warfare and cities under siege that signifies the violence of war but also instills in people an unsettling feeling of being specifically targeted.[6]

In part, this is a question of geographic distance and the forms of paid crossing (translation, intelligence gathering, land and mineral prospecting, and so on) that attempt to translate subjectivities into new forms of social and economic value. The commodification of linguistic difference is part of a larger counterinsurgency effort in which Afghan translators are incorporated. It attributes exchange value and the demand for transparency (the fantasy of a coherent translation) between Persian or Pashto and English; at the same time, translation grounds the work of languages in the experience and arrival of war in unmediated places (usually, but not always, having few connections to television, radio, and Internet services).[7]

Because residents in these places are often less informed about the nature of global events and political changes in Kabul, language is more than a symbolic exchange. It is a powerful foreign code that facilitates the transmission of violence and war. The powers of a language (or what Jacques Lacan describes as *une langue*), and particularly one that demands its own translation (English) into another (Persian or Pashto) increasingly signifies that what Afghans do not know can also be a harbinger of disaster whose origins remain nebulous to those most vulnerable to the often-arbitrary violence of the war. One language, English, brings war. Moreover, translation occurs in contexts of interrogation where speaking and using the pronoun "I" opens dangerous questions of responsibility and agency—such as in the moment the Afghan man said "after two *rakats*" rather than "after I pray two *rakats*."

The condition of being (or imagining oneself to be) far away from the victims of violence (in, for example, aerial bombing campaigns) reveals a form of distance that cannot be equated to geographic boundaries. Carlo Ginzburg describes such distance not as space but as the manifestation of an "inward shift" in consciousness that is subsequently "projected into a geographical scene," becoming the mark of a nonrelation that is crucial to material and ideological violence, including its legacies of torture.[8] The alteration between near and far corresponds to the force of representational practices that are themselves the sites of violent exception and blur the distinction between civilians versus insurgents and foreigners' everyday consumption of war's spectacles versus its video and photographic remainders.[9] This alternation mirrors the perversion of linguistic difference into an index of itinerant danger and the simultaneous pursuit of linguistic translation as a means of seeking clarity and precision amid the lack of distinction between civilians and insurgents.

....

When I first met Zia, he was restless and overwrought. I perceived something had been emblazoned on his mind that he could not put into words which would convey its importance someone like me (who was in Kabul now, but as he said, "could just as easily be gone tomorrow"). When he spoke about the future, he always hinted at a telos of danger and interruption. More than anything else, he wanted a future in Kabul where he could live without the fear that his voice and face would betray him and lead to the possibility of accusation and violence. He explained that there were people like him who lived with the existential threat of being "recognized in the face or by the voice" and others who could move and live without fearing the dangerous consequences of their own physical being.

On his numerous missions in the countryside, Zia understood the existence of dialectal and linguistic differences as the anachronistic danger that would threaten Kabul should those different speakers find his city. He talked about a divided future in which both language and country would be smaller. He spoke with detail and conviction about two possible dramatic outcomes. One of two things will happen, he said. Either (1) the entire country would descend into a long civil war fractured along ethnic and ideological lines, in which men like him would be punished for their collaboration with foreign forces, or (2) a divide in prosperity would manifest and further demarcate urban centers from rural landscapes. But rather than generating conflict, this income inequality would become the accepted situation, resulting in segregated lifeworlds and thus freeing him from the others. In that case, he could return to his own face and voice.

Zia worked as a translator for the International and Security Assistance Forces (ISAF) and learned English in a private language course. When he was a child during the Afghan Civil War (1992–96), his small neighborhood next to Kabul International Airport (an area known locally as "unmapped" because it was not included in the urban development schemes of the 1950s and 1960s) came under direct assault. He described the experience as "very bad days," and recalled how his family took advantage of small breaks in the fighting to buy food or check whether their relatives and friends were alive. Some of them were dead.

> There were always rockets, bullets, and bombs in the air, hitting houses. One night an American cruise bomb flattened seven houses, that's how it was . . . things whizzing in the air. . . . You see, during the Civil War the airport was controlled by General Dostom and so his enemy, Hekmatiyar, would fire rockets at it from the Maranjan hilltop, and then during this war the Taliban would cut off the electricity at night and try to hide in our neighborhood, but the Americans figured it out and bombed them. American cruise bombs would often hit our neighborhood, and one day one of those hit our block. They are very serious and heavy bombs, very dangerous. It fell one house away from my friend's house. It flattened seven houses. We were always in the middle, literally in between the fighting.

But his experience of material violence, which he narrates as the division of tactical space between political parties and industrial weapons, is a division in which destruction is produced through the dialectic of territorialization and deterritorialization. And it quickly develops into the problem of linguistic difference:

> During the Taliban, things became worse. We had even more difficulty because we speak Persian and not Pashto. They ran everything. The whole town. And they were very authoritative about Pashto. They treated northern Afghans and Persian-speaking Afghans badly. They would harass us on the streets. They didn't like people to dress nicely; you had to dress like they did, in traditional clothing, wear your hair and beard like they did. They used to harass my father and beat him in public many times because he speaks Persian and does not dress or look like that. They would make people attend the same prayer session twice, even three times. It was madness.

Zia's entry into the domain of the other occurred through repetition, compulsion, and the loss of divine meaning. It was a repeated act of the body that gave him access to a new symbolic order, but equally important, it was an order of madness that he described as the violence of the monolingualism of the other being inflicted first on his father, and then on the nation and its Persian-speaking population.[10]

He cannot accept linguistic difference as a new cultural form, even though this very difference opens a world of symbolic capital and monetary exchange for him years later, when as a Persian speaker, he becomes a coveted translator, first for the Texas Agricultural Development Team then for ISAF/NATO forces. In that capacity he desires to mediate, find out, question, narrate, and take note of the discourse and place of the other, while the other participates only by virtue of embodying the force of unreason, which is distinct from the powers of reason he sees as his own world of understanding and that he unconsciously accepts as the function of being literate in Persian. This is his poisoned gift.

In one of our early conversations, he described the opportunity to become a translator in distinctly class-related terms. He worked in a military camp inside the Kabul International Airport with people he describes as "middle to upper class and educated." There was social envy around him and in his neighborhood, particularly from those who could not get such jobs because, he said, they came from "the poorer and undereducated families in the city."

After he quit that job, he went to work for a company that I will call "The Company" (TC) and studied English in a private school. Zia explained that TC received a commission for every translator it trained and dispatched to a combat unit (or transferred between units), irrespective of whether the translator knew the dialects spoken in the province where they were sent or subsequently transferred to. He said, "For them, it's about making money from each transfer of translators. So, we often end up in places where people don't speak a common language." He continued, "It was a very popular thing. Everyone knew that Camp Tampa was the place to learn English and become a translator." In class his teachers first spoke in Persian, then in Pashto, which was emphasized because the main battlegrounds were in Pashto-speaking provinces. At the end of his course Zia took a multiple-choice exam of one hundred questions, with four possible answers each. He passed.

The alien experience of feeling afraid and somewhat foreign during the first reign of the Taliban (1996–2001) because he spoke only Persian returned in the form of a transformed power that many translators likened to a gift. The strangeness he once carried was no longer present in his life in Kabul, as the distance between signs and meanings, or in the general impossibility of possessing his "own" language. He had prevailed on all fronts. Instead, those problems were projected onto a remote site that he fantasized as purely spatial (he marked this with the words *there, beyond,* and *far off*) and as the realm of the other. From the outset he categorically placed the other as from "there," (*anja*) and reinforced that the practice of translation meant perpetually speaking from "there," a place devoid of reason or truth. (He emphasized this by saying things like "they are primitive," "totally different," "don't know how to speak," and "you wouldn't believe it.")

For Zia, to speak from the place of Kabul is to possess a voice that is full of reason, life, and worldliness. It is not merely a voice but a cosmopolitan essence that is the gift of language and literacy and the capacity to transcend the fantastical realm of orality he describes as a wondrous condition of backwardness elsewhere. The more he speaks in his own dialect the more he seems to believe what he says is true. Related to this is the image of something that initially seems to be an object of fear, the image of the stranger-invader from the flatlands, but turns out to be a source of desire (for knowledge and commensuration) and, behind that, a fantasy of unity (between word and meaning and between languages) that makes the place of translation so complex and dangerous.

The corollary of this "totally different" and "primitive" image was evoked to me by other translators in different ways. But it was always conveyed through the vision of an ingress from somewhere else and as the related problem of free movement in the country. This is Zia's recurring nightmare, which takes the oneiric form of odd masks, confrontations, or camouflaged individuals who find him when he least expects it. He dreams of surprise and dissimulation, and when he is awake, the problem is still with him because he says you can never trust people or distinguish between their outer and inner state (their *zahir* or *batin*) and thus between being, saying, and doing. This is also his task as a translator.

But representations slip through his grasp. On his missions he seeks a mediating ground on which intervention can occur, but he encounters gaps that make it difficult for him to know what he is seeking or whether he can convey what he understands to others. He confronts the point at which he discovers something is missing from representation and that "the absence of a signified . . . is an unoccupiable point."[11] When we spoke, I sometimes sensed he wanted to say more or share something new, but he would back away from its edge. Instead, he would lean on ambiguous words or trail off or repeat the refrain that I was probably not interested in hearing what he had to say. Or he would say "I don't really know." This backing away was also how he lived in Kabul, away from others and afraid he would be recognized by the enemy, in a manner that is closer to the unformed and unsaid and "contrary to the idealist position that makes form the cause of being" but instead "locates the cause of being in the informe: the unformed (that which has no signified, no significant shape in the visual field."[12] Ideally, I think he would disappear if he could.

For Zia and Matin (whose experience I will turn to in chapter 5), the time between translation and freedom was full of aporetic detours that neither of them could predict let alone control; it had its own ghosts whose voices transformed translation into something very different from the epistemological supplement they both fantasized it could be. In a sense Zia had already realized this. The truth of translation and of a situation being as it is represented by language was spelled out in his dream but eluded him (sometimes dangerously) in waking life. Translation uncovered the split within the other that he did not discern in himself. And to the extent that he recognized no alienating identification within him, no hinterland inside, his speech became a site of purity and presence, undivided by the other's discourse, a foreign discourse in which the repressed always returns.

The dilemma of the other began where the truth of his own being ended. And this idea of the return that occurred only in the speech of the other made it necessary for Zia to repeatedly characterize the others and the places he encountered in opposition to Kabul and his own being. In other words, the object of his translation had to be established as that which could not be known or speak of itself but also as what he could not accept. In separating himself from his task, from everything that he characterized as part of this anachronism, he narrated a monolithic unreason as the recurring problem of social difference and as the interpretive aim of his own language of reason.

This is not a step toward the collective life Immanuel Kant describes as free from the "dread of shadows" and that Michel Foucault later parses as an epistemic-historic frontier by way of an "exit" or "way out" and a new ontology of the self that is a "mode of relating to contemporary reality; a voluntary choice made by certain people, in the end, a way of thinking and feeling; a way, too, of acting and behaving that both marks a relation of belonging and presents itself as a task."[13] It is not about thinking and being with others on a frontier of not knowing. Instead, it is what happens when that space is reduced to the difference between the familiar and the strange, which Matin once likened to the difference between "the ground and sky." It is the specter that is too close, expressed in the idiom of the other and also in the language of national decay, a rot between self and other linked to the necessity of repressing rather than critically reflecting on a national past. Zia characterizes it as something fantastic he still cannot fathom: "You would not believe it." "I could not believe my own eyes." "I had never seen anything like it." "I was in a world of strangeness."

ITINERANT STRANGERS

The notion of the prior is a recurring theme in Matin's and Zia's narratives. It is part of another theoretical problem: the connection to a haunting absence found in the extended space occupied by the other, an absence that finds them despite their attempt to live freely in Kabul. Where can they go from here? What can they hear or relay? Alternatively, how much do those they purport to represent pay to gain access to their mediation? I think if Zia could pose a single judgment or represent his experiences in one theme, it would be the odd-sounding problem of what to do about people who take their dialects with them wherever they go and the related issue of going where you feel you can speak freely. He posed this to me as an unanswerable question that first occurred to him in the province of Ghazni in the southeast, where he encountered a dialect he did not understand and, even more unsettling, where he witnessed the unpredictable pattern of internal migration he fears as the future of strangers forced not to coexist but to exist at the same time in Kabul, a city he would rather keep to himself.

The relationship between language and movement emerges from whether and how it is possible to speak in a certain way. This relationship became part of his missions and waking life but also his dream world and his fear that the people he sought out would come to find him. Zia distinguishes himself from his object of understanding but not from the political context in which he found it. He emphasizes how different places like Ghazni are from Kabul but only insofar as that difference can be narrated and given a fictive rather than contextual or political form. When he speaks of his very first mission in Ghazni, he describes it as a place that is both strange and perfectly suited to being narrated. In other words, it is a place he could affirm and construct as a place unto itself in speech and storytelling: "We were mostly along Highway 1 and on the base but the area surrounding us was very primitive and isolated. It was the kind of place you hear about in stories; it was unlike anything I've seen. Just like in the stories."

He articulates a place that constitutes a bizarre, fantastical scene. And the effect of this difference is intensified precisely when he shifts from speaking about it as an out-of-this-world experience to one he had to parse and relay to others in different languages that wore him down. Speaking to me in Persian, Zia seemed relieved of the weight of a foreign language and happy to speak without resorting to English. "I cannot tell you how hard it is to try to explain why they are this way to others and to translate it all in a different language."

On missions in various villages in the countryside, Zia had to translate between English, Persian, Pashto, and Polish, exchanging borrowed words between them for a wage that peaked at $715 per month and paying farmers in cash for the crops destroyed by the tanks in his arriving convoy. Once again, he describes translation as one of the opportunities offered by the war for literate, settled people such as himself: "These other people who have recently poured into Kabul and cannot read or write will never get a job translating; that's why they call us apostates and traitors, it's just because they can't get work. That's the problem with illiteracy and nomadism; it makes brutes of men."

Zia confronts the absence of reason, but more importantly, also the inability to distinguish between good fortune and apostasy. He sees this inability, and not his own convoy's arrival, as the origin of dangerous confusions that, in turn, necessitate the continued moral intervention of translation and transform the translator's role into determining what can be known and making judgments based on reason and the ability to distinguish between danger and ordinary civilian activity. Yet, in actual moments of encounter, the distinction between civilians and combatants cannot be made. This occurred when Zia was first dispatched to accompany a team of Polish soldiers at Forward Operating Base Aftab (FOB Aftab), in a largely Pashto-speaking area. Zia, who doesn't speak Pashto fluently, made do by learning "through work experience." "I learned Pashto through work experience and English from the course. It's enough to interpret daily and ordinary things. But I was sent to Ghazni with a Polish team, and it was very problematic because they also didn't speak English well, so I had to learn Polish a bit as well."

The problem of linguistic difference and the necessity of learning Polish in order to mediate the tense environment became part of an unexpected transformation of difference into the specter of the mob and deadly violence. The dangerous return of the other was all but guaranteed, something Zia had already intuited and evoked in his descriptions of the provinces but that became more blatant to him on the scene. Once he clearly understood this, there was no way Zia could intervene in the situation.

Zia said his fellow Afghan translators, who were mostly from Kabul, hated the Polish soldiers because they reminded them of Russian soldiers from the era of the Afghan-Soviet War. The Polish soldiers did not want the Afghan translators eating in the same cafeteria or using the same gym as they did. The situation became much worse after a group of injured Afghans arrived at the camp to seek medical care:

> The hardest thing was when they would bring injured people to the door of the camp. One night I was standing guard at the gate, and it was 10:30 at night and the Afghan guards who worked for a private security company and escorted convoys of arms or military supplies had a scuffle in their rooms off base. There was a rocket RPG in the room and somehow, by accident, it went off and several people lost legs and arms. They called us and brought them. It was an awful sight. A horrifying scene. Missing limbs and arms. They had fought over a lost bet; it was after a night of gambling. And somehow the RPG was set off in the midst of it.

Zia does not question that the rocket-propelled grenade went off accidentally. His perception mirrors that of others who fear the continued ability of explosive devices to seize bodies and lives in moments of contact that bear the logic of chance, as in this case when a scuffle accidentally set one off, or when someone inadvertently walks on mined ground.[14] However, what is overdetermined is not that the RPG went off but that the loss of bodily power was transposed as the gruesome perception of enhanced momentum. Zia finds himself captivated not solely by the trauma of the incident but also by the peculiar transmutation in perception that was part of his linguistic imagination.

> But they were refused treatment! This was often the case with civilians, who would be turned away, but the guards? *These* guys were working for *us*. The translator (an Afghan American) who worked for the American Special Forces is the one that brought them inside the base, brought them all the way to the front gate, only to be turned away. The Polandiha were the ones who refused to let them in. One of the young men died that night on the base and we had to send his body back to Kabul. I'll never forget that. But I've seen a lot of that. Drivers, guards, ordinary Afghans come to the base for help. They are in the middle of life and death, and they are turned away. That night, the Polish soldiers refused that group because *several people*

showed up at once and there was commotion, obviously they were in extreme pain, *so the soldiers became afraid of the noise and crowd. They were afraid it would turn into a mob-style attack once they were all inside, even though they were so hurt, missing limbs and arms!*[15]

The vision of a mob converging on the base emerges precisely when the loss of that possibility disperses in bodies before everyone's eyes. But this inversion was already repeated in the domain of speech and writing. It is a form of lack that appears first as excess and then as something to be absorbed or defeated. It mirrors in corporeal form the logic of Zia's own perception of illiterate Afghans who, because they cannot write, do not have access to the kinds of thinking and opportunity that Kabul's booming war economy offers (which attracts people to the city in search of employment). Despite this, they "pour" in from rural hinterlands and mountainous villages and converge on the city without purpose. But recognition of the sacrifices the guards have already made to protect the military base is precisely what does not occur and does not allow this coveted inclusion to fully materialize on the night of the accident. Zia accepts these risks because he deems them a fundamental part of a structure of sacrifice through which he is granted recognition and relief from the *otherwise indiscriminate* forms of violence that occur in war, including in his own neighborhood. In fact, he specifically cites the commencement of the American War in Afghanistan as putting an end to the Taliban regime's generalized forms of death dealing. Zia's entry in the war as a translator is also his protection from random death.

How do a lie and its truth come together in this moment? The Polish soldiers (the gatekeepers to medical care) could not recognize the loss of physical capacity in front of them. Instead, in a collective delusion, they see the Afghans as individuals who refuse to inhabit their bodies and who could at any instant turn into an undifferentiated mob. This is a vision of persons contained neither by rational thought nor the body and, thus, of a momentum that cannot be inscribed into the law or its structures. To let them in once is to consent to being violated repeatedly, and the perceived threat of the mob emerges exactly when it is physically and psychically impossible and when the momentum it requires is displaced by severance.[16]

This situation also entails the betrayal of the translator. Zia's initial interpretation of the limit (to inclusion and medical care) was based on literacy. His literacy was what enabled him to seek employment with foreign militaries, to be at FOB Aftab, to mediate between the local population and military forces, and *then* to access the forms of recognition that resulted in medical care, enhanced safety, access to military gear, cafeteria food, and the like. His trauma consists in recognizing the radical uncertainty of that pharmakonic inclusion. And that recognition reveals another limit beyond the question of literacy or dialect. It is a new limit opened and intensified by the inability to contain the perception of mob violence through the power of translation and, thus, a limit to his belonging to a city or country free from dangerous movement. The mob he encounters at the base will in turn find him in Kabul. And then what?

Zia was not able to intervene or make a difference in getting treatment for the guards. It was a redoubled failure in the same recurring place where translation could not contain the power of orality or the return of the other in a much more literal form that Zia at that moment also embodied, not as a coveted translator but as just another Afghan man on the scene. When we spoke about this, he was still visibly angry because the guards were refused entry "even though they were so hurt, missing limbs and arms." He emphasized that they should have been permitted inside because "these guys" were working for "us." I think two obstacles stood in his way and contributed to why the camp was not a free space. The first is the idea that translation could help clarify an incomprehensible frontier and people, and that doing so would establish (for the translator) a form of recognition and belonging irrespective of local violence and the Afghan state's dissolution in the provinces. In that moment at the front entrance of the camp, when he could do nothing to help the injured Afghans or influence the outcome, Zia understood his notion of inclusion was a lie. The second obstacle is more subtle and is tied to a collective fantasy that a supplement (a logic that incorporates the figure of the translator, the outsider, the disease, the remedy) can contain the chaos of structural violence even as its own ambiguous function (in this case, the translator as a pharmakon) reflects the violence of inclusion. Zia is disappointed in the failure of these bonds but also in his inability to translate and transform the violence of an encounter with radical alterity into a matter of clear distinctions and stable categories that might make those bonds of inclusion legible for him yet again.[17]

HIGHWAY 1

To some extent this was already spelled out in his nightmare of being recognized and in waking life when he fears the vision of a mob closing in on Kabul, a mob that reveals its power and proclivity for movement, first in the domain of speech, then in urban space. It also revealed itself on the road. In 2012 Zia was embedded in a Polish brigade as a translator during a major combat offensive along Highway 1 in Ghazni, a crucial supply line for weapons and personnel and the main link connecting Kabul to the strategic provinces of Helmand and Kandahar in the southeast. Aside from its importance as a logistical and military route, it gave both the Afghan Army and the Taliban access to local villages along the way.[18] Rocket and mortar attacks and roadside bombings were common occurrences on the road and in the villages, where an even deadlier game of middle-of-the night ambushes and retaliatory attacks between Taliban fighters and Afghan and NATO soldiers marked the terror of local life caught between military and nonmilitary units. The price of talking to the Taliban could be interrogation and torture, while the price for talking to Afghan National Army or foreign soldiers could be decapitation.[19] The road became a source of ill-defined fear. But in Zia's narrative, it was linked more to the problem of signification than the violence of battle or movement. In a sense, the road was a "non-center" that failed to connect strategic places but remained inseparable from the problem of monolingualism and dialect he encountered outside the city.

When I hear the name "Highway 1," I think of a very different place. I immediately think of California's six-hundred-mile coastal highway, stretching from the Golden Gate Bridge in San Francisco to Los Angeles, with stunning stretches of road nestled between the ocean and the mountains. It is an intermediary in the middle of the natural world, a concrete passage that both divides and gives in to the chaotic play of its surroundings. There is the forward-going promise of the road but there is also flooding, coastline erosion, fires, and heavy landslides that prevent it from being only what its builders hoped to achieve.

I invoke this image because Zia mentioned Afghanistan's Highway 1 with ambivalence. It was a road he had been on many times and survived; he was proud of its construction because it would function as a crucial artery in the future, but he feared it because of the problem of excess: The road could not contain what lay on either side of it, given that anyone could use it go to Kabul and be in a new place.[20] The highway, like the idea of an Afghan national railway before it, became crucial to fear of the frontier and the invasion of cities by foreigners, or in Zia's case, the specific dread of domestic barbarians he referred to as brutes "who move around and take their language with them wherever they go."

During the early days of the American War, Zia fantasized literacy as a means of access to a moral and practical order beyond contingency. He reinforced this order by claiming to have survived the indiscriminate aerial bombing of his neighborhood so that he could become a translator and help rebuild his nation. Now he describes himself as stuck "in the middle."[21]

> We had a lot difficulty in Ghazni, the locals despised us, both *because we spoke Persian* and because we were interpreting for the Americans. We were stuck. They cursed us, they hated us, and the Pashtuns threatened us. They think that the interpreters are the reason why the troops find and come to their villages. They say things like, "These people would never have found their way, but you showed them, you brought them, you interpreted for them." They think we are responsible for the war arriving to their village, *they think we caused the war*. We would tell them that "without us you are in even greater danger, misunderstanding would become violent all the time if we weren't there to mediate." There is a lot of propaganda. They think we are apostates because the water in Kabul has been poisoned. They will believe anything they hear.

Zia is caught not only between languages but between political forces and violence that cannot be contained through the exchange of words and money but that nonetheless require the speech of the other, unmediated by reading or writing, as a condition of radical uncertainty.[22] The danger and the hidden threat of the Afghan mob are again transformed into a problem of oral credulity and thus a discourse on the inability to distinguish between representation and reality. Yet again, he returns to the problem of orality and particularly the mode of abbreviation he designates as the complete absence of reason and sense:

> The hardest part of this job is we get stuck. We make do this way or that way; we play with words until we finally make the other side understand the basic point. It's very hard . . . but do you know what the strangest thing is? It's the local dialects! The villages have very different dialects, especially the rural, nomadic populations. For example, they use several words for the same thing. They call nomads *bondee* or *aylaq*. It means "nomadic husbandry," and they move to the mountains with their livestock. The rural and agricultural accent is very difficult. So is Pashto; it depends on where you are, Kandahar is different from Khost or from Logar. The accents are very difficult, and it changes depending on where you are, they take it with them. Do you know how they say, "We're leaving tomorrow morning" in Wardak? They say "gahista zu." Fine, but they don't actually say it that way; they don't say it fully, they just say "gista zu." How are we supposed to know

that means "ga-his-ta zu"? That's the main problem we have. It's hardly our fault when things go awry. These people don't know how to speak.

For Zia spoken language was always both the problem and the boon of war. The essential distinction that structured the violence of encounters ranging from aerial bombing to reconnaissance missions and roadside violence was that of orality and literacy and the inevitable confusion caused by those who, as he very directly put it, "don't know how to speak." The problem began with illiteracy and the inability of others (mainly Pashtuns) to acquire translational expertise and carve out a space for themselves in the country's booming war economy, which led to his fantasy of a monolingual horizon under threat from people on the move. In reality, Pashto-speaking individuals were also hired as translators. However, the fact that Zia believed speaking Persian was one of the reasons he was hired as a translator invested his language with a psychological reality that shaped how he (and Matin) confronted non-Persian speakers on his missions.

According to Zia, the others who "pour into" Kabul but "don't know how to live in cities," roam dangerously, and neither read nor write are the ones who make themselves the victims of violence. On the road, however, the distribution of violence took a more elusive form independent of a speaker's native language. In 2010 Zia sustained a near-fatal injury when a land mine went off in the Andar District of Ghazni. The explosion occurred when his convoy activated a roadside mine while attempting to retreat shortly after what he described as an altercation with the locals. Zia said he would never forget the sound and feeling. He carved the date of the attack into his wooden bedpost: May 9, 2010. The medic seated next to Zia almost lost his arm, and Zia sustained a head injury. The land mine was powerful enough that the Mine Resistant Ambush Protected vehicle he was riding in flew into the air and fell into the huge crater in the ground. He said one of its tires was never found.

....

Like poisoned water, language carries a current of signification in what we hear and believe and how we speak. The differences in sounds and words— as in the case of the elided vowel in "gahista zu," pronounced casually as "gista zu"—are not indicative of familiarity or colloquialism but are much more elusive signs that resist localization: "Pashto depends on where you are. The Pashto of Kandahar is not the same as Logar, or Ghazni or Wardak and it is even more difficult because these people are nomadic, always moving with their animals and dialects." These "nomads" are the purvey-ors of dialects they take with them. In essence, they move and speak while believing anything they hear.

Against this trope he positions a non-nomadic discourse that speaks from its rightful place and that he fantasizes as having been the mode of speech that was dominant across the country before the war. But the nomad is still there. The movement Zia fears will occur in space, in his city, and in his dreams, is one of collapse between two symbolic orders he wishes to distinguish. This dichotomy results in misunderstanding across the land-scape that he also fantasizes is his object of knowledge. In this place, deter-ritorialization doesn't manifest through physical or rhizomatic movements but through incomplete meanings. Goin' tomorrow. Maybe. Deferring to another day. Not doing anything at all. This uncertainty, which Zia strug-gles to understand, is the limit of translation as an endeavor that entails both fantasy (about the place of the other, the city, dialect, inclusion) and political force but cannot account for the deferral of signification. This is what encroaches on Zia from a distance. But what is the nature of the dis-placement he would like to define and control? For Zia it is embodied in the other but also in the phantasmatic forms of presence and absence that he cannot predict or situate through narration and that refuse to become translatable objects of knowledge. This is staged in dialogue and encounter with locals in the hinterland but also, more powerfully, in the frontier that he understands to separate reason from its absence, logos from its referen-tial ground and the floating, unpredictable, signifying practices he finds to be the "strangest thing" in war.

To return to Benjamin and the metaphor of the broken, fragmented vessel—the pieces that articulate with each other but do not match up, the fragments that "follow" rather than closely resemble one another—we can situate Zia's anxiety in relation to the power of movement not only in space or between Kabul and its hinterland but as the power of any metonymic sequence that defies binding, resemblance, and inertia.[23] The vessel's frag-ments cannot be part of the constitution of a totality or original; instead, the fantasy of a whole is deferred and meaning is always displaced and fractional, even if we experience it as successive.[24] Paul de Man describes this phenomenon as "movement of the original" in the metonymic series that carries it along but never to a place of return or "home"; it is a state of exile that inhabits all languages "especially the language one calls one's own."[25] Is this movement of the original what is actually strange for Zia, even though he expresses it as the strangeness of an encounter with social difference?

The illusion of monolingualism and the idea that our mother tongue is ours even though we never quite feel at home in it exists precisely in the fragmentation we find in language. And, as we will see, the aim of translation is adapted by the specter of violence, becoming a tool the translator takes into battle, where he foregrounds the fantasy of commensuration that the practice of translation can be a symptom of but also defies.

MONOLINGUALISM: AT HOME OR IN EXILE?

Insofar as Zia hears it, the others' speech is accompanied by a betrayal of reality that he seeks to mediate. This reality is difficult for him to fathom and surveil because it is scattered in discourse and has a proclivity to shift. It imbues the entire terrain with the possibility of mishearing and imperfect translation. It prevents him from positioning himself between words and the meanings that he envisions as the structure of difference between languages. In one conversation, he asked what the process of applying for a US visa was like. He mentioned he had difficulty understanding all the language because he could not read the documents in English. Moreover, like every Afghan translator, he had a "file" in which he said the details of their missions and mistakes were noted: "If we make *even a single* mistake, it will impact us negatively," he said. This is both a problem of the contingent sovereignty of the Afghan state and a threat to his future:

> They would do a biometric scan when we worked for TC, so we are in the system [referring to the US military's Horizontally Integrated Data Environment (HIDE) system, a biometric and personal database]. We worked for a mine clearance unit once, and we also did HIDE with people in the rural districts; they would try to HIDE everyone, they wanted to record everything. We did HIDE on someone in Ghazni who was already in the system but had been registered in Paktika and I asked him why he moved. He explained that he was a student in Paktika. It's good. I like HIDE. It's secure, and you know who and where people are, why they move, where they go. The danger is if it falls into the government's hands. That is our fear. In this political context, you cannot trust your neighbor and our government is deeply divided. So, what happens if the Taliban obtains this information? I wouldn't be able to walk around in Kabul anymore. They'd know everything about me. I'd be in serious danger. I can always escape if I feel threatened, but what about my family? What if the Taliban exact revenge

and kill my father or brother? They have no mercy. They like to make an example of everyone. So, my demand of NATO and ISAF is exactly this, that if things deteriorate in Kabul, they are responsible for getting us out.

For Zia, Kabul is the only place in the country where he can walk around freely. But sovereignty in the city converges on both mobility and archived information in a reversal through which he imagines the Taliban assuming power and parsing the biometric files. Now they can read everything. By turning a biometric technology into a verb, he reinvents it as an act of securing the whereabouts and intentions of others. Zia assumes some of HIDE's technological power as his own to mitigate his anxiety about being recognized or worse, punished, in his own city for collaborating with foreign forces:

> Our lives are in danger. Right now, I am not afraid in Kabul, but I'd never leave for the countryside. I tried to cover my face and wear glasses most of the time, and wear a helmet so I was unrecognizable, but in some meetings, you cannot sit like that, you have to show your face. This was a tactic we translators came up with. And I have a lot of difficulty at the gate of the base, everyone would show up, spies, Taliban, insurgents, *injured and sick people, . . . and people would see my face once they came in, I even changed my name.* Some of us would choose Polish names. Marion was a popular name. I am afraid of the future; it's dangerous for my family and me, even though I have not been threatened so far. But the problem is their illiteracy. That is why they don't understand why people are here, why they do what they do, and that is why they are so brutish with everyone, never kind, never sympathetic.

For the translator, revenge seeking determines the city's future. This is the danger Zia wants to ward off through translation. He fears the millions of people who will move to Kabul but do not know "how to live in a city" or understand the market forces of the economy. He feels the need to change his name because as a signifier it is unsafe, especially if it falls into the hands of dangerous people.

> There will be massive unemployment when the camps close, businessmen are not investing money, and the government makes no effort to jump-start industry. The factories are stagnant so they cannot absorb all the unemployed. Not everyone can become a taxi driver. Who will ride in the cars? People who've come here from the countryside cannot go back. People will hate them and suspect them of having worked with the Americans, which is what Kabul means for those people, so they must stay here out of safety, but what will they do?

The need to hide in the city for fear of revenge adds to the pressures of economic collapse. It redoubles the problem of linguistic difference and transposes the question of orality (as object, mission, goal, problem, and barbarism) onto the divide between Kabul and its rural surroundings. That divide is now filled with the possibility of revenge seeking and crisis. He reflects on the signs already emerging, saying that in Kabul the old factories are stagnant and the camps are closed. As material and economic conditions worsen, the dichotomies he found on missions are transferred onto larger regional-political disputes:

> It will become crazy, and people will leave. I think they will leave for Iran and Pakistan again, another round of international refugees. They already are trying to be smuggled into Iran. A young friend of mine tried to go to Iran, and the Iranian border police shot at their car and twenty-two people died, including him. Everyone assaults us. Iran. Tajikistan. They redirect our water supply. They prevent us from creating dams. They shoot at us. The Iranian government paid the Quetta Shura to disrupt work at the dam and demolish it [because] they need the water, and on another project Indian engineers were killed because they were working on establishing electrical grids. Pakistan wants Afghanistan to cut all ties with India before it considers participating in the peace process. Who can stay here?

The gift of literacy and English that enabled him to become a translator has now been poisoned. He finds himself further and further in its dangerous territory as the force of orality follows him from his missions in the countryside to life in Kabul, making him consider escaping the country, a possibility that is stymied by complex regional and international political dynamics, including battles for natural resources and regional dominance. The danger of deferral he understands as the nonsense of enemy speech becomes the problem of his own future. Unable to pin his hopes on escape, his thoughts return to Kabul, where people are more enlightened than before. Zia can foresee mastering English on the horizon. It is not the violence of monolingualism imposed by war and the market but part of a feeling of cosmopolitanism. It is a new change that elicits in him an almost messianic hope for the future, not as the coming of the other but as relief from linguistic disparity and provincialism.[26]

> Naturally, other countries have experienced and surpassed these challenges and stages, and we will too with time. People are learning English. They have access to the Internet; they know what the rest of the world looks like

and have changed a lot. They have access to media. Media has had a wonderful impact on people's lives. We never had media before; we only had one channel before the Taliban. But people in Kabul are not who they were ten years ago. They are enlightened. People dress differently. They are interested in the world, especially in Turkey. School uniforms have changed. These are all signs that the future will be different. With every shift in a regime, the upper class becomes impoverished and vice versa. It's what time does. It enriches you and then takes it all away. It's a matter of luck. It's the wheel of fate.

Learning to speak English is the difference that makes a difference. English ability and access to the world, in the form of images and information, mark the beginning of an enlightenment and politics as the play of signs, the possibility of enrichment, loss, luck, and fate, rather than the transcendental signified of theological rule. But what does it mean to think we speak or master a language? Or to think others do not fully possess their own? For Jacques Derrida, the way we possess our language is akin to having a dwelling we cannot inhabit. In his account of living with the French language as a French Algerian, he makes the provocative remark that insofar as we think we possess our own language, we imagine it as our all-encompassing home, but we still find ourselves lacking. We have one language that is not ours: "It will never be mine, this language, the only one I am thus destined to speak, as long as speech is possible for me in life and in death; you see, never will this language be mine. And, truth to tell, it never was."[27] The aporia at work here is not reducible to historical or genealogical claims to ancestral or appropriated purity. It is not a claim about fluency or even the trace of an accent or dialect, which Derrida admits, despite all his decentering of phonocentrism, is the mark of foreignness that distinguishes his own speech from the French rendering of the French language he desires but cannot achieve because he is an Algerian Jew.[28]

I think this difference internal to language is precisely what haunts Zia as a fundamentally modern problem that bears on his life in the city. He does not express it in those terms, but he does describe it as something that is coming and cannot be assimilated through exchange. Zia would rather avert his gaze. And yet, like others he holds on to his own speech, his own language, even as the other neither replies nor backs away. He holds on to it in the hope that he is the master and the other a partial reflection of what he seeks to understand; a fleeting specter from another place not here to stay.

CHAPTER FIVE

Between Ground and Sky

Instead of saying that a society is never completely symbolic, it would be more accurate to say that it can never
manage to give all its members, to the same degree, the
means whereby they could give their services fully to the
building of a symbolic structure.
—CLAUDE LÉVI-STRAUSS, *Introduction to the Work of*
Marcel Mauss

Translation and movement, dissimulation and near catastrophe: The
"knowledge" and speech of the translator place him in the middle of battle
and of mimesis, in the jungle, and at the edge of life and death where death
is averted through a gift that Matin, who in that moment is interpellated
as "Mr. Translator," cannot fully see. If for Zia the elsewhere of translation
is about the movement of populations and the metaphor of the stranger as
symptomatic of the crisis of rural life and rhetorical mediation, for Matin
translation pushes him to another incessant elsewhere in language: the
promise of exchange, not between spoken meanings but of self for other,
violence for speech, and the gift in lieu of death. The more Matin seeks
to make a difference, the more he contends with the arbitrary logic of inside versus outside and the forms of deception he seeks to disrupt even as
he fears he will be accused of harboring deception just like the enemy he
surveils. The further Matin takes his task, the more circuitous the detours
become and the more willing he is to assume the attributes of the enemy in
battle, from how and where to hide like an insurgent to striking deals and
unearthing bombs, all in the name of a translation he can no longer grasp.

Through his metamorphosis, we see both the fragmented meanings
inherent in translation and the improvisation it makes possible between
individuals and events that occur not only in experience but through language. In this fragmentation, split by both language and the desire to im-
prove at his task, Matin confronts a form of alterity that is not a singular

fiction but one he must learn to read as two. For him the duality of the other is part of the intensifying difficulty of translation, and it is made more difficult because it evolves into an uncontrollable scene of mimesis in which shifting signs, faces, voices, words, places, and actions mean no condition of knowledge can prevail. This is where he ends up going, and he characterizes the difference he observes between the world of his missions and his own world in Kabul as a gap like the one between "the ground and sky."

For Zia and Matin, the desire to locate and settle this "elsewhere" of language, a place they hear in the dialect of the other and pursue in representational practice and counterinsurgency, represents the impossible challenge of translation. What does this erratic place, both a mark of linguistic difference and a central component of how they conceive of social difference, reveal about the experience of survival in a world defined by translation's misfire? What does it disclose about monolingualism and the fantasy that in one's own language—the "dwelling" Jacques Derrida warned is never truly ours but instead *inhabits and speaks through us*—this unstable outside can be controlled through mediation? Finally, what does it expose about the logic of a pursuit? It is a chase and series of complicated detours in increasingly unknown, forbidden territories, in places where the other hides and where this desire for elsewhere always seems to lead.

As we have seen, translation as linguistic expertise is caught in a crisis of representation in which the outsider is both an object of fear and a source of uncertain but instrumental value. The more the figure of the translator seeks to understand, parse, and narrate the lifeworld of the other, the more the violence of monolingualism becomes symptomatic of a crisis of meaning. This violence shapes Zia's encounters with others and their speech, or more precisely, it transforms the social body he identifies by way of diagnosing its speech. In this chapter, the same paradoxical logic emerges in Matin's experience through a temporal structure of delay in which past violence recurs in the future. Its structure extends from harbingers of violence in speech to the violence of play, in which the first laugh (or "play") begins with words and the last ends in deadly conflagration (as an instance of who gets both the first word and last word), and a particularly striking instance of the misrecognition of a bomb as a gift and a gift as a bomb.

But how else might we account for the aporia of exchange in collective life? What does translation entail when it assumes the logic of a chase to find and assess an object of knowledge that reveals the absence of reason in others? Through Matin's experiences, I follow this chase and the gaps and deferrals that sustain the pursuit of the other who is perceived to lack reason, in both discourse and rural dialect, amid new counterinsurgencies. This reveals moments of closing and opening when signs, words, and translational desire are met with a plurality of meanings that are uncertain, ambivalent, playful, or deceptive, transforming the status of translation from a vehicle of narration and truth-finding to a result of the general failure of the work of culture in times of violent upheaval. And yet, as we will see, there is an excess that cannot be understood as the defeat of exchange; this is the opening and crack that emerges when aporetic gaps are creatively tolerated—for example, when Matin encounters a gift he cannot recognize but nonetheless must accept and repay.

HEARTS OPENING

I first met Matin, a close friend of Zia's, in 2012 when he had just quit his job as a translator for the United States and the ISAF. He lived with his parents in the same poor neighborhood as Zia, next to Kabul International Airport. Zia put me in touch with Matin, and we met in a café in central Kabul. For Matin, the work of translation was part of an enlarged and rousing domain of encounter: "The best thing about these last ten years is that we finally have television! I can see what the rest of the world looks like: Turkey, India, Europe, America all of it. And it looks a lot better than here, and I want what I see, the things people have, and of course I couldn't afford any of it unless I learned English and became a translator. And I did. The same is true for many of my friends." Matin cited Zia as someone he trusted and stated that, therefore, he could trust me too. He initially seemed nervous, like he might betray himself, and would emphatically insert into his stories, "I say all of this only because I trust you like a sister." He recalls the bombing of his neighborhood in 2001 by US forces and using a small propane lantern to help locate the bodies of his dead neighbors.

Images of violence and brutality, whether military, insurgent, or criminal, largely dominated the daily news cycle and a new sense of the scale and proportion of violence took hold of people's thoughts. Matin described his hometown, family, and circumstances as impossibly large to navigate; as he saw it, adversity moved in a large, inescapable orbit, linking people not through goodness but in desperation and confusion. Like Zia he is part of a new era in which the social body is marked by the coexistence of a demand for speech and its perceived absence or senselessness. Speech is a dangerous double bind: the medium of persuasion and belonging and, as I understand its power, an uncontrollable instrument of war that proceeds alongside the translator.[1] When Matin emphasizes that he can trust me, he is gesturing toward this power. The voice is violent, but it is interpretation and the possibility of listening to the voice at any moment or in any place that makes this violence brutal. Matin does not articulate this notion in talking to me, but I believe he intuits the possibility and wants to protect himself from its force by listening and speaking differently to different voices.[2] Thus, even though he fears his own disembodied voice and the displacement of being a subject in dialogue by the power of misunderstanding, especially in Kabul, he still speaks to me, and he speaks to me differently than he did with those he met on the military missions he was embedded in across the country.

Kabul has assumed a privileged position as a metonym for Afghanistan in the imperial imagination of many states (United Kingdom, Persia/Iran, Russia/Soviet Union, United States) for more than two centuries. It has been the scene of dramatic military retreats, intelligence missions, proxy wars, and direct intervention for more than forty-five years of the last century. It is a bustling city situated along the Kabul River and the foothills of the Hindu Kush Mountains, strategically situated with access to the Khyber Pass, one of the main connections between Central Asia and the Indian subcontinent. But residents have seldom had the feeling of pure movement or flow and outpouring. Instead, there are hardened roadblocks, cordoned-off areas, dangerous parts, intelligence and surveillance networks, and entire neighborhoods isolated by fear and poverty. Yet, Matin wants Kabul to represent a purer experience of modern life, perhaps to be as Georges Haussmann once described Paris, an expansive "rendezvous of pleasures," where love, freedom and being go hand in hand.[3]

Matin refers to everything outside of Kabul as the *atraf* (countryside). This is both a place and a scene of vanishing reason he fears and tries hard to repress. Still, it regularly reappears in his life in the city, sometimes as the problem of heteroglossia and excess (as when he exclaims, "rural people don't know how to talk"), and at other times as the problem of lonely abandonment: "There is nothing there to see."

Matin had access to military radio transmissions through wired headphones. On his way to the provinces, to places like Helmand and Kandahar, he would sit inside the armored tank listening to the transmissions to acquaint himself with different languages and with military vocabulary. He possesses a split desire: He wants to know what is being communicated and if there is danger ahead, but it is equally important for him to minimize the possibility of mishearing words while parsing different accents of

English: for example, when working with English, American, and Scottish soldiers. For him, the terrain of war and language are the same; beyond the challenges of being embedded in a foreign military mission in a place he is unaccustomed to, his greatest anxiety lies in the potential for mistakes such as a mispronounced or misplaced word, which if interpreted in a negative way, could lead to serious accusations of spying or speculation that he is involved in a covert "green on blue" plot against his foreign unit.[4]

Speech is different from other instruments of war. It is mysterious and fills the space of encounter with expectation and excess that cannot be contained in a relation of exchange through dialogue. It possesses a transcendental power of which Matin is painfully conscious. This power is even more challenging to control in a foreign language, and thus Matin can only open his heart in his mother tongue when he is relieved of the weight of the foreign. He told me that being able to speak to me in Persian made his heart feel better: "Sometimes I feel like my heart is tight, you know, like my chest is closed, but I feel better when I talk to you," he said. This chest-opening moment is enabled by a common understanding he presumes we share because we share our mother tongue. A common language makes our speech isomorphic and enables us to witness each other's experiences. It is also the doxa (common world, common sense) he sees as a reflection of the spirit of modernity and its rightful place in Kabul, where people know about life and the way the world works. They possess a form of knowledge that imbues their speech and gives them voices capable of openings that lead to more life; their voice is a sign of the fullness of life and intellect.[5] But Matin speaks of and seeks to hear something other than this kind of opening in his heart. When his voice is dislodged from Persian, and therefore from what I imagine he understands as the possibility of control, there is no opening. This is particularly deadly in Kabul, where, ideally, he envisions a city of articulateness and order. He tells me this hope is diminishing by the day. Crime is rampant. The city is dirty and overpopulated. The streets are congested. People speak with various, difficult-to-comprehend accents. His close friend was murdered in his own taxi in the middle of the day when a man, disguised as a woman in a classic blue burqa, stole his cash, shot him, and drove away in the car. "What will become of us?" Matin asks me. "We are not safe in Kabul."

The more he speaks to me in his Kabuli dialect, professing that he is media savvy and knows about the state of global politics impacting his life, the more he seems to feel closer to a "language-of-power" that is part of his sense of national duty but also a duty to life and being.[6]

But these cracks in the fabric of the social, and the possession of symbolic capital that cannot become national, mark the space of the other in contemporary Afghan society, raising the issue of writing and speech serving as one basis for collective life and relationality but also as a form of equivocation and rupture, a cut carried by some and not others. In this sense, Matin's concerns are prescient. Consider a recent comedy sketch on the popular Afghan television channel TOLO. A man enters a shop in the city of Herat, the first city to fall to Taliban forces in August 2021. The exchange (which I've abbreviated) is in Persian:

CUSTOMER: Pardon! Pardon brother! How much are these sunglasses, then?

SHOP OWNER: It's nothing. Just be my guest.

CUSTOMER: Come on, brother, why are we people so full of empty formalities? Just say the word, give me the price, and let's finish the back-and-forth.

SHOP OWNER: In all truth, for anyone else, I would sell this pair of glasses for 6,000 Afs. But you are one of us. So, for you, I can do 5,000 Afs.

CUSTOMER: 5,000 Afs?!

SHOP OWNER: And only because you are one of us.

CUSTOMER: I am one of you? Do you even know me?

SHOP OWNER: Nope.

CUSTOMER: Then why do you speak cheap empty words? Say that I am one of your own and then charge 5,000 Afs for a pair of sunglasses?

SHOP OWNER: These are different in kind. They are a genuine product of Japan.

CUSTOMER: By God, I am not an illiterate. It says right here on the glasses "Made in China." And you tell me these are Japanese. Do you think I am an illiterate?

SHOP OWNER: So you are literate, then? Very well. Show me the evidence.

[The man takes a document out of his blazer pocket.]

CUSTOMER: Yes. Here is my evidence of literacy. I am literate. Now tell me how much.

SHOP OWNER: Oh! You have evidence you are a literate man. OK, let's say 4,000 Afs.

The conversation between the men continues along these lines. The man says he is not stupid, and the shop owner asks for written evidence to back up his empty words. He asks to see paperwork to prove the man is not from a rural village (*atraf*) and merely posing as a city dweller (*shahr nisheen*), to prove his true age, and finally a doctor's note to verify he is sane and can access his rational faculties; in the end, when all the evidence is handed over, the price drops to 50 Afs (70 cents). On one level, the back-and-forth dramatizes the sublimation of social difference as exchange value. But it is also an extended scene of speech sustained by the desire to see and know the reality of writing as a dividing line between self and other, and between reason and unreason. It illustrates the structure of being-in-language and of understanding the power to communicate the linguistic constancy of things despite the loss of confidence in arbitrary signs: for example, the inscription "Made in China," the use value of the glasses, the introductory price, the man's obvious Herat city dialect, his sanity, and so on.

. . . .

In political and intersubjective life, writing and speech never stay clear of each other. The person who possesses writing is rational (*mantiqi*), insightful and illuminated (*rooshan fekr*), civilized (*ba adab*), and crucial to an enlightened future (*ayendeh behtar wa roshan*). These are assertions Afghans commonly make in their judgments of social and intellectual life (*taleem wa tarbia*). In making such claims, they express the idea that illiteracy induces a break in rational thought and that the lifeworld of orality can only lead to excess or madness. In this sense, Matin's problem is the voice and speech of the other. No matter how important the voice is for rendering testimony and indicating a "present corporeality," it is also, as Stefania Pandolfo describes, "an impersonal agent of strangeness, inscription of alterity."[7] This mark of alterity is what Matin hears as the most glaring distinction between people. When he leaves Kabul, he is forced to abandon the voice of reason and speak to people in a different way. It sets him on a path of mimesis but also of discerning the absence of logos in rural places where words and propaganda are readily exchanged to bring those populations under government control but where people are ultimately devoid of sense and life. He tells me, "They are all illiterate," and "They don't know how to speak," and because they lack writing and intelligibility, he believes they misunderstand both image and word. He also tells me they are immune to accountability: They compulsively lie, deceive, and live like violent "brutes."

The rest of the country, and its unpredictable populations, weigh down on him like rocks on his chest. His belief system changes the way he speaks to me. Matin comments on the partial and simple truths of these stories; he tells me these are things I must "already know." He wants to transport me to the world he has recently found, so that I can envision a volatile and vast backwater where people tend to animals and crops in lonely fields and, because of their extreme isolation, "they talk nonsense and are all nomadic." "There is no life there," he adds. He imagines being seen and recognized by one of them. He says, "I look different now, from when I was on missions. But can you imagine if one of them recognizes my face? They'll know. They'll kill me right away." "But what about all of the time you have spent in Kabul without being harmed, and all the relationships and friends you have?" I ask. "That doesn't matter," he replies, and he continues: "Listen. In Mazar-i-Sharif [a city in the north of the country close to the border with Tajikistan] 'they' [the Taliban] caught a guy I knew on the side of the road. You'll never guess what happened. They took his cell phone from him. Poor guy must have been terrified, and he handed it over, of course. They called someone from his recent call list and pretended they were merely helping him out after an accident. An ordinary act of goodwill! They asked about his identity." Matin quickly reenacted the hypothetical conversation on the other end of the line: "'Oh! Dear God! He's my good friend! He's a commander in the Afghan National Army. One of our own. Please take good care of him brother!' Well, they hung up and slit his throat right then and there. They are primitive people, they care nothing for humanity."

Matin speaks in a voice that is not his own.[8] Voices do not speak to him; he wields and uses them while remaining entirely within the order of representation he takes for granted as something we share and mutually understand quite simply for what it is. Thus, his speech is not symptomatic of, for example, the loss of the symbolic or of an imaginary other that shores up his own being; it is revelatory of a reality he thinks I cannot see without his help. His words are the buttress of his claim that the discourse of reason can be imitated or sabotaged or supplanted but never possessed by others. He voices the voice of the other he does not want me to meet or speak to in person to show me that the danger is drawing closer and there will be no place left to go, no other city that will have him, and besides, unlike me, he has no other city.

He faces a peculiar form of failure in the inability to control a space of excess that emerges precisely when words fail to secure a referential ground. This is the space where it becomes difficult, as Claude Lévi-Strauss describes, to "define the social *as* reality" and thus a space where subjects of knowledge who seek to understand, judge, act, and speak are always subverted by a totality they do not grasp even as it invades them, *because* it invades them. This moves in the direction of the other until "we reach a level which seems strange to us, not because it harbors our most secret self, but (much more normally) because, without requiring us to move outside ourselves, it enables us to coincide with forms of activity which are both at once ours and other."[9]

From within his narrative of dialogic voices emerges a pervading strangeness. It extends to his being and even to his face, which looks different in Kabul because it is clean-shaven and free of disguise, and thus no longer ensures that he can traverse between place and mode of appearance. He will be found. And then what? Where will he go? What can he say? What face can he put on? For Matin, the closing is not only of dialogue or moments of translation but also the of the gap between city and countryside; the two atmospheres have become spaces of reciprocal strangeness and dangerous crossings. The protean atmosphere is one of enemies and strangeness and of the quality of feeling Georg Simmel describes as the sense that "he, who is close by, is far, and strangeness means that he, who is also far, is actually near."[10]

IN THE CORNFIELD

Matin grew up in Kabul and had never been to Helmand before. During his mission, among all the elements he encountered, including the infiltration of soldiers via armored vehicles and Chinook helicopters, what struck him the most was the local dialect.[11] He didn't hear it through headphones but with his own ears. By the summer, there was little resistance, and British officials went so far as to compare Helmand to Northern Ireland, hoping the support of the local population would enable a prolonged counterinsurgency. Matin said he felt like things were going well and like they were in control of the area.

One afternoon, while out on patrol by a large cornfield, Matin thought he saw someone. He wasn't sure and was trying to focus his eyes when a shot was suddenly fired at him and his commander. He recounts how bewildered and taken aback he was by the loud bang but also the green of the cornfield and the effectiveness of its camouflage. Then a strange man (*mard-e-ajeeb*) appeared out of nowhere. He was holding a large cob of corn in front of his face and trying to hide what Matin perceived as a sardonic look. Matin admits he didn't clearly see the man's face, but the look he suspects he saw was the inimitable trace of a sinister truth-being. In that instant, the situation became obvious to Matin:

> I knew it was him. I know he shot at us. It was as obvious as day. But he pretended like he had gone into the field to get some corn to eat, he tried to cover his face with a shawl and then he started pretending to be insane, so we just let him go, but I knew it was him. I remembered his face. You won't believe what happened next! A few days later that same man, now clean-shaven, was introduced to us as the local police chief whom we were supposed to support and train. He had trimmed his beard and cut his hair. That's how it is. You don't know who anybody truly is. I confronted him, and he denied the whole thing. He was very articulate, he started to laugh, and he said, "OK. OK. It was me. Let it go." One day they are with the local police force and the next they hide in cornfields and shoot at you. They mock and fool you.

The sense of near and far contained in the stranger is now at the heart of translation. Matin wants me to understand that he faces a particular kind of madness that is impossible to translate, in part because the alteration is so blatant it seems surreal. What he discerns (or "reads") in the landscape and on the man's face is internal to the problem of sovereignty and sense-making. In the moment he thinks he has found clarity—while looking out at an open, empty field in daylight or sitting down for a discussion with the local police—he confronts the absence of stable signification. This proceeds through disguise, first as a feature of the natural landscape, then on the man's face, which is now clean-shaven like Matin's will later be in Kabul, where he no longer has to disguise himself. The man in the field transforms into a mirror image of Matin: now *he* is the false bearer and representative of the Afghan state and its security forces. On the two occasions Matin anticipated being in control—when acting as a watchman in the field and as a translator in the meeting with the police chief—he is instead confronted by the duality of the other. He confronts a form of otherness that isn't singular or unitary but a fiction he must learn to read as two.

For him, this split disrupts the easy exchange he has come to take for granted between language and money, the money paid for destroyed crops or access to village routes, his salary, and so on now evolves into an uncontrollable scene of shifting signs where no condition of knowledge or fantasy of monetary exchange can prevail. He can offer the locals money in compensation for the destruction and be killed; or he can refuse to offer money for the destruction and possibly still be killed. He can look out for the other in a field and be caught by surprise, or he can sit down to mediate between known parties and still be caught off guard by the other's other side.

The uncanny is most powerful when we engage in involuntary repetition, encounter doubles, think others harbor ill will toward us and discover it is true, and so on. And perhaps more powerfully, it reveals that the role of repetition in the psyche is not one of mere symptomatic or illusory effects but a generative, structural feature of unconscious life and collective transformation that Freud went on to connect to the work of the drive.[12] In this sense, the uncanny is that which is familiar but hidden from us and is the name for what "ought to have remained hidden and secret, and yet comes to light."[13]

The uncanny also inheres in the split between the embodied self and its representation: a divide that defies presence and occurs in signification; for example, in the distinction between the "I" and how one talks about oneself to others. In everyday life, we experience it when we speak but are unable to hear our own voice, become estranged from our name, make a slip of the tongue, or experience a gap between what we intend to say and the mode of intention in language. Like ghosts, doubles, and automatons we mistakenly believe are alive, or the experience of being repeatedly lost in the same place, uncanny coincidences are the moments in which we feel a "split" in our encounter with the "real."[14]

To encounter this kind of stranger, or the double that Matin faces, is to want to know something that cannot become an object of knowledge.[15] But what he discovers is also the elsewhere of translation: a side that is impossible to surveil and control, a space where the reality principle is overtaken by the dangerous play of representations. In the gap between his drive to know, read, and reconstruct the other and the proliferation of falsehood, in the space where finding the lie is the condition for seeing the political truth, interpretation becomes impossible for him. This is the aporia he repeatedly encounters, and it leads only to more uncontrollable openings, toward uncertainty and maybe toward death. He recounts his initial bewilderment, a moment I think he recalls later because he should have seen it for what it was at the time. He wants me to hear his belated understanding. He wants me to understand how confusing and difficult interpretation is and why his ambivalent relationship to Helmand and its people becomes a nonrelation.

> I had never been to Helmand before. They are so different! I'd never seen or heard anything like that before, it was my first time, but the difference between those people and Kabulis is like the difference between the ground and sky. They don't know how to speak! I couldn't bear it. They are completely illiterate. There are basic things they don't understand, that they don't know how to say or express. But that's not all. We would give them gifts and in return they would plant IEDs [improvised explosive devices] and land mines by the roads. All they cared about was their crops. Mainly corn and wheat. We would have to use their lands because all the major roads had roadside bombs and mines. Our convoys would pass through their agricultural fields, and of course, the chained tires would destroy the crops and land, and they would come to us for compensation. We always gave them more than the price of their harvest, and sometimes they invited me over for dinner and sometimes they tried to kill us.

Anxiety is about the problem of distance and closeness. And because we can never be certain of what desire intends or moves toward, or how we are seen by others, anxiety is fundamentally about the uncertainty over who one is for others. In facing the other in this direct, face-to-face way Matin wants to distill and narrate for me the lack of coherence, the absence of meaning, in a place where, like the failure of translation, he now faces the general failure of exchange. This excess is what he cannot contain, it goes beyond the words or faces of others, to mark for him the beginning of a cultural scandal that displaces exchange, and thus the practice of translation, from a condition of possibility to the unmitigated experience of failure and political violence.

Violence and retribution for the destroyed fields is not an element of war and counterinsurgency. It is a failure in principle that Matin finds as exasperating as the nonsensical discourse he is tasked to make sense of. Thus, to go to Helmand and speak with the locals is to open himself up, first to the failure of the gift he gives in the form of monetary compensation for the destruction of crops and land, and then to the more general collapse of reciprocity he understands as the logic between war and compensation for its brutal violence.

The situation becomes more uncertain. Matin sees the dangerous mimesis of exchange: the planting of bombs and roadside mines in places where planting crops had become impossible owing to the destruction of fields. But there is another problem. Amid confusion and violence, he cannot escape the voice of the stranger. It's everywhere and different. But he hears it as the truth of what he already knows. It appears familiar, like the opening of a relation of exchange, but it is overtaken by the same remoteness and disruption that characterizes his sense of space and narrative: "They don't know how to speak! I couldn't bear it," he says.

Like Zia, Matin equates the dissonance of the vernacular with a sense of having entered a different and anachronistic time. The hinterland in his country is also a hinterland in his mind. He projects the kind of remoteness that is a hallmark of modern warfare and the willingness to kill those on whose behalf it is his job to speak.[16] The shift is also the terror of an encounter indifferent to shared signs or meaning. From the outset, the encounter is alien to the promise of translation. War is strange and foreign, but Helmand is even stranger because it is foreign to signification as he understands it.[17]

Matin's problem does not relate only to the topographical scene but to a social body that raises unfamiliar difficulties for him, including dissimulation, even as he labors on their behalf to close the gap in meaning between English and the local Pashto dialect. This is his burden and the pharmakon of literacy at work. He characterizes his struggle as "the only way" forward. The task and anxiety are, I believe, the difference he perceives between the "ground and sky" and more generally between social life and violence, but also the overlay of the symbolic and the chthonic lure of drives that find their expression in an intense, mobile power embodied in the other that later "finds" him in Kabul, much like Zia also feared it would.

Given all this danger, he tells me his pay was far too low at $715 per month. When he called home, he had to lie to his parents about his location, so that they would not worry about him being injured or killed. And if he were killed? His parents would have no idea where he was and would suffer the double shock of learning he is dead and is not where they thought he was. And he was not even free to speak his own language. He was anxious about speaking Persian to his family on the phone in case he came under suspicion of cooperating with the insurgents or passing secret information. Unlike when he was listening to military communications through the wired headphones, speaking on the telephone could mean he would be suspected of the same proclivity for violence and sabotage he discerned in the local population. Some of the other translators were even accused of helping plant roadside bombs, so to deflect suspicion he avoided speaking "too much" in his mother tongue. "It was better that I didn't call home," he said.[18]

But he returns to the problem of local speech. It generates confusion that subverts strategic interests on all sides and opens up its own political force. This is the force he would like to silence even as he cautions that it cannot be taken too seriously. The political power of local speech is like a bad dream. With difficulty, he tries to explain this to the foreign soldiers he works with:

> I'd say, Look, these people are different from you. They are uneducated. They don't know how to use language. They don't know how to talk. They talk for an hour and the translation takes five minutes because these people are undereducated. They'll repeat themselves ten times. They never get to the point. They add so much flourish to their words. They absolutely hate responding in a straightforward manner. They will make you dizzy! Running around this way and that way with their words, and after an hour they get to the damn point you wanted from the beginning. They'll repeat it in ten different ways. They don't want to shed light on your questions or give you answers. You have to force them. They daydream while talking.

The oneiric world is awakened for Matin as a feature of senselessness that is distinct rather than inseparable from the function of signification. To daydream while talking and to talk in a mode comparable to dreaming is a collective drive that verges on madness. The figure of the rural person speaks untruth but also stands in the chasm—preventing it from coming together—between the desired effect of speech as a medium of suasion (ideological conversion and military pacification) and the failure of translation to secure a space of meaningful exchange and control.

Matin realizes there will be no straightforward answers to his questions. The people on whose behalf he wants to speak personify an unstable vacillation between violence and speech and reveal the power of his own speech. He still has the power not to say anything at all. He is part of the tactics of counterinsurgency and has access to the tools of battle: He rides in tanks and uses headsets and manuals but also deals with local crops, dialects, and "strange, foreign ways" (*rasm wa rawaj e ajeeb*). But he avoids tragedy at least in part because he has yet to inhabit the aftermath of translation and still wields a powerful foreign code: English. Consequently, he has the power to introduce chaos or language into people's lives, because English demands its own translation, and Persian and Pashto signify what Afghans are either ignorant of or cannot convey through speech alone.

During a mission to Kandahar, a province in the southern part of the country, connected to Kabul by Highway 1, also known as Highway 0101 (the road Zia was patrolling with the Polish brigade) these tensions became impossible for Matin to balance through translation. Rising levels of deceit and violence meant there was no suitable language of exchange. In its absence, Matin and others resorted to excess and the kind of reckless, senseless mimesis he ascribed to the local population but that was now part of his own strategy of survival. His body was a supplement to ground warfare, showing us that sovereignty could not proceed unaided, that it incorporated the danger it sought to neutralize, so Matin used his skill at translation to restructure local life around the twin imperatives of question and answer that he believed were at the core of the logic of translation and his own survival.[19] But he could not do this through words alone.

He told me of specific experiences, in places he plainly described as "surrounded by all land," when the exchange of gunfire replaced what he assumed would be question and reply. Local men rejected this structured interrogation Matin took for granted by taking the first shot in order to communicate the radical contingency of a situation in which reply, rumor, gossip, and answer were all part of a shifting reality in which civilians and combatants became indistinguishable.[20]

This shifting reality weighed on Matin, and the challenge of mediating it felt too big. He recalled his bewilderment over what to do with the double bind of rural life amid an insurgency, when invasion and resistance transformed relations and the idea of mediation. But just as soon as he reflected on this, he remembered that the Afghan translators made do with less: Just as in Helmand, they had less food and fewer supplies than the American soldiers. In Kandahar Province he experienced a second shooting (this time from inside a house, not a cornfield), which he suggested was perhaps the reason things were going wrong. He remembered the road. The road didn't help anyone. In order to secure supplies, they needed to access villages and towns but again, like in Helmand, the roads were effectively closed off by roadside mines and the threat of ambush-style attacks. Matin and his Afghan National Army counterparts (to whom he was conveying information over the radio) were blindsided in yet another place they wanted to bring under government control. Matin did not know where to turn or who to chase. The promise of the translated word led to the surprise of ambush and mimesis in a complicated terrain of moving and fighting. They had to abandon villages and go into the mountains, where the insurgents typically fled for cover. The difference first formulated as one of dialect and language was now the difference between who would attack first in a tightening space.

> MATIN: I went on a lot of missions in the mountains when I was with the special forces. Their missions were almost always in the mountains. We were close to a village, and our mission was to support the local Afghan police. There were a lot of ambushes. That was their tactic, and of course, they laid roadside mines and bombs on the major roads. So, we would go out primarily at night, at two or three a.m., and wait for them in the mountains so they would not attack the Afghan police. They would try to attack every single night. Every single night members of the Afghan police were killed, at least two or three dead, and I'd see their bodies. There were too many dead bodies, sometimes even six or seven of them. Or they would be badly hurt.

> AUTHOR: What did you do?

> MATIN: What did we do? We tried to ambush first. We would try to ambush them beforehand, while they were traveling to the villages, sometimes we got caught by an ambush instead. I got hurt when a mine went off and hit the person in front of me.

Matin is trying to hide in a scene of total collapse. In the mountains, where he went after realizing translation was doomed, the difference between "ground and sky" which he understands as the scope and enclosure of local life—the stubborn anachronism he desires to parse for others—transforms into the domain of translation's abandonment. The play of discourse he first hears as senseless and later understands as the refusal to give a coherent reply is now disseminated as a principle of space and tactic. The local fighter whose opinion is not altered or brought under control in the first instance of interrogation is now caught by surprise by the force of an ambush within his own hiding place. The ambush is a critique of translation and linguistic difference, executed as a matter of counterinsurgent strategy and in the name of the Afghan state. In fact, there is no distinction between milieu and target, the state and terror, imitation and a real event, or even between ideation and the taking of local lives by gaining access to their environment (in this case, the same roads and areas the locals had presumably booby-trapped and where Matin's unit want to attack first).

By the time Matin came down from the mountains, verbal dialogue had come to an end, and the locals refused to communicate what was "in their hearts." Matin and his team tried to engage them: They held local council meetings, encouraged them to open up more, but people were afraid to speak, except to say that they were caught in a dangerous double bind between local and foreign forces. On one occasion a young man who stood up to speak on behalf of Matin's unit in a meeting intended to persuade villagers not to allow the Taliban to plant roadside mines and was later beheaded in revenge. Matin said he was "maybe thirty years old." I understand this man as articulating an aporetic bind. To allow a foreign convoy to stay the night meant appearing to collaborate with them and acceding to future ambush-style attacks, both as retaliation and as a condition for holding territory, a dilemma he was already in since Matin's unit had convened the meeting in his village. In a sense he was trying to communicate that nobody should communicate in such a precarious situation. He was beheaded for bringing into language the reality of a situation in which nobody could protect or trust one another—a situation that the locals and the foreigners shared in the same territory with no resolution in sight.

One afternoon, Matin's unit attempted to play a game of soccer with the local men. The American soldiers laughed at the Afghans for stumbling and not knowing how to play. They recorded videos, took photos, and ridiculed them. The following morning, the local men planted an improvised explosive mine on the side of the playing field to target the American convoy as it left, Matin assumes in retaliation. However, this time Matin comprehended the situation for what it was. He recalled the soldiers all being shocked, and he had to explain the situation to them. They convoy was hit and many of his team members were injured, including Matin, who said he would never forget the experience. But he had to translate the same experience, which all the men had undergone together. He had to translate what their videos and behaviors meant to the locals, to elucidate that making fun of them would have violent repercussions: "They were crying . . . one man was crying a lot and kept asking 'How could they do this? We just played a game of soccer with them yesterday and today they tried to kill us all.' I said to him, 'Take out your phone.' I showed him the pictures and videos he had taken. He was completely unaware of how offensive that had been, how murderous offending someone can be around here. He still didn't understand. 'Why would they kill us for taking pictures?' I had to explain: 'You played music, you made fun, you turned them into entertainment, and they did that in response. You have to respect them.' They listened to me after that, I told them not to walk around with their shirts off or go swimming in their underwear, which they used to do regularly. They only learned to listen to me after something this violent occurred. Otherwise, they were deaf."[21]

The Americans had misunderstood the nature of game-playing in this environment, just as they had misunderstood why the young man spoke out in the village meeting. Who can engage in play? Can Matin? Can the locals? Who is free to speak up? The jouissance of laughter defeats play. It also forecloses the postponement of violence by transforming death into a radical form of reply inscribed as another level of the same game but also not the same game at all. The laughter and images were intended to produce a sovereign moment in a fluid situation where the deferral of death could not be guaranteed, much like James Siegel describes the freeze-frame of a photograph in colonial Indonesia serving not as "a tool for the preservation of a culture, but a technological device devoted to its defeat and to the recording of the remnants of that defeat."[22]

The laugh of the invader *is* an image of defeat and a form of excess that circulates and becomes the scene of another game. This time, it is a game of sheer destruction with no recording or shared laughter. There is only violence intensified by proximity to jouissance, such that laughter becomes explosive and the explosion becomes a new laugh.[23] Matin is the only person in his unit who understands this. He is suddenly capable not only of reading the locals but also intuiting the meaning of shared signs; he enters their discourse and understands that the atmosphere has become impossible to mitigate, no translation will suffice to make the foreigners less "deaf" to the reality of the lifeworld they have structured along the fatal divide between play and annihilation. Translation, the basis of Matin's claim to ethical and national improvement, a claim he shares with Zia, is supplanted by the force of the real nobody can escape in precisely the place where everyone is close but estranged. Matin has become one of them.

THE GIFT

In the absence of viable speech, the gift of giving what one does not have is crucial to knowing how to encounter the stranger.[24] Like everyone else, Matin was outside of himself (a subject *excentric* to its own unconscious) with no solid ground from which he could think or act. He was hiding in what he described (in the same spirit of differentiating Kabul from everywhere else) as the thick of the jungle, close to the agricultural town of Marjah in Helmand

Province. Nightfall had caught up with his unit, and the roadside explosions increased without warning. He described the Taliban fighters who planted the IEDs at night as brazen and deceptive, but they were unaware that Matin and his unit had another gaze on them in the form of surveillance cameras in the surrounding trees. One night, to capture them in the act, Matin and his unit walked through some ponds, into some marshland, and then onto land: They took evolutionary steps in the mire for the sake of the nation. When they reached a clearing, they found only two homes in the area, and Matin, who was wearing camouflage just like the soldiers, befriended the owner of one of them. In return for his friendship Matin promised to protect the elderly man from any retaliatory violence on either end of the battle. He said he could not bear another fatal outcome like the young man who was beheaded in the village. One more time would be too much.

This small area with two homes surprised Matin because of its isolation. But it was known to the Taliban fighters, who sneaked into the old man's yard one night, planted an explosive mine inside an old can of cooking oil, and fled. But there was a third gaze still, because the elderly man would stay up all night guarding his home. He saw everything and went to Matin, whom he called "Mr. Translator," the next morning:

OLD MAN: Hi, Mr. Translator. I brought you something.

MATIN (immediately taking the oil can in his hands, mistaking it for cooking oil or a gift of homemade food): What is it?

OLD MAN: Oh, it's a mine.

Matin said he almost collapsed on the spot, but the old man spoke some more: "Don't worry. I removed the battery, don't worry." Matin alerted the military personnel, and they immediately came out to examine it. The old man kept repeating: "Relax I removed the battery. It doesn't work. Relax. I removed the battery; it will not go off."

He presented the bomb he had defused by hand, but nobody else could see it for what it was without dialogue. It was an empty but suspicious object that required the labor of explanation and friendship to be mistaken as the gift it was but not the one Matin expected it to be. Here, the man gave what he did not have, not in the form of food, but in the form of restoring the mutual recognition that had come undone in this place and the unexpected power of what was still possible between strangers. And he risked his life to defuse the bomb.

By this point, the man's fingerprints were all over the device, and Matin, knowing and perhaps now seriously understanding how readily accusations were made against locals based on biometric evidence, didn't want him questioned or biometrically enrolled.[25] Everyone had to cover their tracks. Matin understood these possibilities because he could read the situation well enough to know that no form of writing or capture, no loss of deferral, could take place without consequence. A new game was being played where the old one left off. Fearing that enrolling the old man would likely result in his interrogation, possible torture, and even deportation to Guantánamo Bay, Matin struck a deal with all sides. They would return to the man's backyard and bury the mine again. They would then watch the house until the perpetrators returned to take back what was left and to remove their own fingerprints from the scene. However, the perpetrator-strangers did not arrive the next day, so Matin went back to man's house and unearthed the explosive himself to spare his friend any further involvement. In the south of the country, he said, "people do support the Taliban, and I was very afraid. They demand your respect, and if you show it to them, they are kind."

This is not to say the final word is "kind." Ironically, in a very serious, and deadly way, Matin understood agricultural life as a signifier of lack in the other, and that the planting of the mine was a substitute for the game of sovereignty and the structures of recognition Matin fantasized would make it possible for him—make it his duty even—to speak on behalf of others. But he could not achieve his objective through words in this agricultural place. Amid the proliferation of false representations, it is the human capacity and gaze (certainly not the camera's) that discerns falsehood for what it is: an opportunity to rescue others from the violence of literalism. To accede to the possibility of exchange in the aftermath of translation's failure and amid the violence of total war still requires one to reckon with the empty places where victims stood to speak, where the defective canister, first mistaken for a gift then for a working bomb, did not detonate. It requires moving across transcripts and places of ambush and disguise—the cornfield, the destroyed agricultural land, and the village fields where men were beheaded—to forge the tenuous link between the translated phrase and maddening dreamwork of local dialect. But alongside these spaces there is perhaps one more, one that requires the opening Matin and Zia desire as the compensation for their survival, but that does not attest to the power of translation so much as it does its inability to capture the kind of saying that is not always said.

A Vita Detoured

Please, sister, take this CV and do what you can!
—ZAHER AHMAD (young man, Kabul)

VITA (NOUN): A BIOGRAPHY OR RÉSUMÉ

I want to apply the idea of a vita as a theoretical metaphor for *extimité*—the intimate yet strange—and for the forms of knowing, meeting, and being with others that traverse the relationships between detours and language that we have been examining. A vita also represents a passage, a life path shaped by encounters that sustain collective existence beyond the illusions of imaginary completion or the confines of tragedy. Perhaps another way to put this is that, when closure is achieved in a conclusion or tragic arc, the vita also ends. And where the vita exists, it carries the possibility of something beyond the tragic, something that moves toward the insistence of the other.

One afternoon, I was sitting in a car in an affluent neighborhood in Kabul, a place where the possibility of becoming rich was visible to anyone through the segregation of neighborhoods and in ostentatious displays of wealth. A young man breathlessly knocked on the window. When I partially lowered the window, he quickly handed me his curriculum vita and implored me, as his "sister," to do whatever I could for him.

CURRICULUM VITAE

NAME: ZAHER AHMAD

PLACE OF BIRTH: HERAT PROVINCE

DATE OF BIRTH: 1972

We are living in Herat. I am very poor and I haven't any money for bread of night and day, please give me a task for me forever. you come here for Peace and Security helping. I hope help with me and we eat bad bread every night and day I haven't any someone that help me you know that the Afghanistan there is not work. My families are sick and I haven't any money for doctor. Please give me a task for me and help me. Please contact me as soon. I worked in ISAF [International Security and Assistance Forces] for Cleaner for 3 years. My days is very bad. Please Help me for a ever work. My families is sick and I haven't money for doctor. Please help me for work You Know that there isn't any work in Afghanistan and give me a work for me. You come here for Peace and Security helping.

How do we read this vita? It is an indictment of the forms of wartime profiteering and violence that rely on a crisis of governmentality and of the idea that the securitization of space and social life has a bearing on economic survival. Perhaps this is why the young man was in Kabul, and in that neighborhood, in the first place. But it is also about *bios*, the life of the human body that can still be shaped by words and action. In the face of wanton destruction and the exercise of power by the other (including the other we encounter by chance), this life becomes all the more political. That vita has moved with me from Kabul to New York to California, where I still have it; a fading testimony in black ink on 8" by 11" paper to the idea that by communicating the extent of one's predicament to others, one might unlock a different condition of possibility. It is a vita that insists on a fresh start, given to the figure of a "sister" as a certain kind of reader; perhaps a reader who can parse the disunity of a letter under revision for the multiple citations it seeks to gather. Where do we find its polysemic opening? Where else has it been used? And because this vita does not reach its recipient, who can give it the reply it seeks?

The textual element of a vita resists clear interpretation and invokes multiple readers across registers of personal testimony and legal and existential claims. It defies the enclosure of meaning and allows for the work of substitution: of seeking out for condemnation, of condemnation for narrative, and of narrative play for logocentric power. For example, in Sohrab's trial, Soraya's written testimony and statement is read aloud on her behalf by her lawyer, who was hired by her brother. Again the question arises of how far one should go for a sibling, beginning as a kind of vita about one's rightful place and direction in life. Soraya's disembodied words stage the study of God's word as her rightful path, rather than the scene of the word, logos, and the forms of truth found in love or in the city.

In a sense, her words are grounded not in a legal truth but in a transcendental signified beyond the contingencies of law and its interpretation, whether that be Sohrab's version of events, the judge's perspective, or our own. Her statement begins with the Quranic invocation *Bismillah ar-Rahman ar-Rahim* (In the name of Allah, the most merciful, the most beneficial), which is written at the beginning of every chapter of the Quran and is also invoked as a blessing of words, to make one's words as impactful and unified as possible through their proximity to divine logos.

Through text she sanctifies her speech: "In the name of Allah, the most merciful, the most beneficial. I live in the Pol e Sorkh neighborhood of Kabul and was very busy with my studies at university . . . while I was engaged in my studies a strange man, unknown to me, somehow obtained my phone number and got in touch with me. He began stalking me on my way to school and threatened me explicitly." This is a kind of vita, one in which the achievement of literacy and the life of studying the Word is interrupted by the desire of the other, a desire that is "unknown," "strange," without truth, and lacking ground and validity in language, appearing like an event rather than a dialectical tie.

Where else can we follow the vita? How does it help us understand *extimité* not as mere repression or forgetting, but as the persistent trace that cannot become the object of knowledge? When I first met a young man named Zaid, he was working as a short-order cook at a private security compound in the city's militarized Green Zone. I came to know him well, and he referred to me as "his sister." He told me he had a vita and letters of recommendation, and that if the compound closed, he would need to find new work, perhaps in a hotel or restaurant, except he worried that the economic downturn would mean those would shut too. Amid all this uncertainty, he hoped his résumé would help him stand out and that perhaps I, as someone he trusted, could help him. Zaid was anxious because he is illiterate, which had already led him to make one catastrophic mistake in his life. When he returned to Kabul from Iran, where he had worked as a day laborer during the first reign of the Taliban (1996–2001), his uncle convinced him to marry his first cousin. Zaid claims he was only fourteen at the time and was not in love, but he found it difficult to articulate a refusal. "I did not know what I could say . . . my family wanted me to get married. My brother was supposed to marry my cousin, but he refused, and my uncle came and told me that I had to marry her, even though I only wanted to play football. I refused but when my father asked me, I couldn't turn him down, after everything he had done for us, protecting us in the war, feeding us, caring for us, how could I say no to him?"

Zaid was at a loss for a way to say no. "So I married my cousin. But she was actually my sister! I never knew that we had drunk milk from the same breast, my mother's. But nobody cared enough to mention that we were siblings. My parents knew we had drunk milk together, but they are illiterate and therefore didn't know the implications of this; they have never read the Holy Quran, and they asked around and other family members said: 'Who cares? Go through with it anyway.' So, they did. My literate family members like my uncle, who knew what these laws meant never bothered to explain them to us."[1]

Because he could not access the domain of scripture and its inscriptions of truth and law, Zaid's life path was irrevocably altered. This marked the onset of new anguish. His body became the site of violent inscriptions beyond his control. He endured daily headaches, rapidly graying hair, and the uncanny opposition of illness and health between husband and wife, brother and sister: "If I was well, she was very ill; if I was ill, she was well. We absolutely could not be together. Eventually, I pressed my thumb on the divorce papers and moved to Iran and worked another four years as a store clerk. The second I was divorced, my headaches disappeared, my health was restored, my hair stopped going gray. Awful things stopped happening to me."

Here lies a different kind of *extimité* beyond the ideal of love or desire. It is fueled by the letter, when the absence of law erupts in excess between brother and sister, but also by an indexical sign that restores the prohibition, liberating him from the marriage and marking the return of his sister. The mark of one's presence through a "thumb sign" brings back the sister, even if the inability to discern alphabetic signs distorts that possibility to begin with. So, what is the sign and who is the sister? These are the moments in which "everything is to be disentangled, nothing deciphered; the structure can be followed, 'run' (like the thread of a stocking) at every point and at every level, but there is nothing beneath: the space of writing is to be ranged over, not pierced; writing ceaselessly posits meaning ceaselessly to evaporate it, carrying out a systematic exemption of meaning" and "by refusing to assign a 'secret,' an ultimate meaning."[2] When Sami tells us about being tortured with a Coke bottle and asks what is in his case file (two objects that capture the reach of the state), he gestures toward the same dispersion. What appears at first to be his state of confusion (Mina's absence) until he finds the truth in his mother's speech (Mina needs to be returned to her rightful place) confronts him later as the material violence of the law and its inability to capture these fragmented experiences (through the charge of terrorism against him).

But the return of the sister is far from conclusive; for Zaid it initiates another fraught detour, this time between his father and uncles, over property and inheritance documents that only his literate uncle can read. Their family meeting, which Zaid refers to as "the garden meeting" erupted into murderous violence when disagreement over the distribution of property and the paperwork resulted in his uncle killing everyone in the house, including Zaid's father, then turning the gun on himself. Not long after telling me this story, he reflected on it as the defining event of his life and remarked that now he had only his brother, the same one for whom he had unwittingly married his sister. He handed me his brother's vita and asked me, this time as his "sister," to help find him work in the city. Once again, the figure of the sister—for him both strange and foreign and unbearably familiar—returns in disguised form, a return made more compelling to me by the fact that Zaid never told me his sister's name or what became of their relationship after the divorce. And once again, in the place where the other is encountered, implored, and called upon, the vita returns as well, gesturing toward revision and other possibilities that Zaid could never fully articulate by saying "He has a vita, he has a vita and all his papers."

How do we understand that these are more than matters of paperwork and reading, and of the circuitous even murderous paths they lead to? Why does the vita become a metaphor for the uncanny turn of events and people? And beyond that, how do the forces of signification perform their most brutal violence precisely when people feel they've hit the mark and escaped its play?

On one hand, this story reveals the power of writing and an experience of illiteracy that is not about something missing, but about something that becomes too much. It is uncanny to me how this story resonates with the anxieties of Nadia's husband, who feared his literate daughter would take the deed to his house and force him out. For Zaid, too, his illiteracy shapes his understanding of the garden meeting tragedy, but it also gestures toward an opening where meaning and people are deferred and disrupt the very boundaries he hoped to secure after his divorce. On the basis of a traceable thumbprint, he is freed from his sister, but what appears instead is another trace, of vita for personhood, that requires him to encounter a sister, once again for the sake of his brother.

For me, the brother's vita represents a particular form of translation between the desire to articulate one's life, one's actions, and the place of desire, and more urgently, more vitally, the desire also to articulate the way in which that life is defined on the basis of what is articulated, written, or enacted through us. One cannot help but return to the figure of the sister, but also to words, to accepting gifts, to heteroglossia, to dreams, and to the forms of improvisation that make relations possible, even as they are caught in the crack.

VITA (LATIN): LITERALLY "LIFE" BUT ALSO "COURSE OF LIFE"

In various settings, including encounters with strangers, the vita became a kind of supplement to the act of sistering and to the idea of a sister not just as someone intimate enough to call upon but also as the other, someone whose presence makes room for the new, the foreign, and the disruption of the predation of the everyday. In their own way, these vitae offer knowledge about specific bodies, sites of ruin, economies, or encounters with others but also reflect the predicament of being a subject in language, a condition that is sometimes but not always tragic, and that entails delayed meanings and inscriptions on the body, the mind, and the socius. They show us a mode of communication that is not about forms of knowledge or recognition that can be satisfied (in either speech or writing) but that point toward the radically unknowable and extemporaneous paths through which understanding is not where we expect it to be, and sometimes is even happily on the run.

But the question of how a sister might respond raises a crucial distinction between understanding tragedy as an error in judgment—like falling in love with the wrong person or taking one's mother's word too seriously—versus misunderstanding your sister or the category of sister in all its power. The latter errors result in tragic actions such as suicide, murder, abduction, or abandonment in prison rather than the ability to see beyond this causal chain toward alternation and possibilities of passage. For me, this movement is not about the emergence of the "tragic" but a certain lengthy and circuitous pathway, a course or way of life filled with encounters that are sometimes tragic but ultimately are part of a movement that makes even a tragic life livable.

I want to be careful about making this distinction. The events I recount—the deadly garden meeting, Sami's attempted suicide-murder, the translator's violence, and the predicament of different sisters—all have elements of conflicting and displaced meanings that proceed toward a tragic downfall. They reveal the structures that sustain these trajectories, like the alternation between two possibilities in a myth, when tragedy seems to conform to the dichotomous framing of two extremes. Here, we can turn to Oedipus not for his tragic self-destruction but for the logic that sustains the plot, logic that reveals how a structural bind moves through a necessary duration in the myth, moving between conditions of possibility with no transcendental resolution. In his famous essay "The Structural Study of Myth," Claude Lévi-Strauss discerns one movement in particular that speaks to what we might see as a tragic crossroad: the over- and underdetermination of familial bonds that either transgress the laws of the social and their grounding in the prohibition of desire (the incest prohibition) or honor those laws in the most radical way possible (Jocasta's suicide and Oedipus's self-blinding as penance).[3]

Again, we can turn to the figure of a sister. Oedipus's daughter Antigone confronts both state law and divine justice in her radical commitment to bury her brother, a decision that costs her her own life but that she makes because of the inviolable sanctity of shared flesh and in the name of a higher law. When she is sent to the cave to be buried alive and hangs herself there, the same over- and underdetermination of blood ties seem to prevail. She acts beyond reason because, unlike her husband or son, her brother is singular and irreplaceable: "that tear in the oneness of the flesh cannot be mended." She must stand by her brother in death: "There is no possible exchange or substitution, no way to fill this gap within the domains sanctioned by the pleasure and reality principles. 'Doing this,' she says, 'it is a beautiful thing to die.'"[4]

But there remains an excess beyond what structuralism identifies as the logic of tragic events, revealing not just the binaries within mythological drama but also the epistemic compulsion to impose them. This excess is about unexpected encounters in language. Even when faced with radical dichotomies (suicide/murder, love/murder, or incest/prohibition) we find that these can be set aside for other possibilities of voicing, writing, dreaming, or deferring that we cannot understand as either the failure or radical valorization of symbolic relations, be they within family, translation or love. These other possibilities gesture toward the much more ambiguous and powerful place of encounters, the unexpected people and experiences we are faced with, and their power to ground collective life despite the experience of political and psychic upheaval.[5]

We can also think of this setting aside as errancy and movement, distinct from the structure of tragedy, because it is part of the erratic, messy quality of language that never fulfills its obligation and thus is always out of place in relation to what we hope to say, mean, or complete. In this logic, one cannot entirely and irrevocably over- or undervalue a relation because every relation is undone by its other. Thus, facing and calling on a sister, and the radical forms of self-sacrifice this unique bond can demand, coincide not only with the predicament of kinship, but with the more powerful law of the other that can neither be repressed nor fully absorbed. Perhaps this is why, after all his revelations and tears, after handing me his brother's vita and other papers, Zaid reversed course and said, "It is OK if you are unable, I only wanted to ask."

In this sense, language-encounters reveal the sister whose absence necessitates the repudiation of collective law and almost causes a suicide-murder, or the sister as ethnographer who can bear witness to the subsequent violence of the state and its corporeal traces, called on by the defendant as he insists that he can speak his truth without being able to read his case file and without his actual sister being present to attest to his story. In other moments, less desperate but also existential, I became the sister to whom Matin could open his heart rather than closing it amid what he describes as the disturbing heteroglossia of voices in which the voices of other others become a source of anguish instead of dialogue. During one of our last meetings, Matin too gave me his vita and asked if I could find him better work or perhaps help him get a visa to go abroad. He told me that his brother, who was also a translator, had been abducted by the Taliban for a ransom of $40,000 and was only released when their family went into heavy debt to raise the money. If that happens again, he laments, there is no money left and no one else to call on for help.

This kind of sistering, and vita-ing, is a translation between experience and narrative and in the case of the ethnographer, it is also the *idea of* sistering between what is heard, understood, and represented anew through the medium of writing for others still.[6] It enables new and old structures of witnessing, radical and ordinary kinds of sacrifice, and those forms of indeterminacy and not knowing that sustain collective life through indefatigable detours, rather than condemning it. Vita-ing, with, for, or against a sister is made possible by the place of the other and by the forms of desire and communication that impel us toward the cracks rather than enclosures, displacing even a tragic story's center such that the fantasy of presence, knowledge, who one can be, or what one can say or achieve or even think all the way through is akin to witnessing what does not happen, and thus of being in the presence of an event that cannot be articulated as an object of knowledge.[7]

What, in the end, can a vita given to a sister tell us? How does it capture those dimensions of knowing and being with others that defy interpretation (or attempt to hold them in place) following a more radical and fugitive proliferation of metonymic displacement but also the realities "of excess, overflowing, of bursting through . . . various conceptual barriers, enclosures, repressions"?[8] Again, I think of Sami addressing me as his sister in court and of what he felt as he drove up the hill to the hotel, planning to kill himself in order to free his sister. I think of Sohrab, happily in love, celebrating at the house party where he was arrested at the behest of his wife-turned-abductee's brother. The primal bond of sisterhood cannot be torn; another sister had to be returned home. And, finally, I think of Zaid's terrible predicament in terms of both kinship and loss, grappling with his inability to write, an absence that makes him cling, one more time, to the vita.

In experiences of oneself and others, something is always withdrawn from knowledge and resurfaces when we least expect it or feel ready to answer it. And again, there will be detours, uncanniness, pain, exceptional vitas, tracing and retracing to reckon with. Learning from this requires attuning oneself to what Walter Benjamin describes as the "caesura in the movement of thought" and the critical flashpoint between knowing and not knowing, the sayable and the said, doubting others and being with them anyway.[9] Here subjectivity is a purely excentric demand, an escapee always found elsewhere, in the dimension psychoanalysis theorizes as a *certain kind of beyond*, where the recognition of our desire and action is tied to a desire for recognition. In other words, in the dimension that emerges within language but can never be held there, the *extimité* where we cannot separate ourselves from those very aspects of language that alienate us, those aspects that make it so we are not in the place where we think, write, or speak from.

Acknowledgments

In an essay on authorship, literary theorist Roland Barthes describes texts as a "tissue of citations," existing in a parallel realm beyond authorial intention, where meaning is ultimately granted by a community of readers. In that spirit, this text bears the traces and voices of others who, over the years, have left countless imprints on my thinking and writing. And because this book has taken longer to write than I anticipated, I have incurred many happy debts. The first I owe is to those who selflessly shared their stories and experiences, including the difficult blows of fate, primarily in Kabul, where an onslaught of economic and political upheaval made their lives more difficult and uncertain than before. My fieldwork took place in 2010, 2011, and from 2012–13, during the peak of the Taliban insurgency against the Afghan government in Kabul and the counterinsurgency across the country. Their candor and willingness to help me learn both from and with them is the backbone of this book. At its heart is an attempt to think ethnographically not only about a place, but about modes of *detour*, collective life and language in our conceptual work. Since that time, another wave of transformation, different in its discourse and conception of sovereign power but also forceful, has rendered life in the city even more uncertain and isolating. As in many other places, this difficulty is often articulated in terms of economic precarity and the failure of exchange: between currencies, between the state and its population, or in access to basic necessities, education, and consumer goods. This breakdown in exchange also unsettles social relationships, which become more strained even as they remain the primary, and perhaps only, ground through which life continues amid upheaval.

The historical inquiries in this book are based on years of extensive archival work, initially in Kabul at the Afghan National Archives, then in England in the British Library's India Office Records in London and the National Archives in Kew, Surrey. I would especially like to thank the dedicated staff in the Asian and African Reading Room of the British Library, for their indefatigable work and caretaking of an enormous, fascinating archive and for their patience as I learned to navigate what at times felt like a towering stack of unconnected files and documents. I would also like to thank the archive director in Kabul, who so generously showed me the various treasures in his care. Over the years, including at uc Davis, I have also received generous financial support that has made possible both the initial fieldwork and the subsequent years of archival work and writing. I thank the Wenner-Gren Foundation for the Hunt Fellowship, which gave me the gift of time off from teaching to write this book. I also thank uc Davis, for generous research support over the years and especially for the Hellman Fellowship, which likewise made it possible to focus on the book.

My ethnography lies at the intersection of the theoretical and empirical and is driven by the life histories, fragmented memories, and experiences of my informants. At Columbia University the Anthropology Department became a place of rich and dialogic exchange and of conceptual freedom that allowed me to understand the discipline's indebtedness to the legacies of literary and philosophical thought that ground its most provocative claims. This spirit of interdisciplinary thought was also something I learned from my teachers. I had the privilege of working with Rosalind Morris, whose conceptual breadth always inspired me to work harder and think more rigorously. Marilyn Ivy has influenced my writing and commitment to think both psychically and ethnographically. Above all, I learned from her the importance of the kind of moral nerve that comes from ceaselessly facing life's unanswerable questions. Nadia Abu el Haj offered incisive feedback and encouragement, including about the importance of clear writing and of laying out one's stakes.

Columbia and New York City were my home for many years, and I was very lucky to share it with and learn from my friends, who offered not only encouragement but also the gift of intellectual exchange and solidarity. In particular, I thank Peter Lagerquist, whose incisive feedback and pushback benefited me a great deal. The writing experience became pleasurable for me only when I started thinking and writing with Victoria Gross and Natasha Nsabimana. I thank them for all of their support and humor, and for thinking with me throughout the years. Victoria has been a steadfast friend and generous presence throughout the years, meeting the world and those in it with humor and warmth. For their friendship, support, and intellectual company I also thank Muriam Haleh Davis, Seema Golestaneh, Jasmine Pisapia, and António Tomás. Maria José de Abreu, whom I did not get a chance to intersect with at Columbia but has since become an inspiration, models the openness of critical imaginaries that are not confined by disciplinary borders but move across theological, affective, political, and philosophical lines.

At UC Berkeley I found a rich and engaging atmosphere and was especially enriched by conversations with Stefania Pandolfo, Patricia Kubala, Michael D'Arcy, Mark Fleming, and Milad Odabaei. Mark has become a dear friend and generous interlocuter whom I turned to at different stages in the writing of this book. For several years now, Michael D'Arcy has helped me think about symbolic life and the collective unconscious; and I am all the better for his company and gift of intellectual and heartfelt friendship. Stefania Pandolfo has been an invaluable source of inspiration and support throughout the years, and I am always edified by the probity of her thought and her generous, dialogic spirit. I am particularly indebted to her for her steadfast support during my postdoctoral fellowship. Rudolf Mrázek, whose feedback on the book I value enormously, has long been an inspiration. I also would like to thank Kriss Ravetto, Robert Crews, Wali Ahmadi, and William Sherman.

In the Anthropology Department at UC Davis, it is my good fortune to have colleagues who are as intellectually probing and expansive as they are kind. Marisol de la Cadena has become a deeply engaging friend, one who said from the beginning that this manuscript should be a Duke book. I thank her for the gift of intellectual friendship and thinking-with that she embodies. Li Zhang is a wonderful friend and mentor whose support has made my time at Davis pleasurable and who has offered both intellectual and much-needed practical advice. Cristiana Giordano has been a dear friend since my arrival in Davis. Our friendship, rooted in a shared love of psychoanalysis and other creative openings, has been an ongoing source of inspiration and intellectual companionship. But just as often, I've turned to her with questions that have nothing to do with work, but rather about life and moving through it. Suzana Sawyer, who I am lucky to call my friend, gave me careful and finely tuned feedback and helped me articulate and give shape to my introduction. I am especially grateful for our shared candor and ability to think across conceptual, historical, and artistic lines of flight.

I would also like to thank James Smith, who has always made time to offer me support while I learned to navigate the numerous processes that both an academic profession and the world of publishing entail, and for always doing so with warm humor and friendship. Tim Choy has been a sensitive, intuitive friend whose company has been both enriching and calming. I value all of our talks, and our walks. Alan Klima, whose own work and prose are an inspiration for me, has been a steadfast colleague whom I've turned to for help and support, in matters of thought and critical edges but also in navigating institutional demands. The graduate and undergraduate students at UC Davis continually push me to think more clearly and broadly, and their enthusiasm for new ideas and no-nonsense exchange has been a source of joy and continual surprise.

I have been fortunate to be surrounded by family and a community that values the written and spoken word and the place of literature in social life. For passing on this wisdom, I thank my immediate family, aunts and uncles, and a very special group of elderly scholars who gather every week without fail to discuss history, language, and culture. They have generously invited me to participate in those conversations, which have given me a new prism through which to understand the legacies of diasporic and intellectual history that unfold before us. For that opening, I especially thank my father. Kiren Chaudhry left this world far too soon, but the spirit of vigorous debate and thought she embodied continues to shape my understanding of global events and pedagogy.

My editor at Duke, Elizabeth Ault, believed in this project and its long conceptual arc, helping me to clarify the stakes and giving me both warm support and good cheer when I most needed to banish doubt. I am also grateful to her for securing two incredible anonymous readers, whose feedback and incisive comments shaped the second draft, especially the introduction and epilogue. I have not been able to do justice to all of their probity, but I am grateful for their deep and moving engagements. I thank my project editor Livia Tenzer for her attention and help with the preparation of the manuscript and all the details and fine-tuning that process requires. I also thank Benjamin Kossak for his care and help with the final preparation of the manuscript. I would also like to thank Diana Witt for her meticulous work on the index.

I began writing this book in the British Library in London, then started it again a few years later in the forested countryside, where I finished the initial and final draft. For opening that world of natural wonder and for their very generous support throughout the years I thank Adele and Richard Holder. Their kindness, our shared walks and conversations has become a source of joy but also a reminder that things can always be otherwise, and that good humor goes a long way in translating the differences of history and culture.

My parents, Naim and Kawkaba Mojaddedi, have been an inspiration for so long that it feels impossible to articulate precisely what, where, and how. I thank them for instilling in me a critical spirit and love of the written word. My mother has given me a sense of courage in the face of power and history; she has shaped the prism through which I have come to understand life and all its transitoriness as, indeed, shelter for the night. In many ways, my attention to language comes from my father's insistence, for as long as I can remember, that it matters a great deal and that in and across language(s) we learn to think and learn from others. I can think of no greater gift than this. At some point, my parents stopped asking when the book would be finished. Instead, they began to ask, vaguely and gently, "How goes the work?" My brothers, Yaser and Salem Mojaddedi, struck a more direct tone and asked when this would all finally be finished. I thank them and Zuhra Ayubzai for the kind of encouragement and banter only siblings can get away with. Jeannie Lee has been a steadfast friend, always there when I needed her in both quiet moments and times of uncertainty. Patricia Kubala is a rarity: a friend whose care extends into the very questions and predicaments that shape my thinking. I'm thankful for her unwavering support, her encouragement, and readiness to celebrate all of life's events, no matter how ordinary or momentous. Little Chucha barked at me indefatigably and hated every moment I spent behind a laptop instead of chasing her around. She reminds me every day of how precious the time and space we share with our kindred animals can be. I would especially like to thank her fairy godmother, Mary Schweska.

Krystyna Holder, you are on an alternate plane. This book and so much more would not have been possible without the endless support, imaginative courage, and gift of wonder you've given me. You shine light wherever you go, into people's lives and the smallest spaces between them. Keep being the gift you are.

Notes

PROLOGUE. OPEN WINDOWS AND HOUSES

1   Nadia and all the other names that appear in this book, including those of military bases and camps, are pseudonyms.

2   Benjamin, "Little History of Photography," in *Selected Writings*, vol. 2, part 2, 510.

3   Benjamin, "A Berlin Chronicle," in *Reflections*, 14.

4   Benjamin, "A Berlin Chronicle," in *Reflections*, 11.

5   Le Corbusier, *Towards a New Architecture*, 120.

6   Benjamin, *One-Way Street*, 47.

7   Le Corbusier, *Towards a New Architecture*, 114.

8   Carpentier, Prologue to "The Kingdom of This World" (1993), 28.

9   Carpentier, *The Kingdom of This World* (1957), 10.

10 Benjamin, "A Berlin Chronicle," 10.

11 Benjamin, *The Arcades Project*, 406.

12 "Shipment of Goods to Afghanistan: Equipment + Material Required for Public Works," L/P&S/12/599, Political and Secret Department Records, India Office Records, British Library, London.

13 "Supply of Goods to Afghanistan: Window Glass," L/P&S/12/608, and "Supply of Goods for Afghanistan: Horse Shoes etc.," L/P&S/12/613, India Office Records, British Library.

14 The Afghan government ordered 77 long tons (172,480 lbs.) of grade A and B window glass and 16,000 yards of window screens.

15 "Supply of Goods to Afghanistan: House Paint," L/P&S/12/636, India Office Records.

16 Arendt, *On Violence*, 4.

17 For Benjamin, in the face of money, social relations are lit up only to crumble: "All close relationships are lit up by an almost intolerable, piercing clarity in which they are scarcely able to survive. For on the one hand, money stands ruinously at the center of every vital interest, but on the other, this is the very barrier before which almost all relationships halt; so, more and more, in the natural as in the moral sphere, unreflecting trust, calm, and health are disappearing." Benjamin, *One-Way Street*, 55–56.

18   Freud, *Civilization and Its Discontents*, 38.

19   McLuhan, *Understanding Media*, 19.

20   Quoted in Barthes, *Camera Lucida*, 20.

21   Benjamin cited in Buck-Morss, *The Origin of Negative Dialectics*, 106.

22   Benjamin, *The Arcades Project*, 532.

23   Farrokhzad, "Gift," *AllPoetry*, accessed April 13, 2025, https://
        allpoetry.com/poem/14330518-Gift-by-Forough-Farrokhzad.

24   Barthes, "The Death of the Author."

INTRODUCTION. CRACKS AND DETOURS

This chapter's opening epigraph is an English translation of the last
lines of the poem "Die beiden Gulden" (The two coins) by Friedrich Rückert. These are, in turn, Rückert's rendition of one of the
Maqâmât of the twelfth-century poet al-Hariri of Basra, in modern-
day Iraq. The quotation and its original source appear as the last
sentence of Freud's *Beyond the Pleasure Principle*, 78.

1   In thinking about these questions, I draw inspiration from Kath-
        leen Stewart's *A Space on the Side of the Road*, a critical, poetic
        reimagining of the other and the ruins of postindustrial America
        as a site of proliferating signs, memories, and talk. Stewart urges
        us to consider how life in "an occupied, betrayed, fragmented, and
        finally deserted place might become not a corpus of abstract ideas
        or grounded traditions but a shifting and nervous space of desire
        immanent in lost and *re-membered* and imagined things" (17). How
        do we scan for signs to read and interpret? What are the "expressive
        signs in all their density, texture, and force" that are also natural-
        ized in the perception of "the world as it is" (20)? In thinking about
        the natural or primal and what is represented by it, *through* it, for
        example, the place of *pneuma*, breath, I am also inspired by Maria
        José de Abreu's *The Charismatic Gymnasium*, an account of the rise
        of "Catholic charismatics" in a setting where political practice,
        media, and bodies merge to reveal contemporary theological and
        political life.

2   I would like to be clear that the gap between the symbolic and real
        refers to the registers of experience either held apart or forcefully
        closed by language and signification. The metaphor of a crack is what
        emerges alongside, beyond, and despite that closure.

3   Fanon, *Black Skin, White Masks*.

4   The Lacanian subject is constitutively "bound up" in the process of
        signification. In "The Subversion of the Subject and the Dialectic of
        Desire in the Freudian Unconscious" he writes about this condition

of boundedness in relation to discourse and the real as the recipient of a cut: "The cut made by the signifying chain is the only cut that verifies the structure of the subject as a discontinuity in the real. If linguistics enables us to see the signifier as the determinant of the signified, analysis reveals the truth of this relationship by making holes in meaning the determinants of its discourse." Lacan, *Écrits*, 678. This is Lacan's attempt to understand discourse as false or fundamentally empty but also to transcend that, to say discourse is the structural bind by which "I" am fractured by language and thus a subject without knowledge that moves toward death.

5   Freud, *Beyond the Pleasure Principle*, 46.

6   For Lacan, the distinction between other(s) as people, objects of desire, ideological commitments, and relationships is distinct from the Other that constitutes the ground of symbolic life; that is, language and the possibility of signification. He famously captures this difference in the claim that "the unconscious is the Other's discourse," meaning that it is structured, enabled, and overdetermined not by what it seeks to possess, desires, or fears but by the very symbolic structure of language. See "The Instance of the Letter in the Unconscious, or Reason Since Freud," in *Écrits*, 436.

7   From 2002 to 2014 the Afghan economy was rocked by a huge influx of foreign money that was distributed in a storm of private contract awards to foreign and "50 percent Afghan National" business arrangements. At the same time, economic activity in the rural provinces and Kabul, including the activities of various politicians, was believed to be connected to global geopolitical interests. In general, economic activity was a metonym for larger political shifts and power relations.

8   On the destruction of public confidence in the banking sector see Emma Graham-Harrison, "Afghan Elite Ransacked $900m from Kabul Bank, Inquiry Finds," *The Guardian*, November 28, 2012, https://www.theguardian.com/world/2012/nov/28/afghan-elite -ransacked-kabul-bank.

9   De la Cadena and Blaser, *A World of Many Worlds*, 5.

10   In seeking to introduce a multiplicity of voices and conceptual registers, I am deeply inspired by Rudolf Mrázek's beautiful undertaking of ethnographic-historical writing as the dialogic form in which the cultural, national, philosophical, or epistemic others can be evoked, especially his evocation of the memories of Jakarta's aging intelligentsia in *A Certain Age*, which is a magisterial example of cultural history in the last decades of Dutch colonial rule and zooms in on the fragmented dreams, anxieties, and languages of desire with which its inhabitants imagine.

11   De Certeau, *Heterologies*, 3.

12   Lacan, *Écrits*, 421.

13   De Certeau, *Heterologies*, 51 (the first quotation is citing Lacan). In relation to practices of academic writing that signify the real, see Klima, *Ethnography #9*. This sense of writing as the space in which the real is conjured and represented but is always fiction informs my understanding of the forms of academic writing we engage in, but more importantly, reflects the idea that writing in Afghan society is a buttress for speech, logos, and other "real" phenomena that are never quite as they seem.

14   By invoking this distance that is moved through or "overcome" I refer to Barbara Johnson's analysis of the Derridean critique of phonocentrism and the sign. She underscores how deconstruction does not seek to reverse the speech/writing binary but rather to show that this conceptual binary and the ability to oppose the terms occurs on the basis of other binaries (presence/absence, immediacy/representation, inside/outside, signifier/signified) and that speech is *equally* (not *only*) structured by deferral and discontinuity. This structuring characterizes the differences that are language (not the difference between languages) and the possibility of signification as such. Johnson writes, "The very fact that a word is divided into a phonic *signifier* and a mental *signified*, and that, as Saussure pointed out, language is a system of differences rather than a collection of independently meaningful units, indicates that language as such is already constituted by the very distances and differences it seeks to overcome. To mean, in other words, is automatically *not* to be. As soon as there is meaning, there is difference. Derrida's word for this lag inherent in any signifying act is *différance*, from the French verb *différer*, which means both 'to differ' and 'to defer.'" Johnson, "Translator's Introduction," ix.

15   Lacan, *Écrits*, 431.

16   Biehl, *Vita*, 18.

17   Pandolfo, *Knot of the Soul*, 4.

18   Golestaneh, *Unknowing and the Everyday*, 5.

19   A masterful example of this kind of ethnographic undertaking is James Siegel's *Naming the Witch*, an analysis of contemporary witchcraft accusations in Indonesia not as the "other" of modern disenchantment but as violence arising from state crises and the failure of socially determined thought to account for death, accident, and dissolution; in other words, as the ambiguous and sometimes violent confrontation between thought (including the fantasy that one can think about the world in order to fully understand it) and the place of detours in collective life.

20   On the role of primordial symbols as a form of political speech and dialectic recognition see Aretxaga, "Dirty Protest."

21   The phrase "itinerary of a signifier" (*Écrits*, 7) appears in Lacan's seminar on Poe's "The Purloined Letter" both as a metaphor for the

movement of the stolen letter in the plot as well as in reference to Freud's conception of the subject not as an ontological reality but as a site, scene, or juncture that receives its arbitrary determination through the process of signification. I also invoke this phrase to gesture toward Lacan's more formal theorization of this process, depicted in his famous graph of subjectivity. The inverted U-shaped image represents a structural process best described as an itinerary through which meaning and subjectivity emerge retrospectively and in relation to others. See Lacan, "The Subversion of the Subject and the Dialectic of Desire in the Freudian Unconscious," in *Écrits*, 681–92.

22   On this and other matters related to modern technology and modernity in Afghanistan see Mojaddedi, "Notes on the Wire," 49–72.

23   Dolar, "On Rumors, Gossip and Related Matters," 146.

24   Dolar, "On Rumors, Gossip and Related Matters," 147.

25   Dolar, "On Rumors, Gossip and Related Matters," 147.

26   Taussig, *Shamanism, Colonialism, and the Wild Man*, 4.

27   Deleuze, *The Logic of Sense*.

28   Mehlman, "The Floating Signifier," 24.

29   Fanon, *Black Skin, White Masks*, 89–90, 91.

30   In thinking about this in relation to narrative practice and an embodied history of political memory, I am also inspired by Allen Feldman's *Formations of Violence*. Feldman explores oral history in Northern Ireland as a site of ideological contention, tracing symbolic, material, and narrative practices that forge political agency. His insight shapes my own effort to integrate sociopolitical and economic contexts with the words, sacrifices, bodies, and desires of my interlocuters.

        On the failure and volatility of representation as a dialogic act see also Mitchell, "Representation," in *Critical Terms for Literary Study*.

31   Siegel, *Naming the Witch*, 1–2.

32   Cadava, *Words of Light*, xviii.

33   Scarry, *The Body in Pain*, 36.

34   This perception of Sami contrasts with that of Pierre Rivière, a twenty-year-old French peasant who killed his mother, sister, and brother and left behind a written statement "in whose beauty some were to see a proof of rationality (and hence grounds for condemning him to death) and others a sign of madness (and hence grounds for shutting him up for life)." See Foucault, *I, Pierre Rivière*, xi.

35   More generally, in Afghan trials during this era, the idea of criminal action was increasingly understood as part of a representational complex in which writing, case file photos, and the meaninglessness of the defendants' oral testimony constitute a hermeneutic complex of guilt. That guilt is read through material and oral signs and the idea, held by most judges, that repetition-compulsion (that is, the defendant's repetitive thoughts and behaviors) are the surest index of

how enemies work against the state and of more insurgent violence to come.

36   I think of this law that inscribes itself on the body of the prisoner as a moment of "justice" without meaning, akin to what Andreas Gailus describes as the machine in Kafka's "In the Penal Colony," which "embodies the fantasy of a symbolism without semantic mediation, of a supreme and transcendent language so pure as to be untranslatable into ordinary words. Gailus, "Lessons of the Cryptograph," 297.

37   Fanon, *Black Skin, White Masks*, 86.

38   Pandolfo, "Testimony in Counterpoint."

39   Derrida, *Of Grammatology*, 112. For Derrida the material violence of writing as historical practice masks two more primary levels of "arche-violence" in which the classification of thought and inscription of difference are achieved. To illustrate this, he turns to Claude Lévi-Strauss's *Tristes Tropiques*, where scenes of "writing" and its absence fail to secure the very distinction as such.

40   Dolar, *A Voice and Nothing More*, 43.

41   I use *Persian* throughout this book to refer to the language spoken in Afghanistan, Iran, and elsewhere, following standard English usage. In Afghanistan, speakers typically use the endonym *Farsi*, while the Afghan state officially refers to the language as *Dari*, a term introduced in the 1960s. Neither *Farsi* nor *Dari* denotes a distinct language. The term *Persian* provides a consistent rendering of this shared linguistic tradition across regional and political boundaries.

42   On what remains of this "voice as the object" after the violence of phonocentrism and the deconstructive turn that "tends to deprive the voice of its ineradicable ambiguity by reducing it to the ground of (self-)presence" see Dolar, *A Voice and Nothing More*, 42.

43   Kristeva, *Black Sun*, 51.

44   Benjamin, *Illuminations*, 76, 77, 78.

45   De Man, "Conclusions," 33. To be part of this exile also means, as de Certeau describes, that every autonomous order is founded on what it represses and tries to exclude, and the remainder that "re-infiltrates the place of origins," is the contradiction that lies between original and translation but also between self and other. De Certeau, *Heterologies*, 4.

46   Kristeva, *Black Sun*, 53.

CHAPTER 1. WHAT'S THE USE BETWEEN DEATH AND GLORY?

This chapter's title is taken from a 2005 song by Babyshambles. The chapter's third epigraph quotes the words of Salar, a failed suicide bomber who was tried in the same court as Sami. Salar, who was also illiterate, spoke this line in response to the charges against him, charges he believed were the direct, material result of writing rather than a reality formally represented through writing and his case file.

1   It is a cultural taboo for Sunnis and Shias to marry, though doing so is not prohibited by Islamic law (*shariat*). The same predicament arises in chapter 2, in the supposed but contested marriage of Sohrab and Soraya.

2   Foucault rejects the idea of a language of the body politic as the discourse of reason in his history of madness, which likewise entails a language that can be a "metaphor or metaphysics of the political realm." Derrida, *Writing and Difference*, 34.

3   Berger, *About Looking*, 35.

4   The meaning and aura of law do not lie beyond the law but come from the mechanical production of that illusion. In his reading of Franz Kafka's "In the Penal Colony," Andreas Gailus illustrates the tension in the opposition of archaic and enlightened justice, showing how both have a conception of law and justice and the fantasy of symmetry between crime and punishment through the "veridical subsumption" of a particular case under universal law. The difference between them is a matter of writing: For Enlightenment justice these are regulative ideas that orient the system but can never be satisfied whereas a premodern machine (expressed in the story by the power of the Old Commandment) converts that principle through writing on the body into physical principles without semantic mediation and therefore, in the penal colony, "radicalizes the Enlightenment conception of justice to the point of crisis." Gailus writes: "From this series of erasures and fusions emerges a Law devoid of any specific meaning. The machine embodies the fantasy of a symbolism without semantic mediation, of a supreme and transcendent language so pure as to be untranslatable into ordinary words." Gailus, "Lessons of the Cryptograph," 297.

5   For Walter Benjamin, the concept of aura implies both a transcendent distance and autonomy. Examples are objects of nature that are autonomous of human agency or intervention and serve as the basis for legitimacy that emanates from a remote origin to historical understanding and appreciation. He states, "The authenticity of a thing is the essence of all that is transmissible from its beginning, ranging from its substantive duration to its testimony to the history which it has experienced. Since the historical testimony rests on the authenticity, the former, too, is jeopardized by reproduction when substantive duration ceases to matter." Benjamin, "The Work of Art in the Age of Mechanical Reproduction," in *Illuminations*, 221.

6   The whole complex was designed to hold five thousand prisoners in total, but under the US-backed former government it contained

more than ten thousand inmates, at least two thousand of them suspected of belonging to the Taliban. Some of the cells, despite poor
sewage and sanitation conditions, held up to twenty-two people.
The Taliban now runs the prison, and many soldiers have even
become the unlikely caretakers of their own former cells, now filled
with a new cohort of men arrested for their suspected collaboration
with US/NATO forces or for serving in the former Afghan military.
See "Once Inmates, Taliban Now in Charge of a Kabul Prison," *Al
Jazeera*, September 14, 2021, https://www.aljazeera.com/gallery
/2021/9/14/inmates-taliban-charge-kabul-prison. On the failures
of a large-scale, $16 million contract to rehabilitate the complex see
Special Inspector General for Afghanistan Reconstruction (SIGAR),
Pol-i-Charkhi Prison.

7   See Siegel, *Naming the Witch*, 78–79. For Siegel, the force of the
witch's voice stems from its demonstration of a nondialectical power
that others (including those in positions of power) do not have
access to. The Zuni witch speaks as a witch and makes his power palpable through his speech by expressing a "foreign power" that speaks
through him and "asserts a nondialectical possibility" (217).

8   Siegel, *Naming the Witch*, 43.

9   Siegel, *Naming the Witch*, 43.

10   For a comprehensive database of suicide attacks from 1982 to 2015
see the University of Chicago's Chicago Project on Security and
Threats, accessed April 12, 2025, https://cpost.uchicago.edu/about
/. See also Watson Institute for International and Public Affairs at
Brown University, "Costs of War," accessed April 12, 2025, https://
watson.brown.edu/costsofwar/.

11   In "Critique of Violence" Benjamin describes the origin of law as the
other and the signifier of fate: "For if violence, violence crowned by
fate, is the origin of law, then it may be readily supposed that where
the highest violence, that over life and death, occurs in the legal system, the origins of law jut manifestly and fearsomely into existence."
Benjamin, *Selected Writings*, vol. 1, 242.

12   In the snowy winter of 1842, when British and East India Company
forces were retreating from Kabul on what is now the Mahipar Highway, they were ambushed by marksmen from the mountains and lost
eighteen thousand troops. See William Dalrymple, "The Ghosts of
Gandamak," *New York Times*, May 8, 2010, https://www.nytimes
.com/2010/05/09/opinion/09dalrymple.html.

13   Neither Sami nor the judges mentioned the deadly suicide and gun
attack that had taken place at the hotel on June 28, 2011, almost a
year before Sami's own attempt. That attack and its brazen tactics

foreshadowed similar attacks in following years when restaurants, businesses, and bustling markets became easy targets across the city. The attackers, armed with assault rifles, grenades, suicide vests, and antiaircraft weapons, launched a coordinated assault on multiple fronts.

14 Baudrillard, *The Spirit of Terrorism*.

15 On the proliferation of image-signs, and how the televisual representation of violence depicts while also displacing its embodied, material effects see Baudrillard, *The Gulf War Did Not Take Place*. Image-events are understood as images to which violence is added to produce horror (awe, fascination, shock): "Rather than the violence of the real being there first, and the *frisson* of the image being added to it, the image is there first, and the *frisson* of the real is added." Baudrillard, *The Spirit of Terrorism*, 29. The question of what happens to the "real event" transforms into a question of understanding the realm of a "fiction surpassing fiction" and thus an imaginary and symbolic moment whose violence is purer and more disturbing than the resurgence of the real. (Baudrillard invokes Borges here, and I also think of "The Garden of Forking Paths.")

16 See also Butler, "Contingent Foundations."

17 On April 7, 2013, a catastrophic airstrike killed seventeen civilians (including twelve children) in Shigal District. This occurred after a February coalition airstrike killed ten civilians (five of them children) in the same district, leading President Karzai to forbid Afghan forces from calling for NATO air support.

18 On the execution of a worker on the Machalgho Dam project in Paktia Province, which has a river as important as the Kunar River and is caught in the regional politics of hydropower, see Mujib Mashal, "What Iran and Pakistan Want from the Afghans: Water," *Time*, December 2, 2012, https://world.time.com/2012/12/02/what-iran-and-pakistan-want-from-the-afghans-water. See also "Taliban Claim to Be in Control of Machalgho Dam Project," *Ariana News*, August 18, 2020, https://www.ariananews.af/taliban-claim-to-be-in-control-of-machalgho-dam-project/.

19 Siegel, *Naming the Witch*, 9.

20 Siegel, *Naming the Witch*, 10.

21 Johnson, "Melville's Fist," 595.

22 Deleuze, *The Logic of Sense*, 8.

23 On the double axis of semiotic representation between the maker and receiver—that is, the "axis of representation" and the "axis of communication"—see Mitchell, "Representation."

24 To discern difference is not only to see how things are empirically different from each other on an extrinsic basis. It is also to

understand what Deleuze formulates as the process through which something "distinguishes itself" from that which does not "distinguish itself from it." To illustrate this, he offers the image of a flash of lightning. Lightning occurs in an instant and distinguishes itself from the dark sky even as it continues to trail the sky. The sky does not appear in the flash, nor does it escape its light. It does nothing. Deleuze expresses this as the postulate that "one does not flee that which flees it." Deleuze, *Difference and Repetition*, 28.

25   Said, *The World, the Text, and the Critic*, 15.

26   Lacan, *Écrits*, 7.

27   Miller, "Lacan's Antigone," 1.

28   Lacan, *Écrits*, 6. This chain that binds and orients is most powerfully evoked by Lacan in his seminar on Poe's "The Purloined Letter," where the formative unconscious work achieved through repetition-compulsion is tied directly to the place of a signifying chain and its principle of movement. He writes, "For the signifier is a unique unit of being which, by its very nature, is the symbol of but an absence. This is why we cannot say of the purloined letter that, like other objects, it must be or not be somewhere but rather, that unlike them, it will be and will not be where it is wherever it goes." Lacan, *Écrits*, 17.

29   Spivak, "Translator's Preface," xvii.

30   By "trajectory" I am also invoking the idea of a detour. For Freud, Thanatos (the death drive) reveals a larger, unconscious goal and the sense of being driven "toward a certain even though not always comprehended goal" that seeks to restore the prior. The tension between beginning and end (or between life and death drives) is sustained by the play of detours and by the movement toward the end under the pressure of delay and alongside a desire to ward off external harm. Freud describes this as follows: "For a long time, perhaps, living substance was thus being constantly created afresh and easily dying, till decisive external influences altered in such a way as to oblige the still surviving substance to diverge ever more widely from its original course of life and to make ever more complicated detours before reaching its aim of death. These circuitous paths to death, faithfully kept to by the conservative instincts, would thus present us today with the picture of the phenomena of life." Freud, *Beyond the Pleasure Principle*, 46. In literary theory the idea of a detour as a circuitous deferral of the ending is crucial to the understanding of a narrative plot as a desire-sustaining structure overdetermined by the "end" of a text but nonetheless made possible through "the way in which metonymy and metaphor serve one another," in a logic not unlike that of Freud's two drives. Brooks, "Freud's Masterplot," 295.

31   Brooks, *Reading for the Plot*, 23.

32   Literary journalism calls for a similar ethics. In an essay entitled "On Morality," Joan Didion depicts the scene of a fatal car accident in Death Valley and a talc miner who decides to stay with the victim's body throughout the night. He watches over the dead man so that animals do not prey on his body and, in doing so, fulfills a primal duty to the dead that Didion considers a singular and powerful manifestation of the moral conscience in modern life. Didion, "On Morality," in *Slouching Towards Bethlehem*.

33   Brooks, *Reading for the Plot*, 29.

34   This is what Barthes and Duisit, following Valéry, call "dilatory signs" in "An Introduction to the Structural Analysis of Narrative," 249.

CHAPTER 2. RUMORS OF LOVE

The remarkable dialogue between two dogs, Berganza and Cipión, in this chapter's first epigraph is part of a longer meditation on the place and function of speech in social life in Miguel de Cervantes's "The Novel of the Colloquy of the Dogs" in his *Exemplary Novels*. The story follows "The Novel of the Deceitful Marriage," which deconstructs both the place of desire in marriage and the possibility of knowing the other as a love object. The dogs reference that story and their reflection on rumor and speech can be read as a discourse enabled both by the failure of social institutions and the gift of speech they possess but that also possess them.

1   Sohrab was led to believe the woman's name was Soraya, but it was actually Razia.

2   The word for a hatchback, or any car with extra room in the trunk, is the same as for the part of the house, usually in the back, in which non-related male guests stay apart from the women and the main residence.

3   The verse that is often cited, which is probably the one Sohrab is referring to is, "And one of His signs is that He created for you spouses from among yourselves so that you may find comfort in them. And He has placed between you compassion and mercy. Surely in this are signs for people who reflect." *Holy Quran*, 30:21.

4   The polysemic notion of *ibar*, which means sign, clue, a trace structure, but also to close the gap between persons, to bridge, translate, or transcend comes from Ibn Khaldun's philosophy of time and history. See Mahdî, *Ibn Khaldûn's Philosophy of History*.

5   For Deleuze the importance (and the "distribution") of paradox is contrary to that of hegemonic doxa and the forms of "sense" we attribute to knowledge. Paradox moves in a nomadic space, and often in opposite directions that do not converge on any single or sovereign moment of sense-making. But in Sohrab's struggle to think of and try

to arrive at this sovereign moment (only to find himself adrift), we do not see what Deleuze describes as the "gift of meaning" that emerges in the "guise of the two simultaneous senses or directions" when we lose common and good sense and the moment when "language attains its highest power." Deleuze, *The Logic of Sense*, 79.

6   Lacan, "The Mirror Stage," in *Écrits*, 75–82.

7   Jalalabad is the capital of Nangarhar Province and the largest city in eastern Afghanistan.

8   Taliban forces carried out an operation against is in February 2023. Prior to the Taliban's takeover of the government, during the years of their insurgency against Afghan government forces, the neighborhood's proximity to the Logar Highway in the south both attracted an influx of new residents from Logar and Paktia and turned it into the route insurgents took to reach central Kabul.

9   In May 2004 the United States Agency for International Development (USAID) awarded a $21.1 million contract to the US firm Technologists, Inc., to develop three industrial parks in Afghanistan, including the one in Bagram, to increase employment for the local population and reduce the cost of entry into new markets for manufacturers. The Special Inspector General for Afghanistan Reconstruction (SIGAR) reported in July 2016 that the contractor did not develop the industrial parks as agreed in their contract. See Special Inspector General for Afghanistan (SIGAR), *Bagrami Industrial Park*.

10   Giorgio Agamben understands sovereignty in relation to its exception, and thus in the power to decide both the exception and control over life and death: "The state of exception is not a special kind of law (like the law of war); rather, insofar as it is a suspension of the juridical order itself, it defines law's threshold or limit concept." Agamben, *State of Exception*, 4.

11   Benjamin, "A Berlin Chronicle," in *Reflections*, 11.

12   For a brilliant critique of Occidentalism not as the opposite or inverse of Orientalism but as its condition of possibility see Coronil, "Beyond Occidentalism."

13   These events resonated with a general media discourse on Afghan lawlessness. In the global mediascape, the idea that the political violence occurring was at the old "nexus between Islamist militancy, crime, opium and Kabul's feeble grip on power," represents the idea that for centuries a self-destructive drive has been implacably at work. See "Afghanistan's Wild West," *The Wider Image*, Reuters, June 11, 2015, https://widerimage.reuters.com/story/afghanistans-wild-west.

14   Mrázek, *Engineers of Happyland*, 67.

15   I borrow this term and concept from Wilder, *The French Imperial Nation-State*.

16   In the Indies this "putting matters" in place was a process of urban and architectural standardization beginning in 1909, after which the design of government and nongovernment buildings was subject to an official standard. Mrázek, *Engineers of Happyland*, 67–68.

17   Jameson, *Postmodernism*, 18.

18   Jameson, *Postmodernism*, 40.

19   Benjamin "A Berlin Chronicle," 609.

20   The siege of the traffic police building was sustained by rockets, hand grenades, and suicide vests and only ended when the ANSF killed the men in a grueling battle that left police officers and civilians dead.

21   This security transition was completed by summer 2014, when Afghan forces assumed full responsibility for national security.

22   Feldman, *Formations of Violence*, 4.

23   Mrázek, *A Certain Age*, 3.

24   The Arabic word *tayammum* denotes the Islamic act of a dry ritual of purification using sand or dirt when no running or clean water is available.

25   In thinking about the city in relation to social violence and new forms of movement and desire, I am also invoking Walter Benjamin's description of its scenes of reproduction and ruin; in other words, the layers of time, material form, and disguise that we experience as "new" or out of place: "To construct the city topographically— tenfold and a hundredfold—from out of its arcades and its gateways, its cemeteries and bordellos, its railroad stations . . . just as formerly it was defined by its churches and its markets. And the more secret, more deeply embedded figures of the city: murders and rebellions, the bloody knots in the network of the streets, lairs of love, and conflagrations." Benjamin, *The Arcades Project*, 83, note C1,8.

26   Pol e Sorkh is a middle- to upper-class neighborhood in western Kabul.

27   Benjamin, *The Arcades Project*, 405, note L1,3.

28   Lacan, "The Split Between the Eye and the Gaze," in *The Four Fundamental Concepts of Psychoanalysis*, 73. Crucially, for Lacan, no gaze or fantasy of the gaze as a reflection of consciousness can fully see because insofar as "this relation is constituted by way of vision, and ordered in the figures of representation, something slips, passes, is transmitted, from stage to stage, and is always to some degree eluded in it—that is what we call the gaze" (72).

29   On the relationship between terrorism and symbolic or sacrificial death see Baudrillard, *The Spirit of Terrorism*.

30   The US/NATO Green Zone occupied the center of the city in the residential neighborhood of Wazir Akbar Khan, which fueled anger among the locals who felt betrayed and like "both sides" or "all sides" were embedded around them.

31 Dolar, *A Voice and Nothing More*, 13.

32 Dolar, *A Voice and Nothing More*, 15. Following Wittgenstein's propositional steps, Dolar situates the voice on a similar ladder of instrumentality: The voice begins by possessing an aura much like the aura Benjamin ascribes to historical art. It is then experienced as an instrument or medium of meaning and finally as the materiality that is opposed (and thus discarded) in favor of the ideality of meaning that transcends it in the last rung. This teleology of voice is also the theology of logos as the Word of Christ is mediated through John the Baptist such that his voice diminishes as the Word, logos (and the progression of the soul) increases. It becomes the case that "the progression from the voice to meaning is the progression from a mere—albeit necessary—mediator to the true Word: there is only a small step from linguistics to theology." Dolar, *A Voice and Nothing More*, 16.

33 For Dolar it is important to think about this proximity (the lack of lack) as a historical development of modernity (that raises the question of what the modern subject experiences) parallel to developments in literary history. He suggests that the Lacanian notion of the uncanny stems from knowing too much. Historically, this kind of excess emerges after the waning of fantastic literature, a genre that opens with "the advent of modernity and its scientific background" and recedes with the emergence of psychoanalysis. Thus, it is more accurate to say psychoanalysis replaces the genre to deal directly with what it indirectly suggests such that "psychoanalysis appears to be the most fantastic of all fantastic talks—the ultimate horror story." Dolar, "'I Shall Be with You,'" 23.

34 On this point see also Mehlman, "The Floating Signifier."

35 Dolar, "'I Shall Be with You,'" 22.

36 Lacan, "The Subversion of the Subject," in *Écrits*.

37 Berman, *All That Is Solid Melts into Air*, 164.

38 Even though nearly 80 percent of the electricity was imported from neighboring countries like Uzbekistan, the national utility provider, Da Breshna Sherkat, could not ensure steady production or collect payment from some of the wealthiest users in the country, a staggering debt that totaled $230 million in 2012.

39 Pol e Sorkh is part of the third police jurisdiction and has numerous roadside bazaars, apartment buildings, wedding halls, and perhaps most importantly, a wide paved street that runs neatly through it, connecting the neighborhood to the city center and other commercial areas. The main road, which Sohrab used to get into and out of the neighborhood, was reconstructed in 2016 with $4.49 million from the World Bank's Afghanistan Reconstruction Trust Fund,

resulting in 3.35 kilometers and 15.5 meters of smooth concrete. In 2014, the five-year, $90 million Kabul Urban Transport Efficiency Improvement Project program incorporated Pol e Sorkh into a new large-scale network of infrastructure rehabilitation with the goal of enhancing traffic capacity, the number of people with all-weather roads, and the condition of major road networks. See World Bank. *Kabul Urban Transport Efficiency Improvement Project*, Project ID: P131864, https://projects.worldbank.org/en/projects-operations /project-detail/P131864.

40   The attack targeting his convoy destroyed several neighborhood stores, killed three people, and injured at least thirty others, including six of his bodyguards and a TOLO news reporter.

41   For Feldman, the imaginary configuration of mimetic, antipathic, and contiguous spatial relations organizes the ideological understanding of violence, the place of the sectarian murder victim within an imaginary of bodies (parts of a "disordering whole"), and the transition from an in-between place to an ordered place. Thus, the act of talking about violence is a reply to the targeting of victims based on "spatial and sensory codes of 'telling'" and it "constructs the victim's mimesis with an assumed space." Feldman, *Formations of Violence*, 78.

42   Feldman, *Formations of Violence*, 79.

43   I'd like to mark an important difference between how I understand the place of the symbolic order in a web of differentiation and how Feldman positions it as the other of the more spontaneous and immediate (or unmediated) Real. He distinguishes between the three Lacanian orders (Imaginary, Real, and Symbolic) and argues that lived violence occurs not in between the Symbolic and the Real (that is, between structure and event) but outside all symbolic mediation, and therefore violence is a force that can only be understood retrospectively as an excess and a diachronic feature of the Real rather than as the internal effect of symbolic life. See Feldman, *Formations of Violence*, 78–81. Yet, Feldman's own account of the dialectical progression of surrogate violence (focused most harrowingly in the new space of the body of the sectarian enemy-intruder-pollutant) that occurred after the British Army removed "no-go" barricades and zones in 1972 is legible only when the violence of "stiffing" is situated beyond its function of destabilizing "local territorial designations" and within a metonymic chain of violence and response. That chain inscribes identity and paramilitary power in social space, to be sure, but also within substitutive relations and therefore as a symbolic whole rather than its lack: a neighborhood for a country, a block for a neighborhood, a "no-go" zone for a series of blocks, a body for a "no-go" zone, a detachable body part for a full body, and so on. Thus, it is not

so much that serial violence exceeds symbolic understanding but that it reinscribes that symbolic understanding in increasingly intimate spaces that metonymically function as place amid the upheaval of urban warfare and counterinsurgency.

44 In isolating the voice as a "blind spot" in the possibility of meaning, it is crucial to disarticulate voice from theological truth and the truth of logos captured most palpably by the voice of God and the prophetic voice that is its substitute. Instead, as Dolar suggests, we need to disentangle voice from the progression to the true Word and from the "spontaneous theology, which goes hand in hand with a certain theology of the voice as the condition of revelation of the Word. We have to make our way in the opposite direction, as it were: to make a descent from the height of meaning back to what appeared to be mere means; to catch the voice as a blind spot of making sense, or a cast-off of sense. We have to establish another framework than that which spontaneously imposes itself with the link between a certain understanding of linguistics, teleology, and theology." Dolar, *A Voice and Nothing More*, 16.

45 The distinction between film and photography can be understood as the difference Christian Metz marks between a film playing on fetishism (it creates belief, duration, and a feeling of reality) versus a photograph that is stubbornly attached to the link between an image-moment and its referent and thus can become a fetish in itself. A photograph also has a fixed duration (that, following Peter Wollen, he describes as its "imposed reading time") and a place that is homey, close by, and found in domestic life. This is different from film's status as a collective, public form of entertainment. See Metz, "Photography and Fetish."

46 Barthes, *Camera Lucida*. The "timelessness" of the photograph can also be compared to the timelessness of the ruins Freud depicts in the urban metaphor of Rome in *Civilization and Its Discontents*. Meanwhile, in *Heterologies* de Certeau contrasts timelessness to historiography as a teleological endeavor. He contrasts history with psychoanalytic time which is the time of the drive, of crisis, interruption and the event as the enabling conditions for being and experience. For an analysis of the relationship between photography and death and its place in a mass-media society see Sontag, *On Photography*.

47 Metz, "Photography and Fetish," 84. On the unconscious fixation or halt before a feared absence and the kind of fear that becomes a fetish-attachment see Freud, "Fetishism," 214–19.

48 Metz, "Photography and Fetish," 84.
    For Jacques Rancière the distinction between the two is not always possible to maintain and what is initially felt as a *punctum* can

then function as part of the studium. He describes this as a splitting of the photograph from its subject. Referencing Lewis Hine's photograph of two institutionalized children, he writes that in confronting it, Barthes "must also operate a strange division at the very heart of what links the visual structure of this photograph to its subject—namely disproportion. Barthes writes: 'I . . . hardly see the monstrous heads and pathetic profiles (which belong to the *studium*); what I see . . . is the off-centre detail, the little boy's huge Danton collar, the girl's finger bandage'" (111). For Rancière, the details function here as "detachable elements . . . they correspond to a highly determinate notion: the Lacanian notion of the part object" (111) but they do not account for the effect of death the photograph has on us, a short-circuit he sees repeated in Barthes's confrontation with the 1865 photograph of Lewis Payne awaiting his execution. Rancière, *The Emancipated Spectator*, 111–12.

49   In confronting Koen Wessing's photographs (1979) of the Nicaraguan rebellion, Barthes finds a structural principle of discontinuity (the presence of two different but co-present series) that run through the photographs (revealed by small but powerful details such as the domestic bed sheet on the body of the dead son). For Barthes, these elements correspond to the "extension of a field" (the signifiers of a context, political culture, history and so on) that in turn generates interest based on an average of effects (the *studium*) and the *punctum* (or thing that shoots out of the studium, that is, the accident, uncanny moment) that disturbs or moves us. Barthes, *Camera Lucida*, 23–27.

50   On the relationship of this logic of lack *lacking* and the subject of psychoanalysis see Dolar, "'I Shall Be with You,'" 1991.

51   In the experience of fetish, the absence of something takes on a powerful meaning when lack is replaced by its opposite. Freud begins quite literally with a glance, recalling the case of a young man for whom "shine on the nose" was a fetish but, once translated into English from the boy's native language of German, the fetish revealed itself to be not the "Glanz auf der Nase" (shine on the nose) but a "glance at the nose" and thus a function of the gaze when stopped in a particular moment or on a particular object. Freud, "Fetishism," 214.

52   With regard to the gaze, this presence with an absence is akin to what Barthes describes after seeing an 1852 photograph of Napoleon's brother Jerome as the experience of looking at the eyes that looked at the emperor. Barthes, *Camera Lucida*, 3.

53   For Metz the photograph is like the fetish object and it becomes part of two distinct but inseparable series: It exists in a metaphoric order as a possession, the effect of mana and power, but it also exists in the

metonymic series of displacement, lack, fear, anxiety, and ultimately the overwhelming absence that must be crossed by presence (like the photo in the locket or amulet), even as that presence can only ever gesture toward something else.

On the relationship between vision and modernity and the rise of a new visual culture of observation, see Crary, *Techniques of the Observer*. For an account of the relationship between photographic representation and modernity, including colonial power and the uncanny reception of photographic representation, see Morris, *Photographies East*. On uncanniness in spirit photography, see Gunning, "Phantom Images and Modern Manifestations."

54 This is the mystery of what creates the effect of Barthes's *studium* insofar as every sign included means there are others necessarily left out of the frame.

55 The central power or force of the photograph for Barthes, like for Walter Benjamin, is the force of mechanical repetition to reproduce what would otherwise remain a singular existential and (now) absent or vanished event. Barthes, *Camera Lucida*, 4.

56 Derrida, *Monolingualism of the Other*, 22.

57 The irrepressible in thought and language is the forceful movement and dispersion of meaning within language. Derrida would say the same is true of philosophy, with its claim to be the literature of truth (distinguished from mere literature). This polysemic movement, akin to desire, carries gaps and absences, risking the loss of meaning or preventing the emergence of any single meaning over others. Derrida, *Dissemination*.

58 Johnson, "Translator's Introduction," xiv.

59 Derrida's interpretation of Freud's use of the "mystic writing-pad" as a metaphor for the unconscious reveals this linguistic structure (characterized by difference, delay, and dissimulation) in unconscious life where nothing is self-same and where difference is repressed in the illusion of conscious meaning and presence. Derrida, "Freud and the Scene of Writing," in *Writing and Difference*, 196–231.

60 For Deleuze the paradox of structure is the nonalignment between signifiers and signified (resulting in what Claude Lévi-Strauss calls the "floating signifier") but also a "floated signified," the unknown element (the "it") that has no fixed sense and fills the gap between two series that communicate through difference. This is a relation he describes as moving between the excessive "empty square" of signifying (the "place without an occupant") and the lack of "an occupant" in the signified unknown. Deleuze, *The Logic of Sense*, 50. Is this also the "it" in "rumor has it?"

CHAPTER 3. THE ALTERNATION OF WORLD AND WORD

This chapter's epigraph quotes William Kerr Fraser-Tytler, Confidential Despatch to the Secretary of State for Foreign Affairs, April 19, 1940, "Propaganda: British Measures for Propaganda in Afghanistan During War-Time," India Office Records, British Library.

1   Such rumors reflected wider imperial anxieties in the wake of the Russo-Japanese War of 1904–5, which had unsettled European confidence in the East and heightened suspicions about trans-Asian alliances and insurgent forms of solidarity.

2   Telegram from William Kerr Fraser-Tytler in Kabul to Major W. R. Hey in Simla, May 8, 1940, India Office Records, British Library.

3   Government of India, Department of External Affairs, excerpt from telegram to the secretary of state for India in Simla, October 3, 1941, "Propaganda: British Measures for Propaganda in Afghanistan During War-Time," India Office Records, British Library.

4   For Derrida, semantic and conceptual blurring is not only a matter of conceptual turbulence but is crucial to the relations of force and interpretive violence that characterize American interventionism and counterinsurgency. See Borradori, *Philosophy in a Time of Terror*, 105.

5   For Benjamin, the angel does not see single causes or events but the entire amalgamation of ruins. Benjamin, "Theses on the Philosophy of History," Thesis IX in *Illuminations*, 258.

6   De Man, "Conclusions," 33–34.

7   Following de Certeau it is better to describe this as the repressed that returns in the present "but does so surreptitiously . . . in the form of a phantom, in another scene." De Certeau, *Heterologies*, 3.

8   Benjamin imagines it as the provisional encounter with difference in the mode of supplemental and poetic license, where neither the original nor the translation are for the beholder. Hannah Arendt explains that this purer language is about the place of history in language and that, for Benjamin, language is not "the gift of speech which distinguishes man from other living beings, but, on the contrary, 'the world essence . . . from which speech arises.'" This is the language "whose existence we assume unthinkingly as soon as we translate from one language into another." Arendt, introduction to *Illuminations*, 49–50.

9   Benjamin, "The Task of the Translator," in *Illuminations*, 71. On the eternal life and renewal of language see p. 74.

10   On the way intention informs indigenous and nonindigenous claims to political leadership and the relationship between Spanish and Quechua see de la Cadena, *Earth Beings*, 20–22. On the relationship between translation and conceptual difference in contemporary

anthropological theory see Mojaddedi, "Where It Was, I Must Come into Being."

11   Benjamin, "The Task of the Translator," in *Illuminations*, 74.

12   Ibn Khaldûn's discourse on "group feeling" in *The Muqaddimah* is distinct from Sigmund Freud's understanding of ambivalence and guilt in relation to the dead, but it shares the assumption that warfare possesses a psychic force and requires a bond of relationality or sentiment that is then transgressed or destroyed. See Freud, "Mourning and Melancholia," in *On Murder, Mourning, and Melancholia*. This idea also emerges in Freud's understanding of group and totalitarian formations in *Group Psychology and the Analysis of the Ego*.

       Writing about contemporary warmaking, Juliet Flower MacCannell locates the violence of war in a relationship of exchange in which sacrifice is guaranteed through an extension of identification. Loss and sacrifice are concealed through the "structures of its leadership," which no longer figure the leader as a vengeful father but as a group leader radiating love. See MacCannell, "More Thoughts for the Times on War and Death."

13   Levi, *The Drowned and the Saved*, 88.

14   Giordano, *Migrants in Translation*, 15.

15   Typically, reconnaissance missions entailed military, intelligence, and paramilitary units being deployed to villages and people's homes in search of weapons or, in the case of Taliban-led missions, of evidence that locals collaborated with and aided US or NATO troops.

16   The word *rakat* (from *rakah*: "ensemble," "movement") is derived because the act of prayer has come to represent an excrescence of extremism, the moving channel and ensemble through which men are "inspired" to take up arms in unison. The inspiration achieved through collective prayer turns it into the medium that incites and galvanizes men to launch rockets. Or so the logic goes.

17   Deleuze, *Difference and Repetition*.

18   Several former translators told me that it was common to be dispatched sporadically based on need (for example, when a counterinsurgent movement was intensifying in one place). Sometimes this meant they were sent to areas where they did not speak the local language (either Persian or Pashto) or dialects (such as the Dardic language of Pashai that is spoken in parts of Kunar, Nangarhar, Kapisa, and other places).

19   For a rich account of this type of rocket, its production and uses in war and insurgency see: C. J. Chivers, "Mao's Rockets and the Eastern Afghan Border War," Parts I and II, *New York Times*, October 26 and 27, 2011, https://archive.nytimes.com/atwar.blogs.nytimes.com /2011/10/26/maos-rockets-and-the-eastern-afghan-border-war-part

-i/ and https://archive.nytimes.com/atwar.blogs.nytimes.com/2011
/10/27/maos-rockets-and-the-eastern-afghan-border-war-part-ii/.

20   For a history of the role of explosives and especially the car bomb's
global development, including by state intelligence services and
insurgent groups, see Davis, *Buda's Wagon*, 2008.

21   Chivers, "Mao's Rockets," *New York Times*.

22   In Kabul and across Afghanistan, there are still military-grade land
mines buried in agricultural fields, in water canals, and along dams,
power lines, and roads. There are at least fifty-two types designed
to detonate if anyone comes in close vicinity, including the Soviet-
produced air-dropped "butterfly" mines that are attractive to
children. Antipersonnel mines, activated by trip wires or pressure
plates, shoot hundreds of metal fragments when detonated. See
Fraser, "Landmines," 79; also Jain, "The Prosthetic Imagination."

23   In *The Writing of the Disaster* Maurice Blanchot reminds us of the
danger of granting importance to "isolated words" (106) and hence
of etymological seduction, or the irrational imposition of a filial logic
onto the relationship between words. We are attracted to etymology
for the "form of enigma" it preserves, and this enigma (the enigma of
the word, the root, the origin) is part of the desire to feel connected
to a linguistic and historical past and "the romanticism is to link the
recognition of the religious character of all language to ancient,
primordial times" (110).

24   Lindqvist, *A History of Bombing*, 42–43.

25   Sebald, *On the Natural History of Destruction*, 20. On the same logic
as it pertains to physical torture see Scarry, *The Body in Pain*.

26   Freud, "Timely Reflections on War and Death," in *On Murder,
Mourning, and Melancholia.*

27   The logic of indiscriminate violence in war was enshrined in international law in 1911 with a modification to Article 25 of the 1907
Hague Convention to allow for the dual possibility of destruction by
air and on the ground in accordance with a law of resemblance. This
transformed international law into a buttress for European geopolitical interests and created a culture of warfare based on the refusal
to distinguish between civilian and combatant populations. See also
Saint-Amour, "Bombing and the Symptom," 74.

28   See Morris, "Theses on Questions of War."

29   Weber, *Targets of Opportunity*.

30   This stratagem is partly rooted in the aspiration for isomorphism
between the US military and its enemies. It is part of a larger shift
in military-historical affairs based on the historical experiences
of counterinsurgency in Algeria, Vietnam, and Latin America.
It extends the FBI's 1956–71 Counter-Intelligence Program into a

global counterinsurgency that combines cultural propaganda with the "post-panoptic visuality" of the electronic and digital age. Known broadly as the "revolution in military affairs," it involves a transition from "platform-centric warfare" (centralized, hierarchical, closed system) to "network centric warfare," a flexible organization (with roots in multinational corporate practices) that produces value from the nearly instantaneous real-time sharing of information and enables knowledge of "all elements of battle space and time." Cebrowski and Garstka, "Network-Centric Warfare."

31 For Baudrillard the Gulf War inflicts violence on two orders: the real and the virtual. The latter suspends war in a hyperreal space of deterrence that is always less than war as we conventionally understand it but still destroys certain populations while enabling others to become televisual spectators to that destruction. Baudrillard, *The Gulf War Did Not Take Place*. The totalizing violence of this logic is also part of the representational drive for coherent understanding and a "phantasmatic whole" in contemporary anthropological theory. As Rosalind Morris writes, "The loss of an opposition between attachment and detachment (affective dependency and subjectivism versus rational distance and objectivity) becomes bearable, thereby enabling submission to a discourse of good and bad attachments. The structure of the (psychoanalytic) fetish is everywhere apparent in this argument: the substitution of a part object for a phantasmatic whole and the displacement of a binary difference, the investment of the object with the means to liberate one's energies (Latour is concerned with freedom)—what we might call, following Baudrillard, the political analogue to the libido." Morris and Leonard, *Returns of Fetishism*, 310.

Morris contends that in the 2003 Iraq War we see not desire or fantasy but a demand that the victim perform their own consent and willingness to be violated. This demand for mimesis, depicted in the Abu Ghraib torture photos, illustrates "the apparent vanishing of repulsion on the part of the observers and the torturers who via the circuitry of the digital camera, can anticipate possessing the very gaze that will observe them (selves) in the (slightly deferred) future." Morris, "The War Drive," 123.

32 This is different, however, from the crisis of representation Judith Butler describes in "Contingent Foundations" as the problem of subjectivity in the 1991 Gulf War and as the kind of will that "immediately translates into a deed." This is the utterance (or command) that becomes an action that destroys the possibility of a counterstrike or response. Her argument is that the agency produced by a disavowal of communicative relations becomes the "single origin" of action, and like the role of empire writ large, it acts unilaterally to remake

the world in its own self-image. Crucially, for both Baudrillard and Butler, this crisis of representation occurs in the age of real-time television and alongside the conflation of televisual perception with the on-the-air trajectory of the bomb, in which what is excluded from view is the point of impact (or "address").

33   In *Simulacra and Simulation* Baudrillard argues that there has been a revolution in the sign-function. He describes the historical transition (which he understands as occurring alongside changes from industrial to post-Fordist production) from a referential relationship between sign and referent (its signified) to a relationship between sign and endless indeterminacy. In *Symbolic Exchange and Death* he locates this revolution in the loss of the dialectic and argues, "Neither Saussure nor Marx had any presentiment of all this: they were still in the golden age of the dialectic of the sign and the real, which is at the same time the 'classical' period of capital and value. Their dialectic is in shreds, and the real has died of the shock value of acquiring this fantastic autonomy. Determinacy is dead, indeterminacy holds sway." Baudrillard, *Symbolic Exchange and Death*, 7.

34   On the logic of appearing to consent to be violated see Morris, "The War Drive."

35   On the centrality of the frontier (modern-day Afghanistan, Pakistan, and India) in the regional imagination see Ahmed, "Adam's Mirror."

36   'Government of India, Department of External Affairs, excerpt from telegram to the Secretary of State for India in Simla, October 10, 1941, "Propaganda: British Measures for Propaganda in Afghanistan During War-Time," India Office Records, British Library.

37   Letter from Fraser-Tytler in Kabul to Aubrey Metcalfe, April 20, 1939, India Office Records, British Library.

38   Giles Squire, the British Minister in Kabul, to Ernest Bevin, M.P., and Secretary of State for Foreign Affairs in London, August 30, 1946, The British Library.

39   On the presence of the "other" voice as the outcome of a structural operation Mladen Dolar writes "the voice is not taken as a hypothetical or mythical origin . . . not as a diffuse substance to be reduced to structure, a raw material to be tamed into phonemes, but, rather the opposite—it stands at the outcome of the structural operation." Dolar, *A Voice and Nothing More*, 35.

40   For an account of the role of ethnography in eighteenth-century Russia, when there was an epistemic shift in understanding the natural world and "national spirits," see Slezkine, "Naturalists Versus Nations." By the late eighteenth century all non-Christian, non-Russian subjects were referred to as *inorodtsy* (aliens), and Russian officials in the southern and eastern lands referred to entire populations as

"untamed horses," in a new hierarchical imaginary of the Other that resulted in mistranslations when the Russians interpreted mutual treaties known as *sherts* (from the Persian word for promise, *shart*) as symbolic pledges of submission. See Khodarkovsky, "'Ignoble Savages and Unfaithful Subjects.'"

In a curious letter to Karl Marx, Friedrich Engels describes the relationship between periodic Bedouin invasions and empire building and compares the Babylonian Empire of the Chaldeans to the formation of the "similar giant cities" of Agra, Delhi, Lahore, and Muttan by the "Afghan and/or Tartar invasions." This conflation of two populations and of ethnolinguistic difference with the signifier of a monolithic invader is precisely what the Russian fixation with its eastern and southern borderlands sought to undo and translate into clearer, ontological categories that could be known, written about, and conquered. See Friedrich Engels to Karl Marx, "On Religion," before May 28, 1853: https://marxists.architexturez.net/archive/marx/works/1853/letters/53_05_28.htm

41   The self–other dialectic is also reflected in Russia's literary search for its other, especially in the construction of Caucasia as a site of masculine and imperial prowess (for example, in Alexander Pushkin's poem "Prisoner of the Caucasus"). See Layton, *Russian Literature and Empire*, 84–85.

42   Jameson's literary typology is rooted in a relationship between the experience of capitalist modernity (embodied in the abstract first-world novel) and its peripheral reckoning (the visceral and organic third-world novel), a dichotomy that ignores the differences within and between literary traditions. Jameson, "Third-World Literature," 68.

43   During his family's years of exile in Istanbul, Mahmud Tarzī was exposed to Ottoman revivalism and the pan-Islamist thought of Jamāl al-Dīn-al Afghānī. He also led negotiations in the aftermath of the third Anglo-Afghan War, which secured Afghanistan's formal independence in 1919.

44   On the idea of an alternative modernity and how it inflects ways of being and relating to time and space, as well as the category of the modern, see Mitchell, *Questions of Modernity*.

45   De la Cadena and Blaser, *A World of Many Worlds*, 6.

46   For Clastres the proliferation of the multiple is achieved through war and the refusal of external law (that is, the unifying order of the nation-state). Clastres writes with probing brilliance, "Only fools can believe that in order to refuse alienation, one must have first experienced it: the refusal of alienation (economic or political) belongs to the very being of this society, it expresses its conservatism, its deliberate will to remain an undivided We." Clastres, *Archeology of Violence*, 276.

47 Tarzi's vision of drive and desire as the ground of historicity is close to Lacan's insistence on desire as the ground of being as opposed to the historicist's emphasis on events and appearances. On this notion of desire against Foucauldian historicism see Copjec, *Read My Desire*.

48 In "Third-World Literature in the Era of Multinational Capitalism," Fredric Jameson discusses the Other as "another reader" whose shoulder we read over. This other reader is like a translator who stands "between ourselves and this alien text" (specifically, a text from the colonial world) and understands the sociopolitical relevance that leaves the Western reader at the impasse of cultural and ideological translation. Translation and mediation of this kind is the result of the hegemony of the Western canon and signifies the "radical difference of non-canonical texts" that unsettle the Western reader, Jameson explains, because they confront the reader with another lifeworld and with anthropological difference. For an explicit and deeply problematic valorization of the Western canon see Bloom, *The Western Canon*.

49 In *All That Is Solid Melts into Air* Berman writes that the split between modern thought and the processes of modernization (including in the modern city) occurred in the aftermath of Auschwitz and Hiroshima. At the same time, in the collective unconscious the ruins of atomic destruction forced the symptom to appear before the trauma. This temporal and uncanny reversal marks the loss of futurity as the horizon of thought and being. See Saint-Amour, "Bombing and the Symptom."

50 Jameson, "Third-World Literature," 69. It is also important to point out that his notion of allegory is not totalizing but "profoundly discontinuous, a matter of breaks and heterogeneities, of the multiple polysemia of the dream rather than the homogenous representation of the symbol" (73).

51 Ahmadi, *Modern Persian Literature in Afghanistan*, 9.

52 Schinasi, *Afghanistan at the Beginning of the Twentieth Century*.

53 In using *detours* I am invoking Freud's critical intervention in the understanding of drive not as instinct or pressure but as a circuitous movement like the kind that drives and displaces the narrative of a story, surfaces as the difference between the latent and manifest content of dreams, or constitutes the temporal disunity of the uncanny, the gap between lack and excess. See the introduction to this book and Freud, *Beyond the Pleasure Principle*.

54 Spivak, "The Letter as Cutting Edge," 226.

55 Jacobs, "The Monstrosity of Translation," 762–63.

56 Hannah Arendt asserts that in the angel we see the "final transfiguration" of the *flâneur* who has his back to the modern crowd and to

whom the significance of things big and small is revealed. Arendt, introduction to Benjamin, *Illuminations*, 12–13.

57 De Man, "Conclusions," 33.

58 This is also the point of rupture between history and the natural analogies of maturation, growth, and ripening that lend themselves to the fantasy of origins: "We are to think of history rather in a reverse way; we are to understand natural changes from the perspective of history. . . . In the same way, the relationship between the translation and original is not to be understood by analogy with natural processes such as resemblance or derivation . . . rather we are to understand the original from the perspective of the translation." De Man, "Conclusions," 23.

Hannah Arendt, following Adorno, posits Benjamin's metaphorical statements as a form of transference (*metapherein*) that reveal the poetic "oneness of the world," including between superstructure and base; and that, for example in the relationship between reason and sense/perception "establishes a connection which is sensually perceived in its immediacy and requires no interpretation." Thus, metaphor is not the same as the allegory which requires interpretation and a connection to be drawn where there would not necessarily be one. Arendt, introduction to Benjamin, *Illuminations*, 13–14.

59 On the problem of grounding as internal to language and the idea of "sense" as an escape that is part language and part event—in other words, a new kind of ground that is the translation of one category into the other—see Deleuze, *The Logic of Sense*, 1–3.

60 Berman, *All That Is Solid Melts into Air*, 33.

61 In his account of the transformation of New York City, first by the monumental and dramatic works of Robert Moses and then through the emerging gap between the idea of a modern city and processes of urban modernization, Berman remarks that for the modernists of the 1950s the modernized city became not the other of modernist thought and art but simply an absence that was no longer engaged, a vigorous, lively place that was mute in the life of the mind. Berman, *All That Is Solid Melts into Air*, 309–12.

62 Benjamin, "The Task of the Translator," in *Illuminations*, 70–71.

63 Paul de Man argues that Benjamin did not think translation was possible. This frustration is not due to inadequacy between languages (or the translator's shortcoming) but to a series of disjunctions that lie at the heart of language and meaning-making. These disjunctions exist between (1) the poetic and hermeneutic register, (2) grammar and meaning (*Wortz* and *Satz*), and (3) between the symbol and thing being symbolized. De Man, "Conclusions," 30.

64   On the notion of work (*arbeit*), especially the work of culture, in Freud's conceptual world, see Smadja, "The Freudian Notion of Kulturarbeit."

CHAPTER 4. DISCOURSES OF ANOTHER OTHER

1   On the idea of sense—including good sense, common sense, and doxa—being related to the violence of thought rather than to radical or creative thinking beyond a "transcendental model of recognition" see Deleuze, *Difference and Repetition*.

2   De Certeau, *Heterologies*, 79.

3   The Persian word *ajeeb* comes from the same word in Arabic, which denotes marvelous or wondrous as well as strange. In Persian *ajeeb* means strangeness but also the power of encounter in, for example, the transcendental realm with jinni (supernatural beings) and divine intimations, or collective life in the encounter with alterity. For an ethnographic rendering of the place of wonder and jinni in New Delhi's spaces of Islamic enchantment and democratic belonging see Taneja, *Jinnealogy*.

4   On the relationship between Persian, the endonym *Farsi* and *Dari* see note 45 in the introduction.

5   The following parable of the fox was invoked during the PDPA's rule to refer to the prevalence of intelligence gathering and espionage, including between family members: "A fox emerged from its hole one snowy morning and stretched its front paws out, proclaiming to itself, 'Oh what a wonderful day to be chased by a useless hunter; to take him around and around in circles and outrun him every time, leaving traces of his defeat in the snow.' A few minutes later, a hunter with a dog chanced upon the fox and the hunter ordered his dog 'go get it!' The dog chased the fox around and around, as the fox had wished. Eventually, the fox tired and, reaching its hole, maneuvered its way in. The dog turned around and returned to the hunter. With an exasperated sigh of relief, the fox said to himself: 'Damn, what a time to be alive! One cannot even talk to oneself!'"

6   On the notion of traumatic uncanniness in Japan and the manifestation of the symptom before the event of trauma and bombing see Saint-Amour, "Bombing and the Symptom."

7   I want to distinguish between the existence of different languages (such as Persian, Pashto, and English, which require translation between them) and Lacan's insight that the unconscious is "structured like a language" (or put differently that it is "the whole structure of language that psychoanalytic experience discovers in the unconscious"

and that this discovery cannot be expressed directly in language).
Lacan, *Écrits*, 413. For Lacan, the subject is forged by a network of
signifying chains that evade a direct correspondence to signified
objects through the movement from signifier to signifier: "For the
signifier, by its very nature, always anticipates meaning by deploy-
ing its dimension in some sense before it. As is seen at the level of
the sentence when the latter is interrupted before the significant
term: 'I'll never . . . ,' 'The fact remains . . . ,' 'Still perhaps. . . .' Such
sentences nevertheless make sense, and that sense is all the more oppressive in that it is content to make us wait for it" (419).

8   Ginzburg, "Killing a Chinese Mandarin," 50.

9   For a poststructuralist account of the aggression of photographic
form in relation to both the "possession" it offers beholders and its
role in establishing a form of witnessing predicated on "noninterven-
tion," particularly in the context of witnessing the destruction of life
in war, see Sontag, *On Photography*.

10   The price that the body pays for access to the law and to the
symbolic—for example through "a speech structured like that
of the person praying,"—is when an imaginary identification and
symbolic act come together in what de Certeau describes as the
monotheistic (particularly Christian) archaeology of the Lacanian
Other (and its correlates: the Word, the Son, the Other, the Name).
See de Certeau, *Heterologies*, 58–59.

11   Copjec, *Read My Desire*, 34.

12   Copjec, *Read My Desire*, 35.

13   Kant, "An Answer to the Question," 5; Foucault, "What Is Enlightenment?" *The Foucault Reader*, 34, 39.

14   The accident as trauma occurs through a moment of physical and
temporal rupture. In Persian the word for trauma (*sadama* or *zakhm*,
which is closer to wound) evokes this. The same is true for the
English word *trauma*, which is etymologically linked to the Greek
trauma, which means to be wounded, defeated, or hurt. *Trau* is the
extension of the root *tere*, which means to turn, twist, or pierce.

Trauma is irreducible to the accident itself or the desire to
repress its occurrence. Cathy Caruth argues that it consists "solely
in the structure of its experience or reception," and that this is what
grips the traumatized subject. Caruth, *Trauma*, 4. Citing Freud on
war-caused neuroses in World War I, she argues that, for Freud,
neuroses and the repetitive "bringing the patient back to the situation of his accident" is explained neither by unconscious meaning
nor wish fulfillment. Rather, it is the "literal return of the event" and
this "nonsymbolic literality" is what is responsible for the delay in
understanding that is constitutive of traumatic possession (5).

On the history of agricultural development and the relationship between land mines, improvised explosive devices, and corporeal violence see Mojaddedi, "Ground War."

15   Throughout the chapter, all instances of italics within Zia's quoted words are my emphasis.

16   A mob and a crowd are different things, but the soldiers' perception of an uncontrollable mob forming at the gate can also be understood as what Elias Canetti describes as the "open" crowd that suddenly appears and then erupts. Canetti remarks on how the crowd seems to transmit movement between bodies and that its goal exists before it is brought into language. Canetti, *Crowds and Power*, 16–21. On the place of mutilation, war, and national subjectivity see Ivy, "Revenge and Recapitation."

17   A differentiating element gives a group its coherence through the construction of liminal figures. On this logic and on the place of the pharmakos or pharmakoi in ancient Greece and the relationship between their bodies and the city's "body proper," see Derrida, "Plato's Pharmacy" in *Dissemination*.

18   National Highway 0101 (the Kabul–Kandahar Highway, a key portion of National Highway 1 known as the "Ring Road") is a $300 million road that connects Kabul to its southern provinces. It became infamous for its roadside bombings and extortion as much as its being the main artery to the capital.

19   At the time, the Afghan government was engaged in the formidable task of trying to establish military control in the provinces. Afghans perceived that this was too large of a challenge for the Afghan government to meet despite the deployment of an additional thirty thousand US soldiers in 2010 during the Obama administration, a significant portion of them stationed in Helmand and Kandahar, two provinces connected to Kabul by Highway 1.

20   When I say he survived the road, I mean he escaped the specific phenomenon of roadside bombings, which disproportionately killed Afghan translators riding with military convoys.

21   On military bases, forms of sociality were literally structured by linguistic expertise. The translators were divided into categories (CAT) 1, 2, and 3. CAT 3 required fluency in English. "Local nationals" like Zia comprised CAT 1. They cooked and ate together, played cards, and had tea into the night. The CAT 3 translators rarely socialized with them. Zia had a friend who spoke English so well he was referred to as "the American." The friend learned English while working in a laundry room at a military base but his skills were not sufficient for him to translate one day during a "very important meeting" of military generals. All the translators would tease him about this. CAT

3 translators made a lot more money than the lower-level translators and were only involved in the most important missions and
meetings. For example, an acquaintance of Zia's, a CAT 3 translator
at Forward Operating Base Alpha in Logar, was only sent to work
with high-ranking generals on "intelligence jobs." Zia made $715 per
month and suspected that TC (the company he worked for) charged
the US Department of Defense much more. The Afghan government
had no regulatory control over subcontracting and wages, so Zia had
no recourse but to accept whatever TC paid him.

22   In addition to the $715 per month, Zia would receive an extra $50
if he did land patrol (LP) and another $200 if he did air and land
patrol. If he took a day off, he made nothing. Most of the time, Zia
settled for the $715 instead of going on LP because of the danger. He
recalled an incident where his friend Daud stepped on a land mine
and lost his leg while doing LP. Daud's employer, TC, refused him
compensation at first, but then after what he described as "much
struggle and hard work" the company agreed to give him $27,000.

23   Benjamin uses the vessel image repeatedly in "The Storyteller," where
he likens it to an element of the storyteller's life that is brought out
and clings "to the story the way handprints of the potter cling to
the clay vessel." Benjamin, *Illuminations*, 91–92. He also invokes it
in "The Task of the Translator" (also in *Illuminations*), where he
transforms it from the index of experience (the handprint) into the
more complex problem of fidelity to an original. This is a moment
when Benjamin's essay is itself lost in Harry Zohn's translation. Paul
de Man ("Conclusions," 32) argues that the image of a broken vessel
in fragments is not, as Zohn translates it, about the task of gluing the
vessel back together so that the fragments "match one another in
the smallest details" (Benjamin, *Illuminations*, 78) but is much closer
to Carol Jacobs's translation of "fragments of a vessel, in order to be
articulated together." Jacobs, "The Monstrosity of Translation," 762.

24   The drifting of thoughts and words enabled by fragmentation
recalls what Vicente Rafael describes as the arbitrary "fishing out"
of meaning that occurs in contexts of hierarchical and colonial
speech. Citing a sermon that Father Damaso delivered in Spanish in the Philippines (which the Tagalog-speaking congregation
did not understand and radically reinterpreted), Rafael argues that
fishing out words and attaching them to "imaginings" is both a form
of drifting away and serves to redouble the natives' attention to the
content of the sermon. Rafael, *Contracting Colonialism*, 2. This drifting away from and arbitrarily reattaching meaning is what Rafael
characterizes as a strategy of decontextualizing through which colonial authority is decentered in a context of subjugation (3). It depicts

a social order "premised not on consensus between ruler and ruled but on the fragmentation and hermeneutic displacement of the very basis of consensus: language" (7).

25   De Man, "Conclusions," 33.

26   In responding to Immanuel Kant's notion of a cosmopolitan peace based on hospitality, Jacques Derrida reveals its "other" side to be not peace but identity and the upholding of the threshold of the master (the patron, host, owner, and so on) who maintains authority over place and thus restricts the gift that appears to be freely given. Against this, Derrida distinguishes between the hospitality of extending an invitation versus welcoming an unannounced visitor, arguing that hospitality must exceed its own conceptual and experiential framing to become possible as the "intentional experience that proceeds beyond knowledge toward the other as absolute stranger, as unknown, where I know that I know nothing of him." Derrida, "Hospitality," 8. Derrida elaborates on this distinction in his discussion of Emmanuel Levinas's notion of a nonpolitical peace. He distinguishes between Kant and Levinas, arguing that for Kant war is natural and peace is the instituted purview of social relations, whereas for Levinas it is peace that constitutes a first promise. If Kant calls for universal hospitality, grounded in the natural right of common possession of the earth, then Levinas seeks unfettered and nomadic universality. And if for Kant peace is always threatened by hostility, even if is unconscious, for Levinas war always testifies to an original welcoming of the other's face and thus of radical difference. Derrida, *Adieu to Emmanuel Levinas*, 90.

27   Derrida, *Monolingualism of the Other*, 2.

28   On the relationship between Derrida's intimate confession of the mark of foreignness in his own speech and the opening of difference within language such that there no mastery but only the unpredictable coming of the messianic decision, the other, the future, see Chow. "Reading Derrida on Being Monolingual"

CHAPTER 5. BETWEEN GROUND AND SKY

An earlier version of this chapter appeared as "The Closing: Heart, Mouth, Word," *Public Culture* 31, no. 3 (2019): 497–520.

1   In thinking about the uncontrolled power and transmission of words, I am also thinking with Jeanne Favret-Saada about the nature of "deadly words" in witchcraft when language precludes the fantasy of impartial observation and has the power to "tie or untie a fate." Favret-Saada, *Deadly Words*, 9–10. This notion of a tie between

language and its violent manifestation also reveals how witchcraft speech is about immediate access to unconscious power, a power that James Siegel (following Claude Lévi-Strauss) shows to be metonymic and about the freedom to link "anything with anything even if the result is catastrophe." Siegel, *Naming the Witch*, 50. Thus, translation and witchcraft enjoy the power of combination and a proclivity for excess that begins like logos with the word and is realized in the unbridled links that emerge from the act of saying.

2   Of course, not all voice is reducible to enunciation, but all orders of voicing are open to interpretation; for example a child's cry signifies pain or hunger but is also about desire and anticipating the other. See Dolar, *A Voice and Nothing More*, 28–29.

3   Haussmann quoted in Benjamin, *The Arcades Project*, 128.

4   A "green on blue" attack is an incident of violence that occurs when embedded Afghans turn on their foreign military units, usually in the form of a shooting.

5   I would contrast this sense of voice, which Matin identifies as a signal of the powers of reasoning and lawfulness, with what Roland Barthes describes as the "grain of the voice," or the dimension and materiality of voice that is inseparable from the body and the "encounter between a language and a voice." Barthes, *Image-Music-Text*, 181–82. This singularity of the voice, which is much closer to what Jacques Lacan designates as the enunciating subject of the "I," speaks to the significance of language from within the body while also rendering the symbolic possible; that is, the play of representation Lacan captures in his formulation of the grammatical subject.

       This double sense of voice and the subject, both corporeal and structured by signs, is what Stefania Pandolfo describes as a voice that is (in Amina's experience in the setting of a psychiatric hospital) a "corporeal expression, material and 'insubordinate' . . . yet which is rooted in a field of power of which her voice is the trace and 'condensation.'" Pandolfo, *Knot of the Soul*, 67.

       For a beautiful account of the "grain of voice" and its reemergence at the margin of national culture and its desire(s) in Japan, see Ivy, *Discourses of the Vanishing*.

6   On the history of linguistic assimilation and national consciousness alongside the emergence of technologies of mechanical reproduction and the general experience of reading print language see Anderson, *Imagined Communities* ; see also Rafael, *Contracting Colonialism*.

7   Pandolfo, "Testimony in Counterpoint," 109.

8   On the relationship between voice and capital for Karl Marx, and the relationship of voicing to representation and dialectical thought, see Morris, "Dialect and Dialectic." Morris illustrates that in the context

of the working day "voice names the quality of a saying that cannot be reduced to the said but also of a real that contradicts (speaks against) the concept" (235).

9   Lévi-Strauss, *Introduction to the Work of Marcel Mauss*, 25, 35.

10   Simmel, "The Stranger," 402.

11   In 2009, there was a large-scale military operation involving three thousand British troops and known as Operation Panther's Claw in the strategic province of Helmand. For an account of the operation's scope and strategic aim, see "Deadly, and Maybe Decisive: Officers Hail Panther's Claw," *Guardian* News, July, 27, 2009, https://www .theguardian.com/uk/2009/jul/27/panthers-claw-operation -afghanistan-taliban; and "Mapping Operation Panther's Claw," bbc *News*, July 28, 2009, http://news.bbc.co.uk/2/hi/uk_news/8172556 .stm. For an account of the relationship between policing and the calibration of intensity (the "more-or-less-ness" of things and ethnic identities), which cannot be reduced to the content of a strategy or mission and which moves in crossings between Indonesia and East Malaysia, see Carruthers, "Policing Intensity."

12   For Freud, the uncanny offers a kind of detour into thinking about the work of the life and death drives (a relation he formalizes in *Beyond the Pleasure Principle*) and the relation between repetition compulsion in psychic life and the fundamentally imaginative task of living as a being toward death.

13   Freud, "The Uncanny," 28. The notion of uncanniness is also at the heart of the disagreement between Freud and Ernst Jentsch, for whom the uncanny was largely generated by intellectual uncertainty and novelty.

14   There is also something fundamentally secular about this quality of feeling. It is, as Mladen Dolar contends, the return of excess previously captured by the domain of the sacred but now writ large in the collective imagination. He describes it as the counterpart to the transcendental Kantian subject that, through Lacan's translation of *Unheimlich*/uncanny as "extimité," or an intimate exteriority, is unsettled because uncanniness cannot be captured by the conceptual binaries of subject/object, inside/outside, and essence/appearance that characterize Enlightenment thought. It is this escape and blurring of concepts that "points neither to the interior nor to the exterior but is located there where the most intimate interiority coincides with the exterior and becomes threatening, provoking horror and anxiety." Dolar, "I Shall Be with You," 6.

15   Again, the uncanny emerges as a point of consideration. One must distinguish knowledge from belief to understand the realm of the uncanny, even if belief remains resistant to understanding, as Dolar

captures when he writes, "I know very well but all the same. . . . I believe." Here knowledge doesn't contradict belief, and belief cannot lose power through knowledge "since it is fundamentally situated in relation to the object—which is not the object of knowledge." Dolar, "I Shall Be with You," 22.

16 For Freud this willingness is fundamentally tied to an altered attitude toward death, especially the death of the other, which in the modern era does not haunt the living or generate ambivalence. The loss of this ambivalence, which he establishes as crucial to psychic life in "Totem and Taboo" and elaborates upon in "Mourning and Melancholia" is the same as the readiness to kill in war. Find both essays in Freud, *On Murder, Mourning, and Melancholia.*

17 Thinking of signification and meaning in relation to alterity is also a problem of locating sovereignty and its operation(s), including the force of laughter and the disruption of discourse (for example poetic, possessed, or holy). Derrida, "From Restricted to General Economy" in *Writing and Difference.* See also Bataille, *The Accursed Share.*

18 The Afghan translators also made do with fewer resources and less food. Unlike the Americans, who had access to Chinook helicopters, the Afghans relied on ground transport, which became impossible to use in areas of heavy fighting because the roads were ambushed, cutting towns and villages off from one another.

19 On the place of immunity as a concept and form of incorporation crucial to political life see Esposito, *Immunitas.*

20 On the role of rumor and gossip in guerrilla warfare see Taussig, *Shamanism, Colonialism, and the Wild Man.*

21 Play is crucial to understanding the reality principle and the role of involuntary repetition in psychic life. It serves as a metaphor for the mastery or the anticipation of loss. See Freud, *Beyond the Pleasure Principle.*

22 Siegel, "The Curse of the Photograph," 60.

23 This severance of ties and bodies is an uncanny reminder of the decapitation that took place after the village meeting. It relates to the failure of speech and the jouissance of laughter but also to the photographic form that enables the defeat to be reproduced and shared with others, which redoubles the defeat ad infinitum. This is in keeping with the violence of the photographic form as being the kind of severance that cuts the moment from a continuity of signs (making it an event) and "incites desire to bring something unapproachable closer . . . the photograph 'transcends' time and space as it feverishly circulates, without origin and without final destination." Ivy, "Dark Enlightenment."

24 For Derrida there is no sovereignty without the paradox of the gift and the desire to appropriate what the other does not entirely possess or

cannot give. And, like hospitality, which cannot be realized through the identity of the patron or master (and to this I would add the city dweller), the gift must also be free of the logic of economy (and the fantasy of home, origin, *oikos*) and become "aneconomic"; in other words, a radical, pure gift that cannot be repaid. Derrida, *Given Time*.

25 The biometric system used in Afghanistan was the Handheld Inter-agency Identity Detection System. Men in rural areas were routinely "enrolled" (as were men in Kabul when they sought employment on military bases). Enrollment meant having one's fingerprints and iris scan entered into the system. Enrollment had the potential to produce complicated scenarios; for example, if someone handled a piece of scrap metal that someone else later used to construct an IED, the first person's fingerprints might still be on the metal. If a match for the fingerprint was found in the system, perhaps because the first person obtained a job on a military base, they could easily be accused of both constructing the device and entering the base to plan an insider attack.

EPILOGUE: A VITA DETOURED

1 In Islamic law, individuals who drink the same breast milk (milk kinship) are considered siblings and strictly prohibited from having sexual relations. The other relatives prohibited from marrying are parent–child, brother–sister, grandparent–grandchild, aunt/uncle–niece/nephew. First cousins are allowed to marry.

2 The condition Roland Barthes captures in the image of the stocking (which in French is translated as "mesh-bottom") lies at the heart of the tragic and the multiple meanings, run-ins, and near-misses that occur in language precisely because there is no principle of unity to ensure a communication is received as intended and whether that is enough to forestall the tragic arc. Barthes, "The Death of the Author" in *Image-Music-Text*, 147.

3 Lévi-Strauss discerns another movement between the two possibilities: the myth addressing the problem of autochthony as revealed in figures and monsters that are born of the earth and lack parents versus beings born of two parents. This movement between one and two is also reflected in the formation of ideas, including the analysis of the myth as a reflection of binary principles that are a metaphor for Lévi-Strauss's own analysis of the problem of mythic thought. See Lévi-Strauss, "The Structural Study of Myth" in *Structural Anthropology*; *The Elementary Structures of Kinship*.

4 Miller, "Lacan's Antigone," 10.

5   It is important to distinguish what Jacques Alain Miller describes in his analysis of the difference between "shared flesh" or "primal one-ness" and civic personhood for Antigone (Miller, "Lacan's Antigone," 5, 10) from the imaginary tension of belonging that Edward Said describes as the culmination of filiation in relationships of affilia-tion that can become objects of critical consciousness. For Antigone this difference is the conflict between her human existence and her ethical drive, which represent two orders of being that cannot be reconciled. For Said, however, the difference can nonetheless be-come an object of critical engagement. He writes, "Two alternatives propose themselves for the contemporary critic. One is organic com-plicity with the pattern I have described. The critic enables, indeed transacts, the transfer of legitimacy from filiation to affiliation. . . . The second alternative is for the critic to recognize the difference between instinctual filiation and social affiliation, and to show how affiliation sometimes reproduces filiation, sometimes makes its own forms." Said, *The World, the Text, and the Critic*, 23–24.

6   In thinking about the dilemma of sistering I draw inspiration from literature, particularly from Ismail Kadare's *The Ghost Rider*, which retells "The Ballad of Constantine and Doruntine," an Albanian folk legend, as the dilemma of a medieval detective seeking to understand the tragic downfall of Doruntine's family but also the meaning of displacement, exile, and uncanny returns. For the detective, Dorunt-ine's ill-fated brothers, and also her and her mother's own ill fate, the question of who is a sister and what she can mean, and how far one should go to honor promises made, is a matter of life and death as played out in radical forms of desire.

7   This raises the theological question of how to witness stories and events that cannot be repeated or represented. For Derrida this impos-sible role of the witness is crucial to the structure of divine submission and to the radical call of the Other in the Judeo-Christian-Islamic tradition. In the story of the sacrifice of Isaac, the representation of that event for others would violate the very secrecy that is the foundational condition (a singular demand by God) of the event and its meaning (one must respond). Derrida captures this aporia in the media-inspired declaration "Above all, no journalists," which ex-presses both the secret between God and Abraham and their singular bond (untranslatable to others), and thus the limits of mediation in language. See Derrida, "Above All, No Journalists," in de Vries and Weber, *Religion and Media*.

8   Said, "The Problem of Textuality," 683.

9   Benjamin, *The Arcades Project*, 475.

Bibliography

Abreu, Maria José de. *The Charismatic Gymnasium: Breath, Media, and Religious Revivalism in Contemporary Brazil*. Duke University Press, 2021.

Agamben, Giorgio. *State of Exception*. Translated by Kevin Attell. University of Chicago Press, 2004.

Agamben, Giorgio. *The Work of Giorgio Agamben: Law, Literature, Life*. Edited by Justin Clemens, Nicholas Heron, and Alex Murray. Edinburgh University Press, 2008.

Ahmad, Aijaz. "Jameson's Rhetoric of Otherness and the 'National Allegory.'" *Social Text*, no. 17 (1987): 3–25.

Ahmadi, Wali. *Modern Persian Literature in Afghanistan*. Routledge, 2008.

Ahmed, Manan. "Adam's Mirror: The Frontier in the Imperial Imagination." *Economic and Political Weekly* 46, no. 13 (2011): 60–65.

Anderson, Benedict. *Imagined Communities: Reflections on the Origin and Spread of Nationalism*. Verso, 1991.

Arendt, Hannah. "Introduction: Walter Benjamin: 1892–1940." In *Illuminations*, edited by Hannah Arendt and translated by Harry Zohn. Schocken, 1968.

Arendt, Hannah. *On Violence*. Harcourt, Brace, Jovanovich, 1970.

Aretxaga, Begoña. "Dirty Protest: Symbolic Overdetermination and Gender in Northern Ireland Ethnic Violence." *Ethos* 23, no. 2 (1995): 123–48.

Asad, Talal. *On Suicide Bombing*. Columbia University Press, 2007.

Bakhtin, M. M. *The Dialogic Imagination: Four Essays*. Edited by Michael Holquist. Translated by Caryl Emerson and Michael Holquist. University of Texas Press, 1981.

Barthes, Roland. *Camera Lucida: Reflections on Photography*. Translated by Richard Howard. Hill and Wang, 1981.

Barthes, Roland. "The Death of the Author." Translated by Richard Howard, 1967. https://writing.upenn.edu/~taransky/Barthes.pdf.

Barthes, Roland. *Image-Music-Text*. Translated by Stephen Heath. Fontana Press, 1977.

Barthes, Roland, and Lionel Duisit. "An Introduction to the Structural Analysis of Narrative." *New Literary History* 6, no. 2 (1975): 237–72.

Bataille, George. *The Accursed Share: An Essay on General Economy*. Vol. 1, *Consumption*. Translated by Robert Hurley. Zone Books, 1991.

Baudrillard, Jean. *The Gulf War Did Not Take Place*. Indiana University Press, 1995.

Baudrillard, Jean. *Simulacra and Simulation*. Translated by Sheila Faria Glaser. University of Michigan Press, 1994.

Baudrillard, Jean. *The Spirit of Terrorism*. Translated by Chris Turner. Verso, 2002.

Baudrillard, Jean. *Symbolic Exchange and Death*. Translated by Iain Hamilton Grant. Sage, 1993.

Benjamin, Walter. *The Arcades Project*. Translated by Howard Eiland and Kevin McLaughlin. Harvard University Press, 2002.

Benjamin, Walter. *Illuminations*. Edited by Hannah Arendt. Translated by Harry Zohn. Schocken, 1968.

Benjamin, Walter. *One-Way Street and Other Writings*. Translated by Edmund Jephcott and Kingsley Shorter. NLB, 1979.

Benjamin, Walter. *Reflections: Essays, Aphorisms, Autobiographical Writings*. Edited by Peter Demetz. Translated by Edmund Jephcott. Schocken, 1986.

Benjamin, Walter. *Selected Writings*. Vol. 1, *1913–1926*. Edited by Marcus Bullock and Michael W. Jennings. Harvard University Press, 2004.

Benjamin, Walter. *Selected Writings*. Vol. 2, part 2, *1931–1934*. Edited by Michael W. Jennings, Howard Eiland, and Gary Smith. Harvard University Press, 2005.

Berger, John. *About Looking*. Vintage, 1992.

Berman, Marshall. *All That Is Solid Melts into Air: The Experience of Modernity*. Penguin, 1988.

Biehl, João. *Vita: Life in a Zone of Social Abandonment*. University of California Press, 2013.

Blanchot, Maurice. *The Writing of the Disaster*. University of Nebraska Press, 1995.

Bloom, Harold. *The Western Canon: The Books and School of the Ages*. Riverhead, 1995.

Boas, Franz. "On Alternating Sounds." *American Anthropologist* 2, no. 1 (1889): 47–54.

Borch-Jacobsen, Mikkel. "The Freudian Subject, from Politics to Ethics." Translated by Richard Miller. *October* 39 (1986): 109–27.

Borges, Jorge Luis. "The Garden of Forking Paths." In *Ficciones*, edited by Anthony Kerrigan, translated by Emecé Editores. Grove, 1962.

Borradori, Giovanna. *Philosophy in a Time of Terror: Dialogues with Jürgen Habermas and Jacques Derrida*. University of Chicago Press, 2003.

Brooks, Peter. "Freud's Masterplot." *Yale French Studies* 55–56 (1977): 280–300.

Brooks, Peter. *Reading for the Plot: Design and Intention in Narrative*. Harvard University Press, 1984.

Buck-Morss, Susan. *The Origin of Negative Dialectics: Theodor W. Adorno, Walter Benjamin, and the Frankfurt Institute*. Free Press, 1977.

Butler, Judith. "Contingent Foundations: Feminism and the Question of Postmodernism." In *Feminists Theorize the Political*, edited by Judith Butler and Joan Scott. Routledge, 1992.

Cadava, Eduardo. *Words of Light: Theses on the Photography of History*. Princeton University Press, 1997.

Canetti, Elias. *Crowds and Power*. Translated by Victor Gollancz. Continuum, 1973.

Carpentier, Alejo. *The Kingdom of This World*. Noonday, 1957.

Carpentier, Alejo. Prologue to "The Kingdom of This World." *Review: Literature and Arts of the Americas* 26, no. 47 (1993): 28–32.

Carruthers, Andrew M. "Policing Intensity." *Public Culture* 31, no. 3 (2019): 469–96.

Caruth, Cathy. *Trauma: Explorations in Memory*. Johns Hopkins University Press, 1995.

Cebrowski, Arthur K., and John H. Garstka. "Network-Centric Warfare: Its Origin and Future." *Proceedings* 124/1/1,139 (1998). https://www.usni.org/magazines/proceedings/1998/january/network-centric-warfare-its-origin-and-future.

Cervantes, Miguel de. "The Novel of the Colloquy of the Dogs." In *Exemplary Novels*, edited by Roberto González Echevarría, translated by Edith Grossman. Yale University Press, 2016.

Chow, Rey. "Reading Derrida on Being Monolingual." *New Literary History* 39, no. 2 (2008): 217–31.

Clastres, Pierre. *Archeology of Violence*. Semiotext(e), 2010.

Copjec, Joan. *Read My Desire: Lacan Against the Historicists*. Verso, 2015.

Coronil, Fernando. "Beyond Occidentalism: Toward Nonimperial Geohistorical Categories." *Cultural Anthropology* 11, no. 1 (1996): 51–87.

Crary, Jonathan. *Techniques of the Observer: On Vision and Modernity in the Nineteenth Century*. MIT Press, 1992.

Daniel, Valentine E. *Charred Lullabies: Chapters in an Anthropology of Violence*. Princeton University Press, 1996.

Davis, Mike. *Buda's Wagon: A Brief History of the Car Bomb*. Verso, 2007.

de Certeau, Michel. *Heterologies: Discourse on the Other*. Translated by Brian Massumi. University of Minnesota Press, 1986.

de la Cadena, Marisol. *Earth Beings: Ecologies of Practice Across Andean Worlds*. Duke University Press, 2015.

de la Cadena, Marisol, and Mario Blaser, eds. *A World of Many Worlds*. Duke University Press, 2018.

Deleuze, Gilles. *Difference and Repetition*. Translated by Paul Patton. Columbia University Press, 1994.

Deleuze, Gilles. *The Logic of Sense*. Edited by Constanin V. Boundas. Translated by Mark Lester and Charles Stivale. Columbia University Press, 1990.

Deleuze, Gilles, and Félix Guattari. *What Is Philosophy?* Translated by Hugh Tomlinson and Graham Burchell. Columbia University Press, 1996.

de Man, Paul. "'Conclusions on Walter Benjamin's 'The Task of the Translator.'" *Yale French Studies* 97 (2000): 10–35.

Derrida, Jacques. *Adieu to Emmanuel Levinas*. Translated by Pascale-Anne Brault and Michael Nass. Stanford University Press, 1999.

Derrida, Jacques. *Dissemination*. Translated by Barbara Johnson. University of Chicago Press, 1981.

Derrida, Jacques. *Given Time: I. Counterfeit Money*. Translated by Peggy Kamuf. University of Chicago Press, 1994.

Derrida, Jacques. "Hospitality." *Angelika* 5, no. 3 (2000): 3–18.

Derrida, Jacques. *Monolingualism of the Other: Or, The Prosthesis of Origin*. Translated by Patrick Mensah. Stanford University Press, 1998.

Derrida, Jacques. *Of Grammatology*. Translated by Gayatri Spivak. Johns Hopkins University Press, 1997.

Derrida, Jacques. *Writing and Difference*. Edited and translated by Alan Bass. University of Chicago Press, 1978.

de Vries, Hent, and Samuel Weber. *Religion and Media*. Stanford University Press, 2002.

Didion, Joan. *Slouching Towards Bethlehem*. 1968. Reprint, Farrar, Straus, and Giroux, 2008.

Dolar, Mladen. "'I Shall Be with You on Your Wedding Night': Lacan and the Uncanny." *October* 58, no. 5 (1991): 5–23.

Dolar, Mladen. "On Rumors, Gossip and Related Matters." In *Objective Fictions: Philosophy, Psychoanalysis, Marxism*, edited by Adrian Johnston, Boštjan Nedoh, and Alenka Zupančič. Edinburgh University Press, 2022.

Dolar, Mladen. *A Voice and Nothing More*. MIT Press, 2006.

Esposito, Roberto. *Immunitas: The Protection and Negation of Life*. Translated by Zakiya Hanafi. Polity, 2011.

Fanon, Frantz. *Black Skin, White Masks*. Translated by Richard Philcox. Grove, 2008.

Favret-Saada, Jeanne. *Deadly Words: Witchcraft in the Bocage*. Reprint, Cambridge University Press, 2010.

Feldman, Allen. *Formations of Violence: The Narrative of the Body and Political Terror in Northern Ireland*. University of Chicago Press, 1991.

Foucault, Michel. *I, Pierre Rivière, Having Slaughtered My Mother, My Sister, and My Brother: A Case of Parricide in the 19th Century*. University of Nebraska Press, 1982.

Foucault, Michel. "What Is Enlightenment?" In *The Foucault Reader*, edited by Paul Rabinow. Pantheon, 1984.

Fraser, Marnie. "Landmines: An Ongoing Environmental Health Problem for the Children of Afghanistan." *Journal of Rural and Remote Environmental Health* 2, no 2 (2003): 76–89.

Freud, Sigmund. *Beyond the Pleasure Principle.* Translated and edited by James Strachey. W. W. Norton, 1961.

Freud, Sigmund. *Civilization and Its Discontents.* Translated by James Strachey. W. W. Norton, 1961.

Freud, Sigmund. "Fetishism." 1927. In *The Psychology of Love*, edited by Philip Rieff. Collier, 1963.

Freud, Sigmund. *Group Psychology and the Analysis of the Ego.* Translated and edited by James Strachey. W. W. Norton, 1959.

Freud, Sigmund. *The Interpretation of Dreams.* Translated and edited by James Strachey. Basic Books, 1955. Reprint, Basic Books, 2010.

Freud, Sigmund. *On Murder, Mourning, and Melancholia.* Edited by Adam Philips. Translated by Shaun Whiteside. Penguin, 2005.

Freud, Sigmund. "The Uncanny." In *Studies in Parapsychology*, edited by Philip Rieff. 1963. Reprint, Collier, 1971.

Gailus, Andreas. "Lessons of the Cryptograph: Revelation and the Mechanical in Kafka's 'In the Penal Colony.'" *Modernism/Modernity* 8, no. 2 (2001): 295–302.

Garcia, Angela. *The Pastoral Clinic: Addiction and Dispossession Along the Rio Grande.* University of California Press, 2010.

Ginzburg, Carlo. "Killing a Chinese Mandarin: The Moral Implications of Distance." *Critical Inquiry* 21, no. 1 (1994): 44–60.

Giordano, Cristiana. *Migrants in Translation: Caring and the Logics of Difference in Contemporary Italy.* University of California Press, 2014.

Golestaneh, Seema. *Unknowing and the Everyday: Sufism and Knowledge in Iran.* Duke University Press, 2023.

Goux, Jean Joseph. *Symbolic Economies: After Marx and Freud.* Translated by Jennifer Curtiss Gage. Cornell University Press, 1990.

Gregorian, Vartan. *The Emergence of Modern Afghanistan: Politics of Reform and Modernization, 1880–1946.* Stanford University Press, 1969.

Gunning, Tom. "Phantom Images and Modern Manifestations: Spirit Photography, Magic Theater, Trick Films, and Photography's Uncanny." In *Fugitive Images: From Photography to Video*, edited by Patrice Petro. Indiana University Press, 1995.

Han, Clara. *Life in Debt: Times of Care and Violence in Neoliberal Chile.* University of California Press, 2012.

Ibn Khaldûn. *The Muqaddimah: An Introduction to History.* Translated by Franz Rosenthal. Edited by N. J. Dawood. Princeton University Press, 1970.

Ivy, Marilyn. "Dark Enlightenment: Naitō Masatoshi's Flash." *In Photographies East: The Camera and Its Histories in East and Southeast Asia*, edited by Rosalind C. Morris. Duke University Press, 2009.

Ivy, Marilyn. *Discourses of the Vanishing: Modernity, Phantasm, Japan*. University of Chicago Press, 1995.

Ivy, Marilyn. "Revenge and Recapitation in Recessionary Japan." *South Atlantic Quarterly* 99, no. 4 (2000): 819–40.

Jacobs, Carol. "The Monstrosity of Translation." *Modern Language Notes* 90, no. 6 (1975): 755–66.

Jain, Sarah S. "The Prosthetic Imagination: Enabling and Disabling the Prosthesis Trope." *Science, Technology, & Human Values* 24, no. 1 (1999): 31–54.

Jameson, Fredric. *Postmodernism or, The Cultural Logic of Late Capitalism*. Duke University Press, 1992.

Jameson, Fredric. "Third-World Literature in the Era of Multinational Capitalism." *Social Text* 15 (1986): 65–88.

Johnson, Barbara. "Melville's Fist: The Execution of 'Billy Budd.'" *Studies in Romanticism* 18, no. 4 (1979): 567–99.

Johnson, Barbara. "Translator's Introduction." In *Dissemination*, translated with an introduction and additional notes by Barbara Johnson. Athlone, 1981.

Johnson, Barbara. "Writing." In *Critical Terms for Literary Study*, edited by Frank Lentricchia and Thomas McLaughlin. University of Chicago Press, 1995.

Joyce, James. *Ulysses*. Introduction by Declan Kiberd. Penguin Modern Classics, 1992.

Kadare, Ismail. *The Ghost Rider*. 1980. Reprint, Canongate, 2010.

Kafka, Franz. "In the Penal Colony." In *The Complete Storie,* edited by Nahum N. Glatzer. Schocken, 1971.

Kant, Immanuel. *An Answer to the Question: What Is Enlightenment?* Translated by Ted Humphrey. Hackett Publishing, 1992.

Khodarkovsky, Michael. "'Ignoble Savages and Unfaithful Subjects': Constructing Non-Christian Identities in Early Modern Russia." In *Russia's Orient: Imperial Borderlands and Peoples, 1700–1917*, edited by Daniel R. Brower and Edward J. Lazzerini. Indiana University Press, 1997.

Klima, Alan. *Ethnography #9*. Duke University Press, 2019.

Kristeva, Julia. *Black Sun: Depression and Melancholia*. Translated by Leon S. Roudiez. Columbia University Press, 1992.

Lacan, Jacques. *Écrits: The First Complete Edition in English*. Translated by Bruce Fink. W. W. Norton, 2006.

Lacan, Jacques. *The Ethics of Psychoanalysis, 1959–1960: The Seminar of Jacques Lacan Book VII*. Edited by Jacques-Alain Miller. Translated by Dennis Porter. W. W. Norton, 1986.

Lacan, Jacques. *The Four Fundamental Concepts of Psychoanalysis: The Seminar of Jacques Lacan Book XI*. Edited by Jacques-Alain Miller. Translated by Alan Sheridan. W. W. Norton, 1998.

Layton, Susan. *Russian Literature and Empire: Conquest of the Caucasus from Pushkin to Tolstoy*. Cambridge University Press, 2005.

Le Corbusier. *Towards a New Architecture*. Translated and with an introduction by Frederick Etchells. Dover, 1986.

Lentricchia, Frank, and Thomas McLaughlin. *Critical Terms for Literary Study*. University of Chicago Press, 1990.

Levi, Primo. *The Drowned and the Saved*. Translated by Raymond Rosenthal. Vintage, 1988.

Lévi-Strauss, Claude. *The Elementary Structures of Kinship*. Beacon, 1971.

Lévi-Strauss, Claude. *Introduction to the Work of Marcel Mauss*. Translated by Felicity Baker. Routledge and Kegan Paul, 1987.

Lévi-Strauss, Claude. "The Structural Study of Myth." In *Structural Anthropology*. Basic Books, 1963.

Lévi-Strauss, Claude. *Tristes Tropiques*. Penguin, 1992.

Lindqvist, Sven. *A History of Bombing*. Translated by Linda Haverty Rugg. New Press, 2003.

MacCannell, Juliet Flower. "More Thoughts for the Times on War and Death." In *Jacques Lacan and the Other Side of Psychoanalysis: Reflections on Seminar XVII*, edited by Justin Clemins and Russell Grigg. Duke University Press, 2006.

Mahdī, Muhsin. *Ibn Khaldûn's Philosophy of History*. University of Chicago Press, 1971.

Marx, Karl. *The Eastern Question: A Reprint of Letters Written 1853–1856 Dealing with the Events of the Crimean War*. Edited by Eleanor Marx Aveling and Edward Aveling. Kirstasbooks, 1897.

Masco, Joseph. *The Nuclear Borderlands: The Manhattan Project in Post-Cold War New Mexico*. Princeton University Press, 2006.

McLean, Stuart. *The Event and Its Terrors: Ireland, Famine, Modernity*. Stanford University Press, 2004.

McLuhan, Marshall. *Understanding Media: The Extensions of Man*. Signet, 1964.

Mehlman, Jeffrey. "The Floating Signifier: From Lévi-Strauss to Lacan." *Yale French Studies* 48 (1972): 10–37.

Messick, Brinkley. *The Calligraphic State: Textual Domination and History in a Muslim Society*. University of California Press, 1993.

Metz, Christian. "Photography and Fetish." *October* 34 (1985): 81–90.

Miller, Paul Allen. "Lacan's Antigone: The Sublime Object and the Ethics of Interpretation." *Phoenix* 61, nos. 1–2 (2007): 1–14.

Mitchell, Timothy, ed. *Questions of Modernity*. University of Minnesota Press, 2000.

Mitchell, W. J. T. "Representation." In *Critical Terms for Literary Study*, edited by Frank Lentricchia and Thomas McLaughlin. University of Chicago Press, 2010.

Mojaddedi, Fatima. "Ground War: Soil, Supplements, and Suffering in Afghanistan." *Ethnoscripts* 24, no. 1 (2022): 201–18.

Mojaddedi, Fatima. "Notes on the Wire: Telegraphic Opening and Ideology in Modern Afghanistan." *Afghanistan* 6, no. 1 (2023): 49–72.

Mojaddedi, Fatima. "Reading the Global Disorder with Maḥmūd-i Tarzī." *Comparative Islamic Studies* 13, nos. 1–2 (2019): 179–88.

Mojaddedi, Fatima. "Where It Was, I Must Come into Being." *Hau: Journal of Ethnographic Theory* 12, no. 1 (2022): 265–76.

Morris, Rosalind C. "Dialect and Dialectic in 'The Working Day' of Marx's Capital." Special issue, *boundary 2* 43, no. 1 (2016): 219–48.

Morris, Rosalind C., ed. *Photographies East: The Camera and Its Histories in East and South-East Asia.* Duke University Press, 2009.

Morris, Rosalind C. "Theses on Questions of War: History, Media, Terror." *Social Text* 20, no. 3 (2002): 149–75.

Morris, Rosalind C. "The War Drive: Image Files Corrupted." *Social Text* 25, no. 2 (2007): 103–42.

Morris, Rosalind C., and Daniel H. Leonard. *The Returns of Fetishism: Charles de Brosses and the Afterlives of an Idea.* University of Chicago Press, 2017.

Mrázek, Rudolf. *A Certain Age: Colonial Jakarta Through the Memories of Its Intellectuals.* Duke University Press, 2010.

Mrázek, Rudolf. *Engineers of Happyland: Technology and Nationalism in a Colony.* Princeton University Press, 2002.

Musil, Robert. *The Man Without Qualities.* Translated by Sophie Wilkins and Burton Pike. Vintage, 1996.

Pandolfo, Stefania. *Knot of the Soul: Madness, Psychoanalysis, Islam.* University of Chicago Press, 2018.

Pandolfo, Stefania. "Testimony in Counterpoint: Psychiatric Fragments in the Aftermath of Culture." *Qui Parle* 17, no. 1 (2008): 63–123.

Pina-Cabral, João de. *World: An Anthropological Examination.* HAU Books, 2017.

Pina-Cabral, João de. "World: An Anthropological Examination (Part 1)." *HAU: Journal of Ethnographic Theory* 4, no. 1 (2014): 49–73.

Rafael, Vicente. *Contracting Colonialism: Translation and Christian Conversion in Tagalog Society Under Early Spanish Rule.* Duke University Press, 1993.

Rancière, Jacques. *The Emancipated Spectator.* Translated by G. Elliott. Verso, 2009.

Riley, E. C. "Cervantes, Freud, and Psychoanalytic Narrative Theory." *Modern Language Review* 100 (2005): 91–104.

Said, Edward. *The World, the Text, and the Critic.* Harvard University Press, 1983.

Said, Edward. "The Problem of Textuality: Two Exemplary Positions." *Critical Inquiry* 4, no. 4 (1978): 673–714.

Saint-Amour, Paul K. "Bombing and the Symptom: Traumatic Earliness and the Nuclear Uncanny." *Diacritics* 30, no. 4 (2000): 59–82.

Santner, Eric L. *Stranded Objects: Mourning, Memory, and Film in Postwar Germany*. Cornell University Press, 1993.

Scarry, Elaine. *The Body in Pain: The Making and Unmaking of the World*. Oxford University Press, 1987.

Schinasi, May. *Afghanistan at the Beginning of the Twentieth Century: Nationalism and Journalism in Afghanistan, a Study of Seraj Ul-akhbar (1911–1918)*. Intercontinentalia, Naples, 1979.

Sebald, W. G. *On The Natural History of Destruction*. Translated by Anthea Bell. Random House, 2003.

Siegel, James T. "The Curse of the Photograph: Atjeh 1901." In *Photographies East: The Camera and Its Histories in East and South-East Asia*, edited by Rosalind C. Morris. Duke University Press, 2009.

Siegel, James T. *Naming the Witch*. Stanford University Press, 2006.

Siegel, James T. *A New Criminal Type in Jakarta: Counter-Revolution Today*. Duke University Press, 1998.

Simmel, Georg. "The Stranger." In *The Sociology of Georg Simmel*, translated and edited by Kurt H. Wolff. 1950. Reprint, Free Press, 1964.

Slezkine, Yuri. "Naturalists Versus Nations: Eighteenth-Century Russian Scholars Confront Ethnic Diversity." In *Russia's Orient: Imperial Borderlands and Peoples, 1700–1917*, edited by Daniel R. Brower and Edward J. Lazzerini. Indiana University Press, 1997.

Slocum, John W. "Who, and When, Were the Inorodtsy? The Evolution of the Category of 'Aliens' in Imperial Russia." *Russian Review* 57, no. 2 (1998): 173–90.

Smadja, Eric. "The Freudian Notion of Kulturarbeit." *Psychoanalysis* 24 (2013): 71–77.

Sontag, Susan. *On Photography*. Picador, 1977.

Special Inspector General for Afghanistan Reconstruction (SIGAR). *Bagrami Industrial Park: Lack of Adherence to Contract Requirements Left This $5.2 Million Park Without Adequate Water Supply and Sewer Collection and Treatment Systems*. SIGAR 16-48-IP. SIGAR, 2016.

Special Inspector General for Afghanistan Reconstruction (SIGAR). *Pol-i-Charkhi Prison: Renovation Work Remains Incomplete More Than 7 Years After the Project Began*. SIGAR 17-46-IP. SIGAR, 2017.

Spivak, Gayatri. "The Letter as Cutting Edge." *Yale French Studies* 55–56, (1977): 208–26.

Spivak, Gayatri. "Translator's Preface." In *Of Grammatology*, by Jacques Derrida, translated by Gayatri Spivak. Johns Hopkins University Press, 1997.

Stewart, Kathleen. *A Space on the Side of the Road: Cultural Poetics in an "Other" America*. Princeton University Press, 1996.

Taneja, Anand Vivek. *Jinnealogy: Time, Islam, and Ecological Thought in the Medieval Ruins of Delhi*. Stanford University Press, 2017.

Tarzī, Mahmud. *Maqālāt-i-Maḥmūd-i Tarzī, by Maḥmūd Tarzī.* Compiled by
    Rawān Farhādī. Muʾassasa-i Intišārāt-i Baihaqī, 1977.
Taussig, Michael. *Shamanism, Colonialism, and the Wild Man: A Study in
    Terror and Healing.* University of Chicago Press, 1987.
Weber, Samuel. *Targets of Opportunity: On the Militarization of Thinking.*
    Fordham University Press, 2005.
Wilder, Gary. *The French Imperial Nation-State: Negritude and Colonial Human-
    ism Between the Two World Wars.* University of Chicago Press, 2005.

Index

United States, war in Afghanistan and, 121–23, 215n30

United States Agency for International Development (USAID), 206n9

violence: angel of history and, 116–18, 213n4; Feldman's analysis of, 100, 209n41; Kabul urban development and, 77–80; language and, 19–22; law and, 21–22, 44–45, 200n35, 201n36; literacy and risk of, 149–53; play as, 19–22; as retribution, 170–76; symbolic-material aspects of, 46–47; translation and, 24–25, 123–28, 141–46, 160–61; war and logic of, 122–23, 215n27, 216n31; writing as, 198n14, 200n39

Vita (Biehl), 13

vita (biography), 179–87

voice: as blind spot, 102–3, 210n44; capital and, 226n8; as object, 31, 200n41; power of, 41; speech and role of, 165–67, 226n2, 226n5; subjectivity and, 92–95, 208n32; translation and paranoia, 124–28

war: in Afghanistan, 120–23; Afghan perceptions of, 4–5; language-encounters in, 1–4; logic of violence in, 215n27; translation as weapon of, 10; US perceptions of, 121–23

Wazir Akbar Khan (Kabul neighborhood), 80, 100, 207n30

weapons production in Afghanistan, 119–20, 214n19, 215n20

Wessing, Koen, 211n49

witchcraft, 42, 54–55, 198n19, 201n7

words, language and danger of, 215n23, 225n1

World Bank, 208n39

writing: freedom linked to, 20–22; reality *vs.* fiction in, 11–12, 198n13; speech and, 165–67; violence of, 198n14, 200n39

Young Afghans writers group, 132–33

Zia (pseud.): dangers faced by, 146–50, 155–58; translation experiences of, 136–46; violence experienced by, 150–55

www.ingramcontent.com/pod-product-compliance
Lightning Source LLC
Chambersburg PA
CBHW020314290526
45785CB00007B/2788